You
Deserve
to Be
Rich

You Deserve to Be Rich

MASTER THE INNER GAME OF WEALTH	AND CLAIM YOUR FUTURE

RASHAD BILAL
TROY MILLINGS

Profile Books

First published in Great Britain in 2025 by
Profile Books Ltd
29 Cloth Fair
London
EC1A 7JQ

www.profilebooks.com

First published in the United States by Crown Currency,
an imprint of the Crown Publishing Group,
a division of Penguin Random House LLC

10 9 8 7 6 5 4 3 2 1

Printed and bound in Great Britain by
CPI Group (UK) Ltd, Croydon CR0 4YY

A CIP catalogue record for this book is available from the British Library.

ISBN 978 1 80522 534 8
eISBN 978 1 80522 536 2

CONTENTS

◆ ◆ ◆

You
Deserve
to Be
Rich

The American Dream Remixed

The American Dream is a lie.

And it's a lie that's been exported around the world. Everywhere, people are working towards that dream, hoping that if they just grind hard enough, they'll get there. But for too many people, especially those of us from marginalised communities, hard work alone isn't enough to land a house with a white picket fence or the financial security it symbolizes.

For too many of us, dreaming is all we can do.

We've followed the rules, played the game—clock in, work hard, clock out, repeat—in the pursuit of a dream that remains just out of reach. We've listened to older generations tell us to get a good job and not lose it. And we've watched as those same elders we love worked until their bodies broke down, robbing them of the opportunity to enjoy the fruits of their labor. Even though they fought it, the money made them do it. The need to work, sometimes harder and longer than others in order to take home the same paycheck, took more from them than they realized or were willing to admit. There was little to no room for luxuries such as brand-new cars, furniture, or vacations. Money was solely for the purpose of taking care of the basic necessities, and we knew better than to complain. On some level, we knew our elders wanted more for us, even if they couldn't always articulate what "more" looked like. They wanted us to be gainfully employed, able to provide for our families and the generations coming after us. But they also hoped we'd be able to thrive in ways they couldn't.

Everyone, no matter where they're from, wants the safety and comfort of knowing they can take care of themselves and their families. For so many in our community and those who are reading this book, the stress of not having enough money is suffocating. Living paycheck to paycheck, wondering if you have enough to rob Peter so you can pay Paul, is not financial freedom. Many would say it is its own kind of prison, consuming all of your energy—physical and mental. Once you make it through one week, the only thing you can do is focus on the next week. The nonstop money stress can push you into all kinds of debt traps and jobs that crush your soul, just to keep the lights on. Battling all that—the uncertainty, the indignity, the shame—takes a toll on you, throwing your nervous system off-kilter, messing with your sleep, and breeding constant anxiety, always wary because the game feels fixed.

These kinds of wounds cut deep across generations—the direct result of systems taking so much more than they give back. Where we come from in the States, discriminatory housing policies have kept Black families from getting the credit and loans that serve as the backbone of financial stability, one reason the average Black family today owns just 10% as much wealth as its White counterparts. Over in the UK, historic discrimination and policy failures like the Windrush Scandal have contributed to a reality where Black families are twice as likely as their White counterparts to have debts that exceed their assets, and the fact that in 2023 only 9% of owner-occupier households were from ethnic minorities. In South Africa, almost thirty years after apartheid ended, over 20% of the population still don't have access to a bank account or similar—and this number comes disproportionately from Black communities. Everywhere we look, the gap between the super-rich and the rest of us is widening. In 2023 in Australia, just 20% of the wealthiest people owned 82% of the value of all investment property, while in India, over 22% of national income went to the top 1%: a historic high. For too many of us, the system is broken, biased and based on false promises. Then those same institutions and systems turn around and label our financial challenges the result of "poor decisions," as if the game weren't rigged from the start.

A lot of the knowledge about finance taught to MBA students and the White middle class is never taught in many working-class communities of color. This disparity leaves many parents without the means to educate their children about critical financial tools such as stock options, real estate investments, debt management, and the significance of homeownership and life insurance, depriving us of economic resources that are readily available to others. But too often, that lack of resources is framed as ignorance or irresponsibility instead of the outcome of discrimination.

When we look back at our lives, we were always in pursuit of the kind of **financial freedom** our elders wanted for us. As Black men, we have always been keenly aware of how vital freedom is to our people. Many Black and Brown people can trace our collective histories back to a moment when the desire for freedom was so potent that the only thing to do was to fight for it. We are able to enjoy many liberties and opportunities because someone else fought on our behalf. And our mission as the founders of the educational platform Earn Your Leisure has always been to level the playing field for our community. That means fighting for the freedoms denied to us and highlighting the need for policy interventions, from increasing access to capital in underserved communities to granting reparations to Black people to atone for slavery and systemic discrimination, while also providing Black and Brown communities with financial knowledge. Because applied knowledge is power.

We were both born in the Bronx and grew up in Westchester County, New York, playing basketball together since grade school. From an early age, both of us were fascinated by finance, curious about the stock market and how money moves among systems and pockets. After high school, Troy went into education, spending a decade working in the public school system, while Rashad became a financial adviser. Both of us became passionate about spreading financial literacy. One summer, we teamed up on a six-week program for high schoolers to educate them on how to "earn their leisure," the very thing we believed our elders were pushing us toward. Like Whitney Houston, we believe that children are our future and that teaching them economic principles will reshape the financial habits of a generation. We started using clips from the classroom to share on social media—mini-lessons on credit, stocks, student loans, and more—and noticed that people of all ages were watching and commenting on them.

But we couldn't shake the feeling that we could do more.

One day, we grabbed an iPhone and a few shotgun mics. Why not start a podcast that brought together two of our favorite things: long talks about personal finance, investing, passive income streams, and the kinds of business opportunities you can pursue outside a nine-to-five alongside barbershop-style conversations about hip hop, sports, and entertainment? We dug deep into barriers to wealth within communities of color, the fact that White households hold significantly more of their wealth in equities, which is a huge contributor to the racial wealth gap, and gave advice on how people could start making their money work harder for them, no matter the status of their bank account.

The next few years were some of the most gratifying and exciting of our lives. A slow trickle of attention turned into a torrent. Within two years, tens of millions of listeners across the globe propelled our podcast to the number one spot on the Apple charts. We heard countless stories of people getting out of huge financial debt, investing for the first time, and finally being able to extricate themselves from exploitative corporate and service work jobs. Our little podcast turned into a financial revolution for the culture, a larger platform that provides tangible and digestible information on building wealth to the overlooked, underserved, and underrepresented.

When we are given the proper tools and allowed to build the careers and lives we want with those tools, the impossible becomes standard operating procedure.

Financial Freedom

You deserve to be rich. You deserve to be able to make a purchase and not hold your breath in fear that your check will go into overdraft. You deserve to go on vacation, simply because you have a headache and need a change of scenery, without having to second-guess your financial decisions for the next year. You deserve a life free from wondering what things could have been like had you not spent an additional $200 on Amazon. You deserve to be able to care for your ailing parents without being concerned about medical bills. You deserve to live the way you want, without reservations or fear. You deserve to be rich. If you agree, we're glad you got your hands on this book.

This book is our answer to the thousands upon thousands of people who have asked us for a detailed blueprint for earning their leisure. **That means having the active and residual income that affords you the freedom to control your time and live a life on your terms.** Let's break down this definition.

> **Active and residual income:** This refers to all the ways you're creating wealth. Notice we said "ways." If your desire is to create wealth for yourself and/or others, you're going to need more than one stream of income. While entrepreneurship is a path to wealth building for some, it's important to note that it may not be for you; that's okay, too. We'll explore a range of wealth-building strategies, from real estate to stock market

investing, and help you identify the most productive streams based on your personal goals, risk tolerance, resources, and more. But for now, remember that **building wealth requires more than one stream of income.**

Control of your time: There is one currency that none of us can replicate, and that is time. Once it's lost, we can never get it back. Many of us watched our loved ones miss out on enjoying life's little moments and creating memories because they had to work. A benefit of building sustainable wealth is being in control of your time, and that control isn't limited to taking a vacation whenever you want. It could mean creating the freedom to attend your daughter's recital or son's game without worrying what bill might be impacted because you took that time off. **Controlling your time is about curating the moments in your life that are most meaningful to you.**

On your terms: One of the biggest lessons we stress in Earn Your Leisure is that you should craft the life that *you* want to live. Financial freedom doesn't matter if you're going to use it to live out someone else's vision and dreams. That's not freedom. At every turn, we're going to push you to ensure that the leisure you're trying to earn is your own.

That means recognizing what works for you and what doesn't. If you don't want to be an entrepreneur, the worst thing you can do is start a business. If you have no desire to get involved in real estate, the last thing you need to do is buy a rental property.

If you're a freelancer with variable income, you might focus on building a larger emergency fund before investing aggressively, while someone with a stable salary could start investing right away. If you're passionate about technology and have a high risk tolerance, you might focus on investing in individual tech stocks or sector-specific exchange-traded funds (ETFs), while someone more risk averse may prefer a balanced index fund. If you have a knack for spotting undervalued properties, flipping houses could be a lucrative side hustle, while someone without that skill set may prefer passive real estate investing through a real estate investment trust (REIT).

When you have the active and residual income that affords you the freedom to control your time and live a life on your terms, you have officially earned your leisure. Many people think that means having enough to retire to an island and live in peace. That's possible, and ever since Derrick retired from the local police department and purchased a vacation home in the Dominican Republic, he has definitely enjoyed spending half the year there and the other six months stateside. But earning your leisure can mean so much more. It can mean what it's meant for Leonard, an only child who now has the ability to care for his aging mother without compromising the household budget that cares for him, his wife, and their two sons. It means that Shareka doesn't have to sit out a college semester and get a job because her family had the resources to pay off her account balance from the previous semester. We're not opposed to making money simply for the sake of having more money. At the same time, we want you to create a vision of financial freedom that shifts patterns and enables both you and others to truly be free.

Wealth building sounds much more intimidating than it actually is. In its simplest form, it is **a system of avenues and opportunities that yield the economic benefits to secure your financial future**. Here's where, with the proper education and information, you can be creative and select the wealth-building opportunities that best reflect who you are and where you want to go. If you're exhausted by trying to maximize your income by working long hours, we'll show you how to avoid sacrificing your time and mental health by learning how to make your money itself do the heavy lifting.

We know how easy it is to read all this and think, "Yeah, but half my income goes to childcare costs just so I can work." We don't take such economic constraints lightly. As working parents, we once lived them, too. Add to that the fact that we inherited many of the financial traumas that we saw in families that look like ours. Troy witnessed firsthand what it looked like for his family to lose their home, due to the complications of an adjustable-rate mortgage, and carry that trauma with them for over a decade. It was hard to get his parents to make any financial decisions concerning their home for a long time after that. And Rashad, who was committed to becoming a financial planner for his people, has experienced the rough side of making the wrong investments. Even knowing better, he didn't always take the time to fully vet an opportunity, and it cost him thousands of dollars. It's not easy to secure your economic future with so many odds stacked against you. Both of us had to buckle down with tighter budgets, apply the lessons of investing, and refuse to play small. More than anything, we had to bet on ourselves in a way that was the biggest investment in our dreams. In this book, we'll meet you where you are and lay out a tailored, step-by-step system that can work for any income level.

Take Sonia, a single mom of three who was once earning just $14 an hour as a home health aide, which barely covered food and rent. After yet another personal loan denial, she took control and started following the principles she'd been learning about for the last year. First, she transferred her outstanding credit card balances to a lower-interest debt consolidation account and tremendously reduced the amount she was paying in interest every month. When she looked at her past bank statements, she was shocked to see how much she was spending on her phone, cable, and streaming services. She spent time researching a cheaper cellular service, finally cut the cable she wasn't watching anyway, and reduced her streaming services to the ones she found herself using on a daily basis. Those small changes added up, saving her $1,400 annually. Realizing that certifications would yield her a higher salary, she went back to school. Over the next nine months, she acquired three care certifications through community college evening courses. Each cost $500, but she qualified for subsidized federal loans with deferred interest to pay for them. Those certifications allowed her to provide higher-level services and bill for $6 more hourly. Suddenly she was earning $768 more per month. She funneled 40% of that extra cash into paying off the loans over the next five months.

Then came the long, grueling process of building an emergency savings fund for the "what-ifs" life inevitably throws at single moms: $12,000, enough to cover six months of expenses. When every cell in her body wanted to pull the money out and take the kids on a vacation and her brain rationalized "We deserve this!" or even "We *need* this for our mental health," she'd run to find her journal and write a reminder to herself of what financial security would feel like: *If something happens, I'll be able to breathe rather than panic. I won't have to ask anyone else for help and be disappointed when they can't or won't help me. I won't feel ashamed for not being in a better position for my kids. I'll be able to give them what they need and want instead of watching them look at what other children have. I'll be able to give them the life I didn't have. I'm showing them the way. And I'll be able to sleep at night knowing that I won't have to worry about whether the lights will be on in the morning. By making the sacrifice and saving this money now, I'm creating the financial freedom that we deserve.*

It took two years, but she did it—and in the meantime, a promotion came her way. With her emergency fund in place, she started tucking away whatever she had left at the end of the month into index funds, and in three years, she'd built a nest egg of over $13,000. Now, with a diversified stock portfolio earning 12% annually and her retirement funds growing, she can afford to do things that would've been inconceivable a few years ago—such as putting her kids through four-year colleges and still retiring by age sixty. Building wealth takes discipline, but it pays exponential dividends.

Unfortunately, we know that some of you have already looked at Sonia's situation and picked apart how that was "easy" for her but will be impossible for you. We get it. So many painful and shameful experiences with money have clouded our judgment and our belief that we can do and have better. Add to that the fact that when the cards of systemic inequality are stacked against us, there's enough reason to believe that it's not worth the effort of trying. But here's the truth: This book outlines every step Sonia took to get to where she is and breaks down how it will be possible for you, too. Sonia isn't an isolated case, and you won't be, either. When you apply the principles in this book, you'll be living proof to those connected to you that anyone really can achieve financial freedom.

When you read this book, you'll be able to identify your growing areas that will lead toward financial freedom. People who have been able to secure their financial freedom had to spend time confronting their "money demons" so they wouldn't jeopardize the wealth they'd begun to create. They also put a team of financial professionals into place who were committed to their financial future. These are small steps, but they are also major strides toward the life you want, and we're going to walk you through how to take them.

Remember those Sears Christmas "wish books" from back in the day? Or those Eastbay shoe catalogues? You remember how you circled all the things you wanted to get? If you were like us, you might never have gotten anything from that wish book for Christmas nor had your choice of shoes from that Eastbay catalogue for the first day of school. But that didn't stop you from seeing yourself with all of it. That's the level of imagination you need to have as you craft your financial future.

Elevating your imagination to become consistent with your idea of financial freedom creates a different understanding of money, its power, and its uses. Your money should always be working *for* you, through various investment strategies or simply by being properly budgeted, even when you are not. Think of it this way: You are the CEO of your life, and you've employed your money. As a dedicated employee, your money works first, second, and third shifts—as well as overtime—to ensure that the company (your life) meets its goals. And **money has four uses: saving, spending, sharing, and investing.**

It's easy to form an emotionally reactive—and ultimately unhealthy— relationship with money when your choices are driven by your economic circumstances. When we're navigating feelings of panic or shame, we often make impulse decisions that give us a temporary sense of safety, security, or dignity, even if they aren't in our best long-term financial interest. Maybe that looks like eating out at an expensive restaurant after a rough day, because you believe you deserve to feel better, even though you *know* that meal is going to cause a chain reaction in your budget. Or maybe it means day trading with borrowed money to regain what you believe is a sense of control over your finances—and life. These are perfectly logical responses in the face of overwhelming stress and repeated experiences of disempowerment. It's extremely mentally taxing to go through life worrying constantly about making ends meet. In order to stop that stress from compounding, however, you have to put in the courage and work to break the cycle—something we'll talk about in the next chapter. As you invest in developing a healthy relationship with money, financial freedom will come closer and closer within your reach.

What does a healthy relationship with money look like? What are the keys to any healthy relationship? **Information, communication, and mutual respect.**

Many of us think that we're born with or just "pick up" the skills that sustain strong relationships, such as emotional intelligence, perspective taking, and attunement—but the truth is that the vast majority of us have to develop those skills by **actively seeking out information** and practicing, practicing, practicing. The same is true when it comes to your finances. Carving out time to become well versed in investment opportunities, attending financial seminars, or watching YouTube videos to gain a deeper level of financial literacy sets apart those who are serious about their financial future from those who are hoping that their cycles of financial dysfunction will resolve themselves on their own. One approach is active; the other is passive.

Communication looks like always knowing how much money you have: being aware of what's coming out of your account and when it's scheduled to be deducted, as well as when incoming deposits will arrive. When it comes to your money, nothing should catch you by surprise. Do you know exactly how much cash you have right now? Is the loose change all in one place? Where's the receipt for the last purchase you made? Do you maintain a log of your expenditures? How often do you look at it?

Last, respect is the key to any productive relationship. Some might suggest that it's impossible to "respect" money. We beg to differ. Treating money well looks like pausing before you book an expensive vacation and resisting the urge to "just deal with the credit card payment later." You worked hard to earn what's in your bank account! Respecting money means defining what's truly important to you and outlining the role financial resources play in your life. Is it security for your family, travel, or maybe early retirement? Set specific, measurable financial goals that align with these values. This will help shift your perspective from seeing money as something to be spent to using it as a tool for your empowerment. Before making nonessential purchases, ask yourself: "Is this a need or a want? How will I feel about this purchase tomorrow?" Respecting your money also means celebrating when you reach financial milestones. Paid off a credit card? Saved enough for that special purchase in cash? These victories, big or small, should be acknowledged and celebrated. **When you respect the money you have, you honor what it can do for you and don't create scenarios where it has to work against you.**

This brings us to the **EYL Thesis of Wealth: Increase your income. Lower your expenses. Invest the difference.**

Increase income

Invest the Difference

Lower expenses

You can increase your income in a number of ways. Yes, there is the option of getting a raise, a higher-paying position, or a second job. But there are ways of working smarter that don't require you to work quite so hard or that require only a small up-front investment of time before, for the most part, you get to sit back and relax—and by the end of this book, you'll know all of your options.

For many people, lowering their expenses can be a double-edged sword. It's the one thing we've all been told we need to do if we want the economic stability that we desire. At the same time, for people who haven't had much, cutting things out can seem like taking a step backward. Growing up in a single-parent home, Shayla knew the sting of her mother telling her that she couldn't afford something or would have to cut back on expenses even more this month. Shayla vowed that when she grew up, she'd get a good job and make enough money that she wouldn't have to make the same painful concessions her mother had. Now, as she looks at a mountain of bills and dwindling money, she feels as though she hasn't made any financial progress and is right back to living the kind of life she wanted desperately to leave in her childhood.

We get it. We know what it feels like to believe that you're hustling backward. However, it helps to think of it this way: Minimizing your basic expenses gives you more resources that you can use to create and consume the best life experiences. You may not *want* to do it, but you also know, deep down, where you *need* to get your act together. Don't worry; we'll help you! The ultimate goal is to have as much money to invest as possible, and you'll get there by following small, actionable steps that will compound over time. The interest on your investments can accrue more quickly than you'd think, especially if you follow our advice for making savvy money moves based on cold facts rather than emotions. Math may not lie, but anxiety clouds judgment.

First Things First

It's important to see the EYL principles at work in real-life scenarios. We've heard thousands of your stories—whether you DMed or emailed us, stopped us as we were headed to the subway, talked to us until it was time to board the plane, or came up to us at InvestFest. Your experiences truly moved us, and your questions helped shape this book. We couldn't cover every unique situation, so we've created characters that represent the most common scenarios in our community. These folks aren't real, but their stories are. As you read, pick the one that feels most like you and follow their journey. As they earn their leisure, we hope you'll do the work alongside them to earn yours, too.

Meet Tracy

Tracy is a thirty-three-year-old single mother of a beautiful three-year-old. After high school, she started college, but life got in the way. Since then, she's started and stopped college twice. Now a mom, she would love to go back to school, finally get her degree, and be a role model for her daughter. However, with no financial support from her daughter's father, Tracy doesn't have much time to do anything but work. She's been struggling financially ever since taking leave for her extremely difficult pregnancy left her behind on bills.

As an assistant at a small law firm, Tracy makes $45,000 a year. When she took the job, it was a major step up from her previous employment. She moved from a job with hourly wages to a full-time salaried position with benefits and a solid career path. After spending years watching high school friends and family members pass her by, accepting that position gave her a real sense of pride. However, she quickly realized that her paycheck still wasn't enough. She's finding it difficult to pay all the bills, tuck away money for emergencies, and save for a down payment for a home.

For her two-bedroom apartment, Tracy pays $2,200 a month, and she just received notice that her rent will increase at the end of the current lease. She's already gone through three rent increases and can't afford a fourth. When it comes to her car, she's upside down on the loan and owes much more than the car is worth. With her credit score of 510, her loan options are severely limited to the point where many healthy ones simply don't exist.

If Tracy could get a part-time job, she would. A second check would definitely help create some breathing room. But working another job presents its own challenges—namely, who will watch her daughter? Paying for daycare would defeat the purpose of bringing in extra income. Currently, she pieces together care among discounted church daycare, sympathetic supervisors who allow a flexible schedule, and her daughter's Head Start preschool. She manages to cover the gaps by working through lunch and staying late when her daughter can attend aftercare. It's mentally exhausting to keep the patchwork system working, but she's mastered the art of the makeshift, always staying one step ahead of catastrophe.

While Tracy has a supportive family and friends, she's not exactly been forthcoming to them about her financial situation. Though they may suspect that something is wrong and she needs help, she hasn't volunteered that information, and they're not going to pry. Tracy's aunt did offer to babysit anytime, but something inside Tracy couldn't bear to say "yes." Pride demanded that she tackle her situation alone. But lately doing it alone has felt impossible—between the soul-crushing job, unpaid bills, and a daughter begging for simple activities beyond their means. Most mornings, Tracy's anxiety wakes her long before the alarm. *What emergency awaits me today?* She feels as though she's drowning.

Growing up, she sold homemade bracelets up and down the street; she always had a knack for spotting the styles and materials that kids coveted each season. For years, she's been toying with the idea of starting a virtual business offering college admissions consulting. She knows that the overstretched counselors at most public schools rarely provide deep application essay editing or granular financial aid package comparisons. With counseling services out of reach for many low-income families, she could help expand their access. Yet without a completed bachelor's degree, she knows her credentials won't cut it. Every tuition payment she diverts to cover childcare represents lost potential—both for her business dreams and for the students she hopes to help. **The idea of earning her leisure seems more like a far-fetched dream than a tangible reality.**

Meet Dre

Dre, the third of five children, just turned twenty, and the world is at his feet! He was a decent enough high school student to know that college wasn't for him. And his parents weren't going to push him to go and ultimately waste money and incur unnecessary debt. Dre's family got by. Both of his parents frequently experienced unemployment and underemployment, but they always found a way to keep the lights on and food on the table. Dre's main objective was to get a job so that he wouldn't be a financial burden on his parents and could help with bills.

Currently, Dre works full time and makes $17.50 an hour. Meanwhile, his parents ask only that he pay his cellphone bill and the home internet bill (because when he's not at work or out with friends, he's at home playing Call of Duty). But even with being responsible for only two bills that total less than $250 a month, Dre is finding it hard to save money. As soon as he gets it and pays his two bills, he is shopping, going out to eat and kick it with his friends, or buying new video games. He has less than $100 in his savings account, and as soon as he turned eighteen, he got two credit cards—and he's now carrying high balances on both.

His parents warn him to watch his spending before the interest compounds, but he brushes them off. *I gotta live it up while I'm young.* If you were to ask him what his credit score is, he couldn't tell you. He doesn't know. Living at home has given him a false sense of security.

Even though he hasn't narrowed down a career field yet, he knows that he doesn't want to work his current job long term. He's already begun looking for another job that pays a little more. *Once I level up at a real company, I'll handle these bills.* Still, doubt creeps in. *Jordan got a condo already. Andre's flipping houses. And I still live with my folks.* **He knows he has to start making moves to secure his financial future.** But like most young people, he doesn't like to be told what those steps need to be and thinks the older people telling him—namely, his parents—are out of touch with the times.

Meet the Williams Family

The Williamses are a beautiful family of five. Married for sixteen years, Gary and Morgan have three children: one in high school and two following behind in middle school. With Gen X parents raising Gen Z kids, there is never a dull moment in the Williams household.

Gary works as an audio engineer for a recording studio, while Morgan handles PR for a nonprofit. Together, they make $225,000 annually, and it's been a long time coming. When they think about how far they've come, they attribute the growth to God and hard work. The increase in their income has helped them tremendously. It's allowed them to make Morgan's monthly student loan payment without fear of the other bills. They've been able to get nicer cars and take better vacations, and they're not saying "no" to the kids as much as they used to. While they don't give in to every whim their children have, it's important to Gary and Morgan that their children experience a childhood not completely framed by their parents' financial situation. They don't want their kids to go through what they did.

But with college quickly approaching, Gary and Morgan have begun to think more about generational wealth and financial legacies. It's something they couldn't afford to think about for a long time, and their increased income has now provided that opportunity. They're not naive; they know that $225,000 isn't a lot for a family their size. While it feels good not to have to say "no" to the kids so often, balancing the day-to-day wants and needs has been tricky. Just yesterday, their teen's fourth cracked iPhone screen led to a tense disagreement, with Morgan ready to replace it and Gary calling her overly indulgent. To provide for their children in the way they want to, they'll need more. Thankfully, they've not maxed their earning potential on their jobs, and though it took some time, their credit score of 700 gives them room to explore investment opportunities and low-interest business loans. Extra cash could not only help them get the kids started in adulthood but also help pay for the trips they've already put on their vision board for once they become empty nesters.

With Atlanta becoming its own creator hub, Gary also knows that it's an investor's dream. He really wants to take the leap to invest in high-quality equipment, becoming a rental service for musicians and podcasters. However, convincing his wife, Morgan, will take some work.

The goal of the Williams family is to create the kind of financial freedom that will shift their family's narrative and trajectory. They've got something good going and believe it can only get better. And if they get this right, it won't take their children sixteen years to get onto the path to financial freedom. That's Gary and Morgan's ultimate goal.

Meet Corey

Corey is forty-five and doing well. Being single with no children has its advantages, as he's been able to keep his debt-to-income ratio very low. While he donates to specific charities and will give his mother whatever she needs, don't ask to borrow money from him or have him cosign on anything. The answer will be "no." Working hard to get and maintain a credit score over 800, he learned that people aren't always willing to do what they need to do to put themselves into the best financial position. Say what you will, but he will be no one's safety net.

Although Corey enjoys having the means to take trips whenever his schedule permits as well as the other benefits of the single life, he's ready to settle down. In thinking about the future and starting a family, he's begun to seriously consider his financial outlook. It was always enough for him, but bringing others into the equation will eventually mean needing more resources. And in considering his financial future, he looked at his retirement plan and realized that it doesn't really cover his current quality of life *if* he remains single. Even though his company matches his contribution to his 401(k), his account will have only about $200,000 in it when he retires. And daily, he's reading about how Social Security benefits won't be guaranteed once he reaches retirement age. Doing the math, he found that he might actually have to delay retirement to maintain his lifestyle.

For as long as he can remember, Corey has wanted to get into real estate. His dream is to own at least fifteen rental properties. Owing less than $100,000 on his home, he's excited about finally paying that off so it can become his first rental property. He's read the books, listened to the podcasts, and watched the videos. But when it comes to investing in real estate and getting started on that dream, he has been dragging his feet. **Growing up, he was taught that investing is too risky and saving money is the only way to ensure you'll have it later.** Yet even with his $115,000 annual salary, he recognizes that investing is the only way he'll create the financial freedom he desires.

Meet Edwin

Edwin is a thirty-nine-year-old single father of two kids: a twelve-year-old son and an eight-year-old daughter. When Edwin graduated from high school, he knew he was done with school. He worked some small jobs for a few years until he got the opportunity to become a party promoter. There were several things working in Edwin's favor: He was well known in the city, he lived in a college town, and he knew how to throw a party. Edwin's parties were always packed and the talk of the town. As a promoter, Edwin was making more money than he ever thought he would.

After the birth of his son, Edwin was given the chance to buy a local club from its owner. Because he mainly promoted parties at this location, he thought owning it made sense. However, Edwin quickly realized that owning a club was not the same as hosting parties. While he was ready for something more stable, Edwin was spending more than he was bringing in for upkeep. At the same time, Edwin's club was open only on the weekends. He had ample enough time during the week to get another job.

Edwin is an entrepreneur through and through, though, and working for someone else just wasn't his vibe. So Edwin took out a loan and expanded the club, which already had a small kitchen, to become a restaurant that was open Tuesday through Sunday with live music and an open mic during the week. He added hookah as another attraction. For the first year after the changes, business for Edwin boomed. Now in its third year, the business has steadied to his weekly regulars and weekend crowd.

Edwin's spot brings in around $400,000 a year, but after paying salaries and with the rising costs of food and upkeep, Edwin is bringing home only $75,000. Though he and his daughter's mother live together and split the bills, it's still not enough to cover Edwin's lifestyle. To attract clientele to his restaurant, Edwin has felt he had to look the part, placing him in debt by about $40,000. Edwin is also paying $925 a month in child support for his son. Although it's tight on his bud-get, he and his son's mother are on good terms and the child support goes toward his educational fees and extracurricular activities.

As he gets older, Edwin is ready to move away from the club aspect of his business. However, it's a large moneymaker, and until he can find something to replace it, Edwin can't let it go. Edwin actually loves the restaurant aspect of his business and has been considering opening a fast-food franchise. He's also been thinking about getting a few real estate properties. Ultimately, Edwin is a serial entrepreneur and wants to find another opportunity that will be his.

Edwin wants to be financially secure and confident in his entrepreneurial journey. Traditional in his values, he wants to make enough money to cover all the major bills in his house-hold. If his fiancé wants to work, that would be her money and not what they needed to stay afloat. More than anything, he's ready for his career opportunities to reflect his own growth and maturity.

EXERCISE: WHO ARE YOU?

Here's an opportunity to introduce yourself . . . to yourself. Don't laugh; hear us out. This is a chance for you to sit with all the things that make you who you are and contribute to your current financial situation. How does money function in your life? What has changed for you in the last three to five years that has impacted your economic circumstances—good and bad? Is there anything on the horizon that will impact your circumstances—good and bad? Where do you want to be, and what do you want? Asking these questions will help you begin to frame what financial freedom needs to look like for you.

Earning your leisure is possible for Dre, Tracy, the Williams family, Corey, Edwin, and *you*. No matter where you're reading this, whether you're in Los Angeles, London or Lagos, this book is designed to help you achieve your vision of success. There isn't a magic formula; you just need to create a plan and work it. Just as you do, our EYL community reps have goals *and* fears. If you stick with them—and us—throughout this book, you'll see how they transformed those fears into actionable steps toward their goals. You can do the same thing. Everything you need is right here.

This book—consider it your financial empowerment mixtape—is divided into two sections. "A Side" is all about your mindset. We'll introduce you to the EYL practice of operating at your highest financial level, discuss healing from financial trauma, and break down our "Assets over Liabilities" principles. We'll also help you determine your financial baseline, take a closer look at our EYL Money Principle, show you how you should think about structuring your money, and walk you through how to budget the EYL way.

In "B Side," we'll break down wealth building. In addition to distinguishing between short-term and long-term wealth-building strategies, we'll be transparent about the risky business that is investments and wealth building. We'll also offer steps to help you practically—and realistically—begin wading into the wealth-building waters. We'll also give you all you need to earn your leisure through side hustles and entrepreneurship, and we'll break down the most profitable businesses and industries to watch, as well as key business practices and strategies. Along the way, we might use the occasional US-specific financial term. In most cases, it'll be obvious what they mean from the context—and you can find the equivalent in your country with just a quick internet search (for example, a 401k is a pension fund; a 1099 employee is a freelancer).

The one thing we ask of you is not to let this book collect dust. Grab a notebook and take notes. Create a plan to build your dream. Then work that plan so you can relax. Because that's the point of it all. We put in the work so we can make the money, never letting the money make us. Matter of fact, we put in the work so that the money can make itself.

A Side

Shifting Your Mindset

Earning your leisure is possible only when you change the way you approach your financial past, present, and future. This section works to address everything that holds us back from fully living in economic freedom. Many of those obstacles are due to no fault of our own; they are the work of systematic oppression. And then there are the times when we've known better but didn't necessarily do better. We'll work through all of that.

Shifting your mindset and the way you frame your relationship with money is not just the key to economic freedom; it also unlocks other character traits that are essential to a life of great value and integrity. As you journey through the chapters in this section, we invite you to take your time and soak it all in. Use the margins to write additional notes, and when the notion hits you, feel free to pick up the phone and chop it up with your family elders and leaders. Hearing their stories and asking them questions will help provide context for many of your behaviors and decisions.

Whatever you want, it really is possible for you to achieve. Even if you don't get anything else we say, we want you to know that we believe in you and your ability to be great. That greatness is on the other side of misinformation, trauma, and poor decision making. As of right now, all of that is in your rearview. It's time to focus on the road ahead.

CHAPTER ONE

◆ ◆ ◆

The Highest Level

Remember when we defined earning your leisure as having the active and residual income that affords you the freedom to control your time and live a life on your terms? Well, the key to financial freedom is knowing what you want. The reality is that not many people do. Sure, most people can tell you that they want to be debt free or be rich. But when you ask them exactly what they'd do with the money, it turns out that they've never thought about it in great detail. And it's not their fault. We've been conditioned to think that spending our time thinking about money is frivolous and shallow. Only snobs and people who are severely out of touch do that. But in fact, if you're clear about what you want, you can gain clarity about what you need.

For instance, if you want to send your retired parents on a trip every quarter without their having to touch any of their money, you'll need the kind of money that comes from a dividend investment that will supplement your parents' income and give them extra spending money—a strategy we'll discuss in much more detail later in the book.

We've told you to dream big and take the limits off yourself and your financial future. Here's where you'll put this into practice. Many people call it "vision casting." Take a few moments to ask yourself these questions.

- **Why do I *want* money? Why do I *need* money?** Our wants and needs matter. Many of us were taught to live a life strictly focused on our needs, and if a few wants slipped in, that would be its own blessing. Regardless of how you feel about capitalism, we all need money—and unfortunately, a lot of it—to deal with inflation and the rising cost of living. But it's important to understand why money has to be a part of our lives specifically. Here's an opportunity for you to list all the reasons you want and need money. Think specifics, such as knocking out that $10,000 credit card debt by next Christmas or stashing away $5,000 for a dream trip in two years. Write them down, make them real. Is there any difference between why you want and why you need money? If you find yourself with few to no wants, it's time to evaluate why you've taken the position that you don't deserve to have money for the sole purpose of joy and pleasure.

- **If I had financial freedom right now, what are the first three things I would do?** This isn't just an exercise in daydreaming—imagining the money in your bank account and asking yourself what in your life you'd change first reveal a lot about what's truly important to you. If caring for a loved one found its way onto your list, it matters a great deal to you to find a way to make life easier for them. And if your thoughts ran straight to a vacation, we get it—you probably need to hit that reset button. Whatever your top three are, they should help you understand what financial freedom really means to you—and what roadblocks are currently standing in your way.

- **What does my dream life look like?** Be specific as possible. Where do you live? What do you drive? What kind of clothes do you wear? Do you hire extra hands to help you with the household duties such as cooking, cleaning, and day to day with your children? What kind of school do your children attend? Do they participate in any extracurricular activities? How often do you vacation, and where do you go? Do you have traditional employment, or are you self-employed full time? Do you own a business? What kind of charitable footprint do you have?

In order to achieve your dreams and goals, you need to know what you have and what you need. Notice we didn't just say "needs"; that's because we want you to get in the habit of incorporating your desires and things you want into your financial planning. For some of you, this may take a little work, considering that we're not used to thinking about money or ourselves in this way. But as a strategy for overcoming your hesitance, consider this affirmation: **I deserve to have my needs met, and I deserve to experience all the things that bring me joy. Money is not an obstacle for me.**

Nope, you say. We already know that some of you skipped right over that. You're asking "What are Troy and Rashad talking about? Money absolutely is an obstacle for me. It is *the* obstacle." In no way are we trying to minimize your circumstances. We understand that working to get to a point where you can combine your wants with your needs is difficult when your needs aren't being met. We're not asking you to dismiss the reality of your current circumstances; we're asking you to trust us as we work with you to craft the financial structure that will enable you to overcome your current financial circumstances and get onto a solid foundation for the future.

The Highest Level

Operating at the highest financial level means creating the terms and conditions that will hold you accountable to earning your leisure.

It's what Simeon did when he traded in his Audi for a Toyota with a more sensible car note because owning a home began to mean more to him than stunting in his dream car. Operating at her highest financial level was what led Kelly to ask her parents if she could move back in with them for eighteen months, enough time for her to save and get a handle on her debt because she couldn't do that and maintain her own apartment at the same time.

This level of hustle separates those who *talk* about what they're going to do from those who actually get it done. And there's nothing that's possible for them that's impossible for you. Like them, if you can see it, you can have it. Shifting your mentality to believe that your financial dreams are within reach is the first step.

Here's the thing: Once you accept that your goals are achievable, you'll see much more clearly what's been holding you back. Maybe you've been avoiding looking at your bank statements because you're afraid of what you'll find. Or maybe you've been telling yourself that you'll start saving "someday" instead of taking action now. Holding yourself accountable in this way often means that you've got to reckon with some counterproductive behaviors on your part. Facing these behaviors can be tough. It might make you feel guilty, ashamed, or even a little panicked.

But here's the good news: The people who achieve their financial goals aren't perfect. They don't have some magical ability to resist temptation or stick to a budget. What they do have is the willingness to be honest with themselves, even when doing so is uncomfortable. So if you find yourself feeling some fear or resistance as you start to believe in your own potential, don't worry; it's a normal part of the process. Embrace the discomfort as a sign that you're growing and evolving. It's always easier to look as though you've got it together than to actually do the work of having it together. But because you deserve to be rich, you'll no longer be taking shortcuts; you'll be doing the inner and outer work to get there. It won't always be easy, but it will always be worth it.

This isn't the time to hide behind facades and personas. Regardless of what we may look like to others and how things may appear, none of us has it all together. While there are some who are in a better financial position than others, we are all striving to reach our goals. That means we are all learning. And we will all make mistakes. But even with those mistakes, we will not fail—because when you can learn from your mistakes, there are no failures; there are only lessons.

Let's look at some of the other characteristics and behaviors of people who operate at their highest financial level—and how you can start adopting them yourself.

They have clarity about their goals and what it will take to achieve them.

They pull up their bank statements, credit card bills, and anything else that tells the story of their money. They lay them all out—literally or figuratively—and see what they're working with.

When you're in survival mode, living paycheck to paycheck, it's extremely difficult to think ahead and process things. We can't tell you how many times people have told us that our financial advice is easier said than done and doesn't take people like them into consideration. They're frustrated because they always feel as though they're in a never-ending cycle of bad financial decisions, fueled by the simple fact that they don't have enough money to break free.

This exact cycle had ensnared Tracy, who found herself increasingly reliant on payday loans just to make it through the week. With her modest salary as a legal assistant, every dollar was accounted for, but still she didn't have enough. The gap between her income and her expenses had widened dramatically after her rent hikes and the ever-increasing cost of childcare. On days when her paycheck hit, Tracy had to make a hard choice: Pay down some of the growing interest on her loans or buy necessities. At the end of the day, she had to do what she needed to do for her daughter.

What would it look like for Tracy to start operating at her highest financial level? Her goal is to become a homeowner, build an emergency savings account with at least $10,000, and start a college fund for her daughter. While she's used to doing everything on her own, she is going to have to let people in and ask for help if she's going to make her goal a reality. After much internal debate, she reaches out to her aunt, explaining that her aunt's babysitting her daughter on the weekends could allow her to pick up a part-time job. She also confides in a colleague from work, who helps her map out a detailed budget and connects her with a debt consolidation adviser who can negotiate with payday lenders on her behalf and coach her through the most effective steps for increasing her credit score. These new support systems not only lift some immediate financial pressures off her shoulders but also reduce her sense of isolation.

We absolutely understand the harsh realities faced by people like Tracy, who are pressured to make short-term decisions that jeopardize their long-term financial health. It's not just about making poor choices; it's about having to choose from limited, often detrimental options.

This book is designed to help people like Tracy break out of the endless cycle of financial emergencies, starting by taking a step back to get clarity about what you have the power to change. Getting a better understanding of what you need to attain financial freedom and the steps you have to take to get there won't cost you more than time, effort, and discipline.

They believe they can make intelligent decisions.

You are smart and capable of making decisions that are logical and serve your highest good. Earning your leisure is about just that: your leisure. Life is meant to be lived and thoroughly enjoyed. We're pushing you to put the work in now so that you will reap the benefits later. We said it before, and we'll say it again: Developing financial discipline will be your greatest asset in life. Whatever you want is possible when you discipline yourself enough to pursue it. Go back to the EYL Thesis for Wealth: Increase your income. Lower your expenses. Invest the difference. It takes being disciplined and holding yourself accountable to the future to make this happen—because the natural inclination is to increase expenses along with increased income. It happens so gradually that we often don't even realize it. If there's a pleasure you'd like to experience that you can't afford right now, put it on the vision board and give yourself something to aim toward. It'll be that much sweeter when you get to indulge in it.

Say you've been working a steady nine-to-five office job, making $45,000 a year, when your manager calls you into their office to tell you that you've been promoted to senior associate, bumping your salary up to $60,000—with the potential to keep moving up! Your mind immediately pictures the number in your bank account ticking higher. Then you realize you can afford to upgrade your reliable old Civic to the brand-new sedan you've had your eye on; nothing too flashy, but a nice step up with some upgraded tech features and leather seats. Your car payment would increase from $500 a month to $750, and that $250 wouldn't feel like pressure at all. But while it may be your dream car, is purchasing it now operating at your highest level? If your emergency savings account doesn't have enough in it to cover your bills for a minimum of six months, you have your answer. Consider taking that extra $250 a month and placing it in a high-yield savings account to get your emergency fund to where it needs to be. In the coming chapters, we'll help you think through these questions: Even as you enjoy life, how can you prioritize your responsibilities so that you don't feel you're missing out on certain things while you purpose your goals? What are the current and future financial burdens that can get you off track? What steps can you implement to address them? Having a structured financial plan that budgets for moments of joy and forecasts for emergencies and life events is key.

They are self-sufficient.

More than deserving to be rich, we deserve to break the cycle of needing others to take care of us. Now, don't misunderstand what we're saying; we need to have relationships with other people in order to thrive. What we don't need is the kind of financial dependency on others that doesn't allow us to stand on our own two feet or hold our head up high.

When you're operating at your highest financial level, you are in a healthy relationship with your money and are making it work for you. The last thing you want to do is stretch your money in ways it can't bend and create added stress on yourself. Financial burdens can easily get away from you and snowball into financial crises. The greater the financial burden people experience, the less likely they are to seek assistance due to shame and guilt. When this happens, a downward spiral is often inevitable. Things come and problems arise; we all know this. But there's no need to create trouble for yourself through poor decision making.

Take John, who found himself always needing to borrow money. It didn't even make sense. He had a good-paying federal job with benefits.

But like clockwork, he always needed to borrow money. He never seemed to have enough for gas or groceries for the next week. And his cellphone was often getting disconnected. It had gotten so bad that he'd begun borrowing money from people to pay other people back. John's family and friends began talking among themselves about what could be the issue. Many of them thought the worst: addiction. But that wasn't John's struggle; he simply didn't have a handle on his finances, and they were spiraling out of control. It caused him to feel shame. Here he was, a grandfather. And instead of John's grandchildren being able to borrow money from him, he was asking them for money.

We wrote this book because we don't want people like John and Dre to stay stuck in guilt and embarrassment. You can't make moves when you're weighed down by shame. It's time to let it go and finally grab hold of the building blocks that will enable you to secure your own future—one that doesn't require you to ask people for money to cover your basic needs.

They have breathing room.

Once you have around 85% of an emergency fund established and have paid off any high-interest debt (that's typically anything with an interest rate over 10%), you can begin contributing to a regular savings account and/or begin investing, depending on your risk tolerance and goals. Keep paying off more than the minimums whenever you can. You know you're stable when you're not losing sleep over bills and your emergency fund is untouched and intact.

In the past few years, Gary and Morgan Williams have done a lot of work to get themselves into a better financial position. There was a time when they were drowning. Then they started treading water. Now they're coasting, and it feels great. And their sense of pride comes from knowing how hard they've worked to get to this place. Currently, their interest lies in maximizing the breathing room they have. It's time for them to put the same effort they put into cleaning up their financial situation into wealth-building strategies, such as investing and entrepreneurship.

With $40,000 in mostly high-interest debt, Edwin is having a hard time creating that breathing room his family needs. Though he's made his payments on time and has a solid credit score, there isn't much room for him to create a savings account. Many entrepreneurs know this feeling all too well and believe this is the reality for the first decade. But this isn't the way it needs to be or should be. Entrepreneurs especially need a safety net, and creating that financial breathing room is the way to do that.

You may be reading this book and find yourself in the exact same place as Gary and Morgan. You've done the work to create the breathing room; that's a great achievement. But we want you to see this room as more than a safety net from financial instability; it's the opportunity to craft the kind of wealth-building strategies that will make that safety net so big that it can catch future generations of your family before they have a chance to fall. And if you're like Edwin and aren't where Gary and Morgan are yet, this book outlines how they got there, and incorporating those same steps, you'll get there, too.

They have flexibility.

Imagine taking a year or two off work because you can, not because you have to. Or being able to help your parents out or invest in a friend's small business. That's freedom. Work your way up to having $50,000 or more saved, so if you want to chase a dream, you can. There's nothing holding you back other than money, and when you understand how to use money and how to make more of it, you will realize that your opportunities are endless.

You might be like Corey: You make good money, you have little to no debt, and you've done well at cleaning up your finances. If that's you, then you're in a prime position to employ the various wealth-building strategies of investing to craft the life you truly want and lean even further into the flexibility you've crafted for yourself. What's the point of having options if you don't exercise any of them?

Too often, we run into people who think that flexibility is what you achieve after retirement and is only for those who are entrepreneurs. They think that it's impossible to possess the kind of flexibility we're talking about and remain a traditional employee. That's absolutely not true. Edwin is an entrepreneur, and without the financial security in place, he doesn't have the flexibility many people assume he does. Building wealth is available to everyone, and when you're a traditional employee, this kind of flexibility empowers you to work on terms that are in alignment with your personal and professional goals. You're no longer working just because you need a paycheck; your work can have a much deeper meaning.

They have financial independence.

The money rolling in from your investments can cover all your living expenses. Whether it's rental properties, dividends from stocks, or interest from bonds, your money is working for you. If your rental properties are bringing in $3,000 a month and your lifestyle costs $2,500, congratulations—you're playing with house money now. It's about having enough not only to live well but also to give generously and set up the next generation. When you're at this stage, think bigger: estate planning, giving to charitable foundations, building a legacy. This is about making your mark and leaving a legacy that lasts way beyond your years.

At age fifty-five, April was able to establish a scholarship fund at her old high school, providing two full scholarships to deserving students. When he became a father, Gabriel established a trust and began collecting assets for his twin girls. It gave Virginia the greatest sense of pride when she was able to help her mother retire five years early. Her mom had invested so much in her and her brothers, sacrificing for them so they could have what they needed.

IF $2 MILLION IS DEPOSITED INTO YOUR BANK ACCOUNT TODAY, WILL YOU GO TO WORK TOMORROW?

If there's one thing that social media does well, it's taking a random topic and making it a trending topic for days! Some of them resurface from time to time. As we were in the process of writing this book, a conversation that started on Twitter and spilled over to other social media apps caught our interest. It posed the question of whether you'd return to work if you mysteriously received a $2 million direct deposit.

Mind you, many of these hypothetical scenarios aren't grounded in logic. The likelihood of receiving $2 million and having no idea where it came from is . . . not great. While that potentially makes for a great comedy, Hollywood doesn't always reflect what's happening in the real world. Yet you'd be surprised at how many took the bait and—yep, you guessed it—said they'd be emailing their resignation, effective immediately. There were some who said that no matter how much they received, they weren't going to give up their steady paycheck (and benefits) for just one $2 million check when another one would never be on its way. The conversation lasted for days, with people who will never meet one another going back and forth about who was making the most ridiculous financial decision. Fun times!

In keeping with the fun, we decided to play along and give you our advice on what to do should $2 million fall out of the sky and into your bank account. *Or* it could come as the result of a very wise and financially savvy friend or loved one cultivating their financial freedom and leaving you the possibility of inheriting generational wealth: No matter how rich you get, **don't quit your day job!**

That is: Stay employed until you have a solid financial plan in place. You want to do this regardless of the amount of any lump sum you receive. If you can wait at least thirty days before spending it, that's even better. You need time to meet with a qualified financial professional who can advise you on a tax strategy that will allow you to keep the majority of your money. This professional will also help you prioritize your needs so that you can take care of your business while also enjoying a nice flex vacation or purchase. Hey, we've never said you have to spend *all* your money on paying bills!

At the end of the day, your goal is to craft and maintain a lifestyle that is not driven by money. Receiving a lump sum should not make you want to jump to spend it. If it does, there's still some financial trauma that you need to address and work through. Look at the deposit, marvel at it for a while (if you must), and let it breathe. And you make sure to breathe while it's breathing. It's not going anywhere. That's the whole point; you're building a life where the financial resources you need will always be at your disposal. So you might as well get used to it.

The Earn Your Leisure Baseline

When Rashad worked in sales, he had a goal of earning $100,000 in commissions annually. When he broke that down using reverse engineering, it equated to making ten successful calls a day. **In its simplest terms, reverse engineering starts with having a goal in mind and working your way backward to get there.**

Reverse engineering your financial freedom starts with determining your *Earn Your Leisure Baseline*. This is the annual income you'll have to make to reach your needs *and* goals. Is there a certain amount you want to save toward a house, new car, or vacation? That needs to be included in your budget. Is there a certain amount of money you want to invest annually? This has to be budgeted.

The best way to determine your EYL Baseline is to take your current income and begin to lay out those financial dreams and visions. Initial EYL Baselines can be calculated based on one-year goals and updated accordingly. Let's look at how Dre, Tracy, the Williams family, Corey, and Edwin determined theirs.

Dre hasn't figured everything out yet, but right now his financial goal is to get his own apartment and move out of his parents' house. He works full time and makes $17.50 an hour, which is roughly $33,000 annually before taxes. In this economy, the average rent of a one-bedroom apartment is around $1,700 a month—and even those are scarce and get snatched up pretty quickly. Even working overtime, he doesn't have enough of a consistent base pay to qualify for the apartment on his own. Most places require that a tenant have three times the rent in monthly income. That means Dre would need to earn around $5,100 a month to qualify for an apartment on his own— which is around $61,000 a year.

Dre will need to pay down his credit card debt before he's even eligible for an apartment. If he pays the minimum, he will never get out of debt or his parents' house. To make a dent in his credit card debt, he will need to pay at least $200 every month. When he looks at how much he's making, he sees that he has three options: (1) get a part-time job and stack that check so he can move out as soon as possible; (2) find a roommate and move out immediately; (3) stay put for now, saving as much as he can. If the goal is moving out now or eventually, Dre's definitely going to have to adjust his spending habits.

Tracy makes $45,000 a year and needs to become a homeowner before her rent becomes more than she can afford. The cost of rent continues to creep up, and she's looking for a more stable housing payment. She's paying $2,200 right now, but she's already gotten a notice from management that the rent will be going up. Staying within her current rental budget, she could afford a house priced at $250,000 or less. Depending on her interest rate, it would put her somewhere between $1,400 and $1,800 for her mortgage payment. Though she's working on improving her credit rating, she wants to be able to put down a substantial down payment to show lenders her commitment to keeping her home. Back in the day, we always heard that people should be able to put down at least 20% toward the cost of their home. However, in 2021, the average first-time homebuyer made a down payment of only 6%. For Tracy, that would be $15,000.

Tracy has an ambitious goal of saving that in one year. She already has $3,000 saved. She'd planned to use it for tuition, but she'll have to sit out yet another semester because she can't afford it right now. Even if she buckles down and gets extremely aggressive with her budget, she can see only where she's able to save $300 a month toward it. To save for her down payment and have enough for new furniture and some breathing room for the transition, Tracy's EYL Baseline is between $65,000 and $70,000 a year.

Gary and Morgan Williams have decided that they want to save $200,000 to assist with their children's college education *and* travel more once they become empty nesters. They have three years before their oldest heads to undergrad and six years before their youngest leaves the house. Combined, they currently make $225,000 a year, and both are scheduled for performance raises this year. They have decided on a monthly amount they will assist each of their three children with while they're in college and want to begin setting that money aside. They've also already planned their first luxury romantic (*kid-free*) international getaway for just two years from now.

Though Morgan still needs a bit of convincing, Gary is convinced that his business idea of renting out high-end podcast equipment is going to be a game changer. They'll need to take the leap, invest in the equipment, and establish the business. When Gary and Morgan calculate what they need to begin the business, save for their children's college fund, and prepare for their dream vacation, their EYL Baseline is about $200,000 a year.

Corey is beginning to seriously consider starting a family. Within his career field, he's beginning to knock on the door of the salary cap. And his current job is stressful enough that he's not looking to add a second one to the equation. That said, he still wants a stronger financial portfolio for his future family. Though he makes $115,000 a year and believes his future wife will financially contribute to the household on some level, he can't shake the fact that the national average cost of raising a child is $17,000 a year. He would feel more comfortable if he could bring in an additional $25,000 toward that cost to ensure that his family has the life he envisions. If he's honest about what his dream life looks like, he'd quit his job and pursue real estate investing full time. So in theory, while his EYL Baseline might remain the same, he has to create a solid structure to achieve it, through real estate investing, before he quits his job. Having a million dollars in investments within the next fifteen years is Corey's financial goal. He doesn't spend wildly and has been incredibly responsible with his credit. But to get to a million dollars by the time he's sixty, he will have to take diverse investing much more seriously—and start as soon as possible.

Edwin already has a family and knows he needs to do so much more to provide for them. While he likes the restaurant aspect of his business, he seriously wants to let the club side go. Working late nights every weekend was fun when he was younger. That's not where he is anymore. Also, Edwin is feeling the itch to try something new to add to his entrepreneurial portfolio. But before he can do that, he's got to clear his $40,000 debt. Edwin's goal of making $500,000 annually is his EYL Baseline, and it's a good distance from the $75,000 he makes now.

When he calculates it, Edwin may have to push out his goal of making the $500,000 annually from two years out to five or seven years. While this may be frustrating, it's a more realistic approach to discovering a new entrepreneurial endeavor and building it up. Even if he opens a fast-food franchise, he's still going to have to actively work toward getting to that $500,000 mark. Though a new business venture and investments will be essential for Edwin to add to his portfolio, his focus has to be on cutting down his expenses and creating a more realistic budget that will allow him to begin saving and establishing the financial breathing room that will enable his family to be okay while he builds a new business.

Here's the truth: Getting to your EYL Baseline will push you completely out of your comfort zone. Even if you're investing in the stock market, you're going to have to do the legwork of researching the best stocks for investments and watching your trends for a while. If you're looking into investment properties, there's still the work of property management. Even if you hire a property management company, it's not as though you're going to give it the keys to your investment property and never check in. And if you're going to start an e-commerce business, you need to market and advertise it. Everything you do is going to take work.

We get that some of you are already stretched to the max and the idea of more work is a turnoff. Remember that all of this can happen at your own pace. This can be as intense as going back to school and getting a degree, or it can be as simple as listening to a financial education podcast on Saturdays while you're cleaning or lounging around the house. Either way, we don't want you to get overwhelmed by the notion of work. This will take effort, but you get to decide what kind of effort it will be. **Remember: Taking realistic steps toward reasonable actions reaps rewards.**

The rest of this book will help you form a realistic plan to get started, including:

- **Building your emergency fund.** Start small if you have to, but start.

- **Saving a portion of every paycheck until you've got a cushion**—aiming for six months of living expenses as your target. Lock it down and keep it sacred; it's only for real emergencies. Start by paying off high-interest debt, since it compounds quickly and can tank your credit score.

- **Setting up automatic payments** so your credit card bills are paid off in full every month, or for the largest amount you can afford.

From there you'll build up to more ambitious goals. If your dream is to pay off all your debt and have a minimum of $250,000 in investments, for instance, what are the intelligent decisions that will get you there? First, you'd start with a plan to pay off your high-interest debt, open a brokerage account (if you don't already have one), and then begin investing with the amount you'd previously used to pay off your debt. This would also be the time for you to explore what medium-term and long-term investments are most optimal to get you to that $250,000 mark.

We'll get into investing strategies in more detail in the second half of the book, but it's worth noting that just because investing can be lucrative doesn't mean you're in a good position to do it. Operating at your highest level means knowing when to make the right moves so they don't become the wrong ones.

By following the steps to financial freedom, you won't be scraping by anymore; you will be building a fortress around your financial future. Each step is a building block to not just surviving but thriving. Remember, all the work you're doing is not just about making money; it's about making a life.

When you can recognize that everything you have experienced—good and bad—has led you to this moment, where you are putting a plan in motion to achieve your financial goals, that is what it means to operate at your highest financial level. So free yourself from the guilt and shame you've held on to for your past poor decisions. Definitely try not to make any more of them—at least not without goals or a plan in place. **Give yourself permission to see yourself beyond existing in the deficit of right now and instead living in the overflow of your financial freedom.** Let you see yourself making wise decisions with money and experiencing a life that isn't weighed down by the trauma of mismanagement. Because as we've told you before, if you can envision it, it can happen.

◆ ◆ ◆

CHAPTER TWO

Dealing with Financial Trauma

Our ability to operate at our highest financial level has everything to do with how we were raised to understand money. Many of us grew up being taught some variation of the principle: **Make *as much as* you can and save *whatever* you can.** In other words, working as much as possible was the only way to ensure that you had enough money to cover household and personal bills. Unfortunately, saving couldn't be the first priority. After the bills were paid and everything was taken care of enough to give you some breathing room until next month's bills rolled around, then and only then could you think about saving.

That mindset put us all behind the eight ball when it came to money and our finances. First, it taught us to be ruled by our jobs and the pursuit of a check. Whenever the opportunity to do overtime was available, we jumped at it. We found ways to fit a second (and sometimes third) job into our already tight schedule. More than anything, it put us into panic mode, believing that we'd never have enough money unless we burned the candle at both ends to get it. When we hustled like crazy and still fell short, we were not only dead tired but also angry with ourselves. Financial instability impacts our ability to see ourselves as worthy and productive human beings.

◆ ◆ ◆

How you *feel* about yourself is reflected
in your relationship with money.

◆ ◆ ◆

Take a minute to sit with that. As you think about it, consider how true it may be for you. Actually, more than considering it, we want you to look at it in black and white. So here's a little exercise. Pull out your banking statements, and examine your purchases for the last three months. Place those purchases into three categories:

- **Needed It:** These are your essential bills and necessities.

- **Wanted It:** These are the indulgences that make life better.

- **What Was I Thinking?:** These are the purchases that can be considered completely unnecessary and/or are a symptom of our financial trauma.

What percentage of your purchases went into each category? How much of your annual income goes to support causes and initiatives beyond yourself? What does your money—the way it comes, goes, and stays—say about you? What's in your savings account? What percentage of your monthly income automatically goes there without your touching it? Do you have an emergency account, completely separate from your savings, that you can access when urgent needs arise? (**Keep** those statements close. **We'll ask you to pull them out again in the next chapter.)**

For many people, this can be an easy exercise to complete because they grew up in families and communities where financial literacy and economic empowerment were cornerstones. They have robust savings. Their checking accounts never even heard of an overdraft fee. And after donating sufficient amounts of money to charities and loved ones, they still have enough for their daily expenses and at least two summer vacations. Their relationship with money is a good one—because they were given everything they needed to ensure it. They feel great about themselves, and their economic circumstances reflect that.

But there are others who weren't as lucky. Their upbringing was much different. One late bill could completely wipe out their savings account. Unfortunately, many of them know what it means to "work in the hole"—needing a paycheck to bring an overdrawn account current, meaning they wouldn't see all the money they worked for and another negative account status was imminent. And while the greatest strength of these communities is how we take care of one another, many people donate and give out of their own deficits. And they don't have time to think about a weekend getaway, let alone a summer vacation.

Understanding that the way we feel about ourselves is reflected in our relationship with money stings a bit, partly because it's true. We know deep down when our financial decisions aren't made from a place of abundance but from desperation or a scarcity mindset. But it stings mainly because it's not our fault. There's a common assumption that people are bad with money because they want to be. Have you noticed how people love to start talking bad about people without money once they get some themselves? Often coming from the same communities and circumstances, these people disparage the very people who didn't get the same opportunities they did. That's not financial empowerment or literacy; that's condescension and arrogance. We've never wanted to be part of that, and we won't be.

If you don't have the tools to cultivate the healthiest relationship with money can you really be blamed for how you feel and what you think about yourself? It's important to acknowledge that our toxic relationships aren't our fault. We can't ignore the history of systemic inequality and the legacy of racism that impacted the ability of minority communities to build wealth. During Reconstruction, the Freedman's Bank was established to create the ability for newly freed slaves to gain economic independence from White slave owners and their businesses. At its height, the bank was home to the current equivalent of $80 million. Though there were concerns about and irregularities in the bank's practices, Black people invested all they had into the promise of uplift. However, when the bank abruptly closed, it was discovered that over $20 million in deposits had just *disappeared*. Whatever intentions of equity and fairness President Abraham Lincoln had had when he had established the Freedman's Bank, formerly enslaved people were crippled yet again when the money was stolen.

In addition to mistrust, the prevalence of banking deserts continues to widen the racial wealth gap. In 2019, the median income of White families was $188,200. For Black families, it was $24,100, and 17% of Black families were unbanked, compared to 3% of White families. **A banking desert is defined as a neighborhood that has no banks or financial institutions located in it or within ten miles of its center.** Prior to the 2020 COVID-19 pandemic, banking deserts severely impacted rural areas. However, financial pressures in the aftermath of COVID-19 forced banks to close branches in urban and metropolitan areas. Banking deserts leave individuals and families with no other choice than to rely on check-cashing institutions that charge exorbitant fees and leave people unbanked.

Carrying Childhood into Adulthood

And then there are our personal experiences. Coming to America from the Caribbean, Troy's parents didn't have any financial literacy. All they knew is that you come here, work hard, and provide the best life possible for your children. For them, that meant purchasing a home. Troy's family followed the traditional journey of those leaving their home country of Jamaica to end up in places like Montreal, Toronto, and New York City. Most of his father's side ended up in the Bronx, while his mother's people settled in Queens. So when Troy's family purchased a home in Greenburgh, that was a game changer. Because the rest of their family lived in apartments, their homeownership was a win for everyone and symbolized that they, too, could be part of the American Dream. The house literally had a white picket fence!

In 1988, the Millings family moved to middle-class suburbia and their home became *the* home. Mr. Millings's friends would come up from the Bronx and watch football games. Troy's cousins would come because everybody wanted to see the house. It was a different feeling; there was space for kids to play. When it was time to have a game of football, Troy, his two brothers, and their friends would meet at the house to play. Being homeowners did undoubtedly provide a sense of pride for Troy's parents and a source of joy for him and his siblings. It was a new way of life, and it felt good.

And then, in 1993, everything changed. Their home went into foreclosure, and he and his siblings had no idea what that meant. But even without having any real understanding of what was going on, they were all living through it. Looking back, Troy remembers the initial emotions of confusion, disappointment, and embarrassment. They were emotions he knew everyone in his family was feeling. To their family and friends, they were the ones who made it out, but now they were heading back into an apartment. People who once admired them were now looking at them like, "Oh, wait, y'all can't afford to live here? What happened? Oh, y'all don't really have money like that. That was quick." And honestly, Troy had the same questions. What happened? It felt like they were moving on up, but now it seemed they were taking more than a few steps backward.

And those backward steps included lying about where they were living so Troy and his siblings could remain in the same schools they were attending. When they left the Bronx, Troy left all the friends he knew. When they moved into their home in Greenburgh, Troy was able to make new friends in the neighborhood. However, now he was about to lose friends again or have to try and make new ones. It was during this time when he heavily relied on the local community center, as a space where he was able to find new friends and maintain relationships.

But losing the house and moving into an apartment wasn't the end of the Millingses' housing instability. The rent became more than his parents could afford, so they ended up leaving the apartment to move into the basement of someone's home in the Bronx. At twelve, Troy had to share a bed with his two older brothers, who were fifteen and twenty-two. At six feet tall, the young men had to continuously hunch down in the basement to move through their new surroundings and avoid hitting the ceiling.

Though they were living in the Bronx, Troy and his brother were still attending school in Westchester. Their father would start his day at 5:30 A.M., driving them to school, and they would take an hour bus ride home. Their parents would give them $3 or $4 a day, and with that, they had to budget for lunch and getting back home. On the days when they got $4, Troy and his brother knew that it was going to take $2 for them to get back home. They figured that, if they didn't eat lunch at school, they could stop at McDonald's and get a cheeseburger and small fries off the dollar menu. Though it was out of necessity, Troy quickly learned the importance of budgeting and being smart with money. For Troy and his brother, it would mean they literally wouldn't be able to go home.

It would be years before Troy learned what actually happened. To get what they thought was the best deal possible and to get in the home, Mr. and Mrs. Millings opted for an adjustable-rate mortgage. Essentially, an adjustable-rate mortgage offers an incredibly low rate the first year that will increase each year, for two to five years, until it's set at the rate that will be maintained for the life of the loan. This could easily double and sometimes triple the mortgage payment from the first year. Troy watched the toll losing the home took on his parents. They were disappointed and ashamed to have what everyone considered the American Dream slip through their fingers. And they never really recovered from it.

Troy's parents didn't purchase another home until 2010. And when interest rates dropped during COVID-19, Troy approached his parents about refinancing their loan to get a lower rate and payment. It was an emphatic "no." It could have saved them around $300 a month, but Troy understood his parents' hesitation. Losing their home was one of the most traumatic experiences of their lives, and they didn't want to risk losing the one that took them so long to courageously purchase. Troy watched the experience of losing their home change his parents. His father, a genuine risk-taker, became more calculated in his financial decisions in a way that essentially kept him from making any major decisions. And his mother began to operate with a sense of fear that whatever they had could easily be taken away again.

And no matter how much Troy tries to tell them that isn't the case, they won't hear it. When he shows them their financial portfolio, which includes a 401(k) and robust savings, Troy tries to get his parents to see that their financial situation is no longer what it was in 1993. Yet he's learned to give his parents the space to be cautious in the way they want to be while he does what he wants to do to show his appreciation for his parents' sacrifices. Though they can afford it, Troy's parents aren't going to take a vacation. So Troy plans it and they go— if for no other reason than they're not willing to waste the time it took to plan or the money that's already been spent on it.

The Most Common Financial Trauma Experiences

There are very real differences between growing up with parents who were squarely in the middle class and with parents who were working poor, underemployed, or unemployed. The lack of mobility limited your family's options. The neighborhoods you lived in weren't always the best. Vacations typically never happened, and there was always little to no money for extracurricular activities. As kids, many felt the pinch the hardest around their birthdays, at Christmastime, and at the beginning of the school year, when there was no money for gifts or new clothes. Many people might romanticize that time by saying things such as "We didn't even know we were poor, because all we had and needed was each other." In theory, this sounds great, but it's a trauma response. It reflects the ways we tried to make sense of how the odds were stacked against us and we made ways out of no ways. We did—and we should be proud of that—but that doesn't mean we came out unscathed. In fact, there are studies showing that adults who grew up in a toxic financial environment are more likely to make unhealthy financial decisions themselves.

Growing up in a one-income household makes for a very different childhood experience from growing up in a home where two parents are contributing. And the types of one-income households can vary. In those that are experiencing poverty, kids learn early on that they need to do whatever they can to bring money into the house and to minimize their needs so that their parents can redirect their money toward other necessities. For example, many sons in single mother–led homes take on the belief that they need to be the "man" of the house, bringing in money however they can. All too often, the focus on education shifts to getting money *now* so that their family can have what they need. The children can internalize the narrative that they're a burden—and then carry that stigma with them into adulthood.

While two incomes are always better than one, there are some one-income households that are not experiencing poverty. They are solidly middle class—or higher—and are thriving. Though money may not be the issue in those homes, the children living in them don't get the benefit of seeing their parents work with another partner to make financial decisions for the household. When it comes to establishing a family in their adulthood, this can sometimes put the child at a deficit. Knowing how to work together for the financial future of a family is important, and many adults, who never saw that in their homes growing up, confess to struggling with this.

When their parents are unstable, children develop various coping mechanisms designed to protect themselves mentally and physically. Maybe they learn to lie about what's happening at home to their friends, wanting to present a happier narrative than the chaos they're experiencing. It could also mean learning never to ask for anything because you know the answer will never be "yes." We can find ourselves developing unhealthy triggers, trauma responses, and avoidant habits because of what we saw our parents do, whether opening bills sends our adult self into a panic attack or we form a shopping addiction to compensate for the years when we had to go without.

We were made painfully aware of this reality through our work with the young people of New York City. In 2009, we ran a summer program that paid participants a stipend, up to $500, at the end of the program. During that program, we taught the students economic principles that we knew the public school system didn't have in its curriculum. Yet every week, our students let us know where we would be able to find them on payday: They were going to the mall to buy new shoes, an outfit, or jewelry with their earnings. They wanted to look good because, at the end of the day, that was what they valued. As some of them came from homes and environments that had limited options, their outward appearance was the only way they felt they could make a statement in the world.

We ran the program at our old school, Woodlands High School in Greenburgh, New York. As a high school educator and a financial adviser, both coming from the same neighborhoods as our summer program participants, we knew what we were up against. We knew the schools weren't teaching what they should, and we knew that financial literacy wasn't abundant in their homes. That was completely different from our experience at a business competition at a high school in

Scarsdale. Those mostly White high school students were quite famil-
iar with Bitcoin, cryptocurrency, and real estate as viable paths to economic success. Financial literacy was already part of their curriculum,
ensuring that they would be light-years ahead of the Black and Brown
students at Woodlands and fully prepared for the future.

It became clear that in order to level the playing field, we'd have to
do it by ourselves. And that was literally what we did. We combined
my experience with structuring a curriculum with Rashad's financial
literacy information and created a lesson about money that the students could understand. On the whiteboard, we drew three columns,
each with the letter S at the top. We didn't tell the students what the S's
stood for until the end. We wanted them to see how their financial
activities were being grouped without telling them. As we described
different financial scenarios and asked the students what they'd do
with their money, we instructed them to write each of their answers
under a specific S column. One column began filling up much faster
than the others, and the students began to guess what the S's stood for.
Smart kids.

Once we completed the exercise, we told them that money ultimately has three uses: saving, spending, and sharing. They came from
families and communities that looked out for one another, and those
ethical commitments were rooted in them, so sharing made sense to
them. But most of their financial decisions fell under the "spending S"
column. What the students saw was that saving money was next to
impossible considering all they were spending. Over time, we've re-
fined this lesson to include "investing" as one of money's uses.

Though they were children, their financial decisions didn't exist in
a vacuum. They really didn't know what to do with money. And when
you don't know what to do, you do what you know. It would be easy
to dismiss those kids as products of their environments and write their
parents off as people who just didn't want any better out of life—what
upwardly mobile, out-of-touch people often say. But the economic behaviors and financial patterns of those kids and their communities

reflect the ways Black and Brown people have been systemically excluded from financial literacy and economic empowerment.

A lack of financial literacy has much larger implications. It prevents poor and working-class people from establishing loans so they can own homes, purchase cars at decent rates, or attend college with minimal to no debt. It makes planning for the future as precarious as overspending on groceries. One financial mistake can set a family back for decades. For these reasons and more, online and phone-based money apps, such as Cash App, have become the primary source of "banking" for many in Black and Brown communities. In 2022, the Pew Research Center found that despite serious concerns regarding the safety and security of money apps, 59% of African Americans and 37% of Hispanic Americans use Cash App compared to 17% of White Americans and 16% of Asian Americans.

Contrary to popular belief, there is enough money to go around. According to the Federal Reserve, $188 billion was printed in 2020. And though the vast majority of that amount is used to replace older bills, it's clear that Americans' problem isn't lack of availability of money—it's access to it. Many institutional programs and grassroots initiatives exist to call out systemic inequalities and work to change laws and policies to produce a more equitable distribution of resources. Community development corporations and church benevolent funds are still some of the greatest sources of financial assistance in our communities. We need them; their work is tireless and often thankless. But more than anything, vulnerable communities need people who will speak truth to power and stand up for what is right.

We also need people who will provide our communities with the education that has long been withheld from us. You didn't pick up this book by accident. There's something in you that recognizes how unbalanced the scales have been. The truth is that we all deserve the opportunity to experience financial freedom. This actually goes beyond earning your leisure and having the right to live on your own terms. It's about righting the systemic wrongs that keep you away from the tools and information that make earning your leisure a possibility. In this way, EYL is an act of resistance. It's as much a commitment to social justice as all other forms of revolution are. When you are learning and implementing the tools of financial literacy, you are rejecting the notion that equality and equity aren't possible. You are living into what many of your ancestors dreamed for you.

Merriam-Webster defines trauma as, among other things, "a disordered psychic or behavioral state resulting from severe mental or emotional stress or physical injury." While we've given you examples of the experiences that lead to financial trauma, it's also important to recognize the ways financial trauma can show up in our lives. Some of them include:

> **Hoarding money:** Many of us either know or have heard stories of family members hiding money around the house, under mattresses, or in Crown Royal bags. And while we've joked about it, these are prime examples of manifested financial trauma. Additionally, believing that you must keep every dollar you earn, never sharing or investing any of it, is often a trauma response. We all know penny pinchers who don't have to pinch as much as they do. Nickel-and-diming everything out of fear doesn't mean you're being savvy with money. The idea that you'll never have enough money causes you to dismiss opportunities to develop a healthier relationship with it. If you're wondering if you exhibit signs of hoarding money, here are some examples of behaviors associated with it:
>
> - choosing not to spend time with family, friends, and loved ones because you feel you need to save money
>
> - deciding against essentials like health insurance or life insurance because you believe you can't afford

them, when you have the financial resources to get
them

- creating an unrealistic and unsustainable budget to save money

- setting incredibly high standards to allow yourself to spend money and then feeling anxious once you spend it

Spending excessively: At the other end of the spectrum, spending like there's no tomorrow is also rooted in financial trauma. It reflects the belief that "Since there will never be enough anyway, I might as well live now." The nonchalant attitude behind this attitude masks a sadder reality; it suggests that you've given up on any possibility that your financial future can be any different from your current experience. Excessive spending can also be a way to prove that you're not where you used to be financially. When you've experienced poverty or financial insecurity at any point in your life, there's a tendency to spend money to show that you've made it— often trying to impress people who ultimately don't matter or care. Unfortunately, excessive spending is often written off as not that important or a behavior that's associated with young age that we'll eventually outgrow. However, if you don't take the behavior seriously, it can snowball and become a serious issue. Examples of excessive spending include:

- shopping without a list or budget

- shopping with a list or budget and purchasing more than what's on that list or exceeding your budget

- overspending during a night with friends

- making purchases five to seven days per week

- keeping expenses in your budget without the
  money to cover them

Shopping emotionally: At some point, all of us have engaged
in a little retail therapy. Whether to console ourselves after a
painful breakup or to celebrate a major accomplishment,
we've made a purchase with a hefty price tag. And we all
know what it feels like to have to brace ourselves to look at
the credit card balance on Monday morning after a weekend
of swiping. Some people even resort to compulsive shopping
as a way to cope with any uncomfortable emotion or strain.
As a trauma response, emotional shopping keeps people in
the loop of having to work to earn as much as they've spent.
While financial freedom leads to greater happiness, emotional
shopping does not. While we all pretty much know what
emotional shopping looks like, it's more important to address
the emotions and experiences that can drive us to it. Here are
a few:

- feeling jealous after someone you know (loved one
  or colleague) experiences a win you've wanted

- being upset and/or heartbroken after a breakup or
  professional disappointment

- being angry with your spouse or partner after an
  argument (also, using their bank or credit cards for
  the purchase as revenge)

If you're experiencing these feelings or think you're engaging in
emotional spending, wait forty-eight to seventy-two hours before making the purchase. This will give you the opportunity to step outside of

the immediate emotions associated with the experience to make a more rational financial decision.

Money and Health

According to the Urban Institute's Center on Society and Health, there is a direct relationship between income and your overall health. On one hand, people with more disposable income have access to better healthcare and all that comes with that. At the same time, more income and wealth also improve your physical and mental outlook because you are not impacted by the stressors related to financial instability and economic strain. This is especially important because all too often people dismiss the origins of many of their health-related issues when the root cause is money.

The greater a person's income, the less likely they are to experience disease or a premature death. Did you know that 77% of adults say they regularly lose sleep because they are worried about money? Or that people experiencing financial stress are thirteen times as likely to have a heart attack as people who do not worry about their financial circumstances? Some of the most dangerous and overlooked financial trauma responses show up in our bodies. Physical, emotional, and mental health challenges have long been linked to financial insecurity. The shame and guilt attached to experiencing financial trauma can cause people to minimize their self-worth and self-care, dismissing the presence of ailments and illnesses. Add to that, who's going to go to the doctor and create another bill? Refusing to acknowledge that we carry financial trauma in our bodies is quite serious, and the result of doing so can't be overstated. Doctors have discovered connections between financial trauma and various health concerns, including diabetes, depression, migraines, and sleep issues. In 2020, Americans listed finances as the top cause of stress in their lives, and those who experience financial trauma are twenty times as likely to attempt suicide—or engage in suicidal ideation—as someone who has not experienced a financial hardship. Ignoring the impact of financial trauma is literally a matter of life and death.

Financial trauma doesn't just impact our relationship with money; it touches every aspect of our lives. It's that invasive, and sometimes we don't even realize it. Being short with our spouses and romantic partners, snapping at our kids—when things aren't right financially, we may take it out on the people closest to us. Declining opportunities to kick it with our friends because we aren't where we thought we'd be financially or refusing to date and open yourself to the possibility of love—financial trauma can rob us of so many meaningful experiences. It's time to take control of our lives and set ourselves on the path toward wholeness and financial freedom.

Healing Financial Trauma

Corey came from incredibly humble beginnings, living in apartments with his parents and three other siblings. He grew up knowing that there was very little money and that their electricity and water would be frequently disconnected. What he never understood, though, was that whenever his parents were fighting, his mother always found money to take him and his siblings shopping afterward. That would always result in his parents arguing even more. As the middle child, Corey did his best to stay out of the way and learned to associate doing nice things for himself as a consequence of something and not as a reward.

As an adult, Corey works hard. He refuses to experience his utilities being disconnected, so he pays the bills on time. He also checks the monthly bill to make sure that his usage hasn't crept up from the month before. And though he may have money to spare, asking Corey for a loan isn't worth the effort. He's always going to say "no." It's not because he doesn't have it; he just never knows if he's going to need the money himself.

Corey doesn't take vacations but, whenever his boss has made him mad, he always finds himself buying a new outfit. To quickly get over his last breakup, he bought a vintage Rolex he'd been eyeing. For him, spending money is an obligation. He knows that he has to pay his bills, so he does that. What he doesn't spend on bills and necessities, he saves, because there was always a time when his parents needed money but didn't have it, and he promised himself that would never be him. Yet he refuses to invest because he can't "see" that money, and every investment isn't guaranteed. The fear of losing any money outweighs the risk of possibly making more. And he spends money on himself only when he's frustrated or upset. Even if the purchases are things he likes, they're not seen as treats. Rather, they are ways to soothe his emotions or avoid dealing with the issue at hand.

As he's working to better his financial position, Corey will need to confront the ways he's internalized what he understands about money based on what he experienced as a child. There will have to be a moment where he deals with how the constant financial instability in his home affected him. Though he may not be able to discuss this with his parents, he might need to sit down with someone who can connect the dots for him and reveal how his frugality, his insistence on only saving money, and his resistance to investing are all rooted in his fear that he will experience the poverty of his childhood again. It will be important for him to look at his current position, his savings, and his retirement accounts to realize that he's come so far from that place in his life, and it would take a great deal from him to get back there again.

Corey will also have to do some extensive work on how he processes his emotions in relationship to money. While this is something that he picked up from his mother, it doesn't suit him or his financial goals. It's possible to deal with the frustrations of life without blowing a bag on something we want. And here's the thing: Even if we want a particular item and can afford it, there's also work that we must do around our worthiness for it. If we're making purchases only when something is wrong, then what are we telling ourselves about what we deserve? We can't make room for joy and pleasure in our spending if that's connected to our trauma and feelings of inferiority.

Corey sees his financial decisions as being responsible, but it's really operating out of fear and not at his highest level. If you don't get anything else we lay out in this book, we need you to get this: It is possible to heal financial trauma. Not only is it possible, but it's also necessary. Before making any major new financial decisions, we encourage you to follow these steps to healing financial trauma.

1. **Watch your language.** We believe in the power of affirmation and positive thought. Some people call it "faking it till you make it," but we truly believe it's important that you are cautious of what you say about yourself and your financial situation. By no means are we telling you to spend what you don't have. We are, however, encouraging you to be mindful of what you call yourself and the things you say. Instead of saying, "I'm broke," consider saying, "That's not in my budget right now." How you view yourself is a crucial part of your new financial framework.

2. **Ask the right questions.** For many of us, our relationship with money is rooted in *someone else's* relationship with money. We watched our parents and grandparents and either adapted their behaviors or did the exact opposite. Again, just as we can't blame ourselves, we can't blame them, either. They likely learned from their parents, and these relationships are a direct response to lived realities. But while the origins of our financial trauma may not be our fault, learning from them is our responsibility. Troy was in his twenties when he learned why his parents had lost the family home. His parents' vulnerability and honesty enabled him to know

what to look for and stay away from when it came to financing his own home. **Having conversations about our financial histories creates the blueprint for stronger financial legacies.**

3. **Seek the help you need.** There is absolutely no shame in asking for help when you need it. As many people have begun to explore healing financial trauma, financial therapy has become a more widely available and acceptable resource. Financial therapists work with their clients to address specific financial traumas that impact their economic conditions and daily life. This is a great opportunity for those who will need more intensive assistance in healing financial trauma. Additionally, certified financial advisers and accountants stand ready to aid you in making better financial decisions. Many banks have them on staff or can refer you to those affiliated with them. Last, seeing a doctor or therapist to address the physical and emotional manifestations of financial trauma is just as important as seeking out financial experts.

4. **Put parameters in place.** Once you've been able to identify the roots of your financial trauma and the behaviors associated with them, instituting boundaries for yourself will be important. Earlier, we offered the suggestion of waiting a specific time period before making a purchase if you're an emotional shopper. If you spend excessively, you may want to consider switching to prepaid debit cards or setting up spending alerts until you get it under control. If you refuse to spend money and it's becoming an issue for you or in your relationships, you may consider instituting a "self-care" or "fun" day every

few weeks that will get you in the habit of spending money and using it for other purposes. These parameters and boundaries will be unique to you and your situation. But it's going to be important for you to create and maintain them.

5. **Hold weekly or monthly "money meetings" with yourself.** More than just going over your monthly or weekly budget, this is also an opportunity to survey your spending and saving habits from the perspective of your experiences and evaluate whether you're operating from your financial trauma. Instead of just asking why you made or didn't make a purchase, sit with the emotional patterns and behaviors that ground your decision making. This is the beginning of developing the strategies you need to cultivate a financial freedom that isn't rooted in your past trauma or mistakes.

6. **Start by saving small, and build from there.** If saving money has been one of your greatest challenges, start small. It sounds simple because it is. We'll talk more about building a detailed budget in the next chapter, but for now, consider starting with a small amount—say, $5 to $15—a week. Set a time when you will increase your amount, by either a percentage or a specific dollar amount. This is one of the easiest ways to begin trusting yourself with your own money.

7. **Buy it and keep it.** For some of us, the issue isn't saving money; it's spending it. It's possible to have experienced some financial trauma that makes spending money seem like the one thing that doesn't make sense. But that's exactly what we want you to do. This may be one of the

few times you'll hear us tell you to go shopping for your financial and emotional health! Consider making a purchase of something you can easily afford but would never buy for yourself because you think it's not worth it. Buying it will be an opportunity to create and solidify your agency in your relationship with money.

8. **Expect and accept gifts.** It sounds crazy, but think about it: So many of us grew up not receiving what we wanted—if anything at all—for birthdays and Christmas, due to financial restraints, and now we answer "Nothing" whenever someone asks us what we want. Growing up with lack or believing we were financial burdens keeps us from having meaningful experiences in our relationships. We all deserve to be treated well and cherished by the people in our lives. Just because your family couldn't afford it doesn't mean you should deny yourself the joy of receiving gifts and other tangible forms of love and care.

Financial trauma should be treated as seriously as any medical or emotional condition. We can't always control what we've experienced, but we can control how it will impact the other aspects of our lives. For people in Black and Brown communities, it can feel like just another way to keep us behind the eight ball—and if we allow others to keep us from accomplishing our financial goals, it can be. But your optimal health and well-being include healthy financial behaviors. Confronting the past can be ugly, but it's necessary. It's time to let all the pain attached to your money go. It's time to move forward.

How you feel about yourself is reflected in your relationship with money. At the end of your journey with this book, we'll come back to this theory. If you found yourself disappointed with the truth of your first reaction, hopefully it will change once you get into the thick of the work we're about to do. You may not have had any control over your initial relationship with money and its impacts on you, but you're making the right decision now. Gaining financial literacy and confronting emotional patterns that affect our finances are the first steps toward achieving economic success and building wealth. You didn't know what you didn't know, but that changes today. The work you will do while reading the next chapters will change your life forever, and it's time. It's time to finally live your life on your own terms.

◆ ◆ ◆

CHAPTER THREE

Creating Annual and Monthly Budgets

Tracy sits at the kitchen table, looking at a stack of bills. Just the sight of them causes a lump in her throat. She doesn't want to open them. In her mind, she doesn't need to. Each envelope contains an amount she owes and a due date by which she needs to pay it, and she already knows she doesn't have the money. She's been here before; she's been here a while. Her anxiety over her mounting debt makes her want to throw the bills in the trash without even opening them. She's done that before.

But unlike before, Tracy is now committed to becoming more financially responsible. That means facing her fears and looking at her bills. She opens each one, jots the amount down in her notebook, and gets to work, looking at her budget to figure out where she can rob Peter to pay Paul. Surprisingly, she's got a bit of room, and it's not as tight as it's been before. She lists her bills, balances her budget, and finds that she has more money left over this month than she did last month. She breathes a sigh of relief.

The reality is that Tracy's been working her new plan, although it's still in the beginning stages. She's trying hard to let go of old habits—including doubting herself and the belief that she can actually become free of all her high-interest debt. Crucial to Tracy's strategy has been her budget, and she's proud of herself for sticking with it. Thanks to her financial blueprints, she's set her goals and made a plan, and now she's gaining momentum.

There is no way that anyone is going to be able to achieve financial freedom and cultivate generational wealth without making up a budget. It's just not going to happen. We know that most people hate budgeting, but it is what it is. If we're being honest, the reality is that most people don't know how to budget. Despite all the online budget templates and how-to videos, for many people it remains one of the most confusing aspects in the journey toward financial freedom.

This chapter is all about demystifying the process. As we break it down, we're going to tell you the truth: Your budget should be one of the most detailed and best-planned documents of your life. It's time to stop getting excited when you find $10 in a coat pocket. You should know where every dime of your money is located and what every penny is doing. Remember when we told you that your money should be working *for* you? Your budget is how that's about to happen. If you're still not sold on the process of making a budget, we'll make it even simpler for you: Every rich person has one. Enough said.

The EYL Money Principle Equation

When it comes to the functions of your money, we've established a formula to help you envision where your money needs to go and what it needs to do:

15% saving

55% spending

10% sharing

20% investing

———————————

100% annual income

Our budgeting framework suggests dividing your income into saving, spending, sharing, and investing. Keep in mind, this is a general framework, not a one-size-fits-all solution. How stable your income is, where you live, and what you're aiming for financially all play huge roles in how you should budget.

For example, if you're dealing with sky-high city living costs, you might have to spend more and save less at the outset. Freelancers or anyone else with a bumpy income should tweak their budget as their earnings fluctuate. Where you are in life matters, too; someone just starting their career will budget differently from someone gearing up for retirement. That's why it's key to keep revisiting and tweaking these percentages to stay on track with your financial goals and life changes.

Using the EYL Money Principle, we're going to give you a template for constructing your overall annual budget and then break it down into a more manageable monthly budget. We'll use our EYL profiles to provide you with real-world examples and give you some opportunities throughout this chapter to create yours along the way. As a matter of fact, if you don't already have a notebook out, we recommend that you grab one right now so you can work alongside us.

Fixed and Variable Expenses

As you create your budget, keep in mind your fixed and variable expenses. Your fixed expenses are the bills you pay monthly that are the same amount. Your mortgage or rent, car note and insurance, and daycare fees are examples of fixed expenses. Your credit card payments, gas, and utilities are examples of variable expenses because the bill and total cost will always reflect the amount of usage. A suggestion for those who are new to budgeting and want to get better control over their finances is to set the amount you plan to pay monthly and not exceed that.

If you set a cap of $250 a month for gas, you know that you're spending roughly $60 per week to fill your tank. That's going to determine where you go and force you to be strategic with your trips and joyriding—and that's okay. The goal is achieving the bigger picture, and keeping it in focus will mean more in the long run.

It's not too hard to figure out how much your fixed expenses are, but it may take a while to catch a rhythm with your variable expenses. The key is to try. This is the only way you'll be able to determine what will or won't work for you. You'll have time to take those evaluations and make the necessary adjustments during your budget review sessions.

Budget Review Sessions

When Damien got serious about his financial goals, he attended a seminar that stressed to him the importance of using the calendar app on his phone as an accountability tool. The speaker said he should set monthly and quarterly reminders to review his budget and track his spending and overall money habits to see if he was still making progress or was falling behind. Damien had never set aside that time to comb through his spending habits before. Once he set those reminders, he noticed himself becoming better informed about his finances and making the necessary adjustments when he saw an issue on the horizon. He found himself checking his account balance less and less out of fear. Tracking his money's movement empowered him and gave him confidence that showed up in other areas of his life. He hadn't realized just how much his financial instability had been weighing on him.

Make up your mind now that you're going to take the time to review your budget and your habits according to the EYL Money Principle. This is the only way to truly track your progress. A budget review session helps you first and foremost to understand that a budget is a living document. The amounts you set in January might need to be tweaked in May; should that happen, you will have four months of data to justify the change.

Budget review sessions also create accountability. The time's past for checking your balance at the ATM with one eye open. You're an adult who wants to be rich and create sustainable generational wealth; it's time to act like one. Remember those "Needed It," "Wanted It," and "What Was I Thinking?" categories from the previous chapter? They will come in handy during each budget review session, and you'll want to keep the list close.

While we're going to work with you to develop annual and monthly budget structures, some people may need to review their budget weekly, and that's absolutely fine. Whatever helps you stay on track of your spending and budget is what you should do. At the same time, if you find yourself checking your account and budget daily and obsessing over the number, it may cause you to develop unhealthy financial behaviors. Start with a week; you should be good. More experienced budgeters may opt for a quarterly review instead of a monthly one, which is fine as well. We also recommend holding the review session for the previous month during the first week of the following month. That way all of your payments from the previous month will have posted and cleared.

Your Annual Budget

Consider your annual budget your road map for the entire year. It plainly and painstakingly lays out everything—and by everything, we mean *everything*. When it comes to your annual budget, there can never be too many line items. As you continue to grow your financial portfolio and embrace wealth as a reality, your line items will continue to expand. This budget should make more sense to you than it does to anybody else. You're living it, and it's your money. Are you ready to get started? Let's go!

Saving

Most people aim to save 5% of their annual income. We'd recommend setting a more ambitious goal of 15%, even if that sounds far off right now. There are a lot of factors that play into why. We've already delved into how past financial traumas impact our money decisions. There's no need to go back there, especially since we're doing what we need to do to heal from those traumas, right? But if you're having a difficult time saving right now, it's important to know that some circumstances truly are beyond our control. Recent studies found that the 15% the average American was saving in 2020 plummeted to around 3.3% in 2023, due to inflation.

Now, here's the truth: Some people *like* to blow money. Even more like to blow money they don't have. Their risky financial behavior reflects a recklessness that they are proud of and want to maintain. But that's not everyone. Most people don't want to live from paycheck to paycheck. It's not fair, when you know you've worked hard, and it doesn't feel good. It takes a toll on every other aspect of your life, and no one deserves that.

We want you to dream big. We can look to the numerous examples of Black excellence to prove that anything is possible. Right now, there's a person in your head whose economic situation is on your vision board. You don't necessarily want to be like them, but their success and financial freedom have created a road map for you to follow. Imagine if they had believed others who told them that achieving their economic dreams wasn't possible. And just as it happened for them, it can absolutely happen for you.

Here's the thing: When you go back to the EYL Thesis for Wealth, you'll see that the ultimate goal is to increase your income. For the majority of us, making more money is a key step in earning our leisure. The problem, though, is that Biggie was right: More money does bring more problems. When you've struggled financially throughout childhood and/or adulthood, there's so much that changes once you begin to make more money. Instinctively, many people will start purchasing the things they've always wanted or taking the trips they never got to take. *Some* of that will be okay. The key word here is *some*. You can't live a current lifestyle of excess and still believe that you'll have enough for your future. It doesn't work that way.

When we say "lifestyle of excess," we don't mean luxury purchases and extravagant spending. Some people will see that and immediately think it doesn't apply to them because they're not buying big-ticket items. But it isn't necessarily about that. **A lifestyle of excess is a pattern of behavior that is ultimately counterproductive to your long-term goals and best interests.** That pattern of behavior can include extravagant spending, but it can be as simple as too many DoorDash orders. Sure, it's raining, you don't feel like going out, and you have the additional $25 and won't miss it. But four DoorDash trips in a month is $100, and a couple of months of that can quickly add up. Nothing is more frustrating than realizing that you spent a dream vacation's worth in food delivery fees in a year, but it absolutely can happen.

Essentially, you should have at least two savings accounts: **general savings** and **emergency savings**. Both should be high-yield interest-bearing accounts to maximize on the return. Look for accounts that offer no monthly maintenance fees and no minimum balance fees to keep your costs down. **Do not put your savings into a long-term investment fund or any account that has a penalty for withdrawal.** The key is to have quick access to your money, should you ever need it.

Emergency savings account: An emergency savings account is just that: for emergencies. This can range from having unexpected car maintenance costs not covered by insurance, such as new tires, or having to go out of town for a family emergency. And because it's solely for emergencies, this savings account should be accessed only for such. The ultimate goal is that an emergency savings account should have a minimum of six months' to a year's worth of expenses available.

If you are just starting an emergency account, you should aim for one to three months. For someone like Dre, who doesn't make enough with his current job and doesn't have any investment or entrepreneurial options to hit his EYL Baseline, we recommend placing a minimum of $100 a month into his emergency savings account. Because Tracy and Gary and Morgan Williams have children, they need to have extra insurance for emergencies. For Tracy, two to three months' worth of expenses might be the max she can save this year, but the Williams household should consider shooting for four to six months. Because he's in an optimal financial position, Corey should be well on his way to a solid six months' worth of expenses saved. Right now, Edwin has less than $200 in his savings account. He really needs to focus on building his.

While you will need to adjust the amount of your emergency savings to any increase in your monthly expenses, we don't recommend going over that six months threshold. Anything additional can be placed in your general savings account or put toward investing.

General savings account: A general savings account is what you'll pull from when your checking account gets low. It's not your rainy day fund; that's your emergency savings. This is where you are actively saving for the things you *want*. It may be where you stash the money you're saving for a new car, house, vacation, or luxury ticket item or your dream of going back to school. Of the two, your general savings account will be the most often accessed.

Though you will be saving for a number of things at once, it's best to allocate your general savings budget based on priority. Dre wants to have a place of his own, so the majority of his budget is going to go toward saving to be able to afford rent. For Tracy, a 70/30 split will allow her to save more for the down payment on her house and still save for new furniture. Gary and Morgan Williams have already set the amount they want to set aside for their children's college fund, and the first won't be heading off for three more years. A year before that, they want to take their first luxury vacation without the kids. Saving more toward the vacation than the college fund is a good strategy because, after the trip, all the money can go toward the kids' college. As Corey begins to think about the future, his general savings account will be centered on an engagement ring and a childcare fund. As Edwin drastically shifts his budget to cut unnecessary expenses, he will need to place it all in his savings.

Here's an opportunity for you to establish your annual savings budget: Decide how much of your annual income, after taxes, will go toward your savings, whether it's the full 15% or you need to aim for something lower. Then break it down further and allocate what will go into your emergency savings account and what will go into your general savings. We recommend placing a minimum of 15% of your total savings budget into your emergency savings account—or more, depending on your risk tolerance and circumstances. If you can save more, do it! This is just a starting point.

FIVE STEPS TO BUILDING BETTER PERSONAL CREDIT

No matter how much we may hate it, the saying is true: Credit is king. How much credit you have and how well you've maintained your credit score will determine if you'll have access to any more credit and will be the difference between a high interest rate and a low one on a credit card or loan. At the end of the day, none of us wants to pay more in interest than we need to. A healthy credit score is an essential component of your financial future and a core component of financial freedom.

Here are five steps to build better personal credit.

1. Evaluate your credit score.

Before you can fix your credit score, you need to know what it is. You're allowed to request one free credit report per year from each of the three major credit reporting bureaus (Equifax, Experian, and TransUnion). You can go to their websites to sign up, and you can also go to Annual Credit Report.com, where you can get access to all three in one place. Additionally, most banks and credit unions now provide links to these services from their website or app. You should never have to pay to check your credit score.

There are five components of your credit score:

Payment history: 35%

Current debt: 30%

Length of credit history: 15%

Types of credit: 10%

New credit: 10%

As you can see, several factors go into your credit score, but none is as important as your payment history and how much you currently owe.

2. Sign up for credit monitoring.

There are several services that will monitor you credit score and report. You can receive an alert anytime there's activity regarding your credit. You can also utilize services that enable you to "lock" your credit until you're ready to use it and then "unlock" it. We recommend using credit-monitoring services that focus more on your FICO score for reporting and alerts.

3. Dispute incorrect charges.

You're going to want to pay off every single balance on your credit report in the hope that it will drastically improve your score. Don't . . . because it won't. Your creditors have to keep updated records that you owe what they say you owe, even if they sell the debt to another company. If they can't prove you owe the amount on your report, they have to cease the collection and remove it from your report. You might be surprised at what's incorrectly on your credit report. When you sign up and pay for a credit report monitoring and dispute resolution service, the service does the work of contacting creditors and cleaning up your report for you.

4. Establish a plan to pay down debt.

If you're going to get into a better financial situation, you've got to do better than you have been. If some of us looked at what we've been spending our money on and how much, we'd cringe. Saving and applying "extra" money to bills never hurt anybody. And you may not like talking to creditors, but you can't avoid them forever. That's how some of us got into this mess in the first place! Start out by setting aside an hour to contact your creditors and ask for lower payment amounts or interest rates. Lower payment amounts will mean your repayment schedule will be longer, but it's okay if that's what you need right now to become more financially stable. Get on the phone and talk to somebody. More people are willing to help you than not. It's also about accountability. We've all got to take some.

5. Use credit-enhancing tools.

To begin to establish more accounts with a positive payment history, you can:

- **Set up a credit-building loan.** Essentially, the loan works as a savings account. You make monthly payments for a set time, and at the end of that period, you receive the loan amount to do with as you wish.

- **Get a secure credit card.** We recommend selecting a credit card that will report to all three credit bureaus as if it is an unsecured line of credit. This will boost your credit score more than reporting it as a secured card will. After making your first five or six on-time payments, an unsecured credit limit increase is usually possible.

- **Ask a family member or trusted friend to include you as an authorized user on their credit card.** Admittedly, this is a bit trickier because it requires someone else's consent, and folks don't play around about their credit! In this instance, you're asking them if you can be listed as an authorized user on their credit account so that as they pay their bills, your credit score will increase. You're not asking them to be allowed to use the account; you don't even need access to it. You just need to be *on* the account. If you have someone in a solid financial position with a really good credit score and a history of making payments on time, don't be afraid to ask them. Make them aware of your goals and the steps you are taking to clean up your credit and establish your financial freedom. Reiterate that you're not asking for access to their account. You may even offer to kick in a set amount each month toward the bill for a year to show your commitment. Most important, if they say no, don't take it personally. You can still get to where you need to be without doing this.

You can get a financial adviser to coach you through these steps, or it's possible to do them on your own. Regardless of what option you choose, know that it will take some time and discipline, but healthier credit and a higher credit score are attainable. Where you are now isn't where you have to remain. All you have to do is put in the work!

Spending

How many times has the money you spent been productive? By productive, we mean spending money in ways that make sense. In the exercise in the last chapter, you'll remember that we asked you to divide your spending into three categories: "Needed It," "Wanted It," and "What Was I Thinking?" Those are placed in the order you should be spending. The "Needed It" category is self-explanatory. Bills and essentials are always going to go there. "Wanted It" spending is important, too. Even as we're working to earn our leisure and build our financial future, we deserve to have good things. The key here is not to have more "Wanted It" purchases or money spent in that category than "Needed It."

"What Was I Thinking?" spending trips us all up. It can be everything from completely blowing your Homecoming budget to post-breakup emotional shopping to swiping and swiping that debit card without a care in the world, because you know the money's there. Spending without any purpose or function is equivalent to throwing money away. When you're trying to secure your financial future, you can't afford to spend aimlessly.

Productive spending is ensuring that your basic needs are fully covered and that your wants are enjoyed in moderation. This might mean that you become your own barista at home and enjoy Starbucks just two or three times a week instead of every day. DoorDash can become a biweekly or monthly indulgence instead of what you're doing now. Every dollar you make isn't going to be spent (because you're saving some of them). At the same time, every dollar you spend should be respected.

Depending on how much you're putting into your "Savings" and "Sharing" budgets, your "Spending" budget will range between 55% and 70% of your annual income. We're going to assume that you're using the standard EYL 55%. That means that if your annual income is $75,000 after taxes, your annual "Spending" budget will be $41,250. As you're going through this exercise, you might want to begin with the amount of your annual "Spending" budget. Remember, you're adjusting from your "Saving" and "Sharing" budgets. You want to keep your "Investment" budget at the minimum 10%, eventually increasing it to the EYL standard of 20%.

Just like your annual "Saving" budget, your "Sharing" budget should be extremely detailed. Everything should have a line item. Keeping additional checking accounts to categorize your expenses may be really helpful. Again, whatever helps you make sense of your money is what you need to do to make sense of your money. Here are the categories to include in your annual spending budget.

Personal expenses include all expenses directly related to you. They include your personal cellphone bill, car note, insurance, organization membership dues, clothing, physical fitness memberships and activities, personal maintenance, student loan payment, food delivery, and entertainment. Anything that is an expense that is solely applicable to you and/or that you are responsible for should be listed here.

Household expenses include all expenses related to the upkeep of your home. They include rent or mortgage, utilities, groceries, and other household needs. We understand that you may be responsible for all of these bills yourself. However, separating them from your other expenses will enable you to see how much of your "Spending" budget is being allocated to the house.

Family expenses include all expenses related to your family and its needs. They include daycare, before and after school care, child support, insurance, and other family-related costs. If you have school-aged children, we suggest budgeting for field trips and other miscellaneous expenses that may arise throughout the school year. If you are caring for an aging or ill parent or family member, your contribution to their care should also be a line item here. Note that this is different from the resources dedicated in your "Sharing" budget; that is only to help family members when needs arise. Any support that you are consistently responsible for should be budgeted.

Using the EYL template of 55% of your annual income, create your annual spending budget. Separate your expenses into "Personal," "Household," and "Family." Write down every expense for each category and what they would total for the year. This is also when you can revisit the concept of variable expenses to set the total amount of a particular expense that you don't want to exceed for the year.

Sharing

Whenever people from our community win an award, who are the first people they thank? God and their mamas. They know that their success would have been impossible without a higher power and the sacrifices of loved ones. None of us got here on our own. Even those who claim that they're "self-made" had assistance along the way. Whether a family member or a friend, a teacher or a community leader, somebody loved us and somebody believed in us. We are able to live our dreams and operate at our highest capacity because of that love and belief. This truth is what grounds the principle of sharing money.

Sharing your money includes giving tithes and offerings to churches and religious organizations, donating to local organizations and universities, and helping family and friends in need. For the most part, what you share should not come out of what you're saving—unless it is an extreme emergency and you can't access the amount needed from your general checking account. And those instances should be few and far between.

Your annual "Sharing" budget **is your giving threshold.** Unless the circumstances are unprecedented, you don't want to go over this amount. Many people choose to make this about 10% of their annual income. For someone making $75,000 a year after taxes, that means their annual budget would be $7,500. Traditionally, Christians give 10% of their annual earnings, $7,500 in this instance, as a tithe, and Muslims offer 2.5%, or $1,875 in this case. The additional money in your annual "Sharing" budget gives you the ability to donate to various charities and organizations of your choice.

It is also from this budget that you will help your family members *first*. Unless the circumstances require that you dip into your spending or savings (this should be your last option), you should pull from your "Sharing" budget to assist others. This is the only part of your budget that is set aside to give other people money. It ensures that you don't overextend yourself. And when the money's gone, it's okay to say "no."

For those of us who come from marginalized families and communities, there will always be a need. And while someone will always need help, you can't help everyone. Creating an annual amount for assisting others and refusing to exceed it will be key. We know this will be hard in the beginning. Here are two habits to consider employing.

1. **Never feel pressured to give 100% of what's requested.** This will allow you to help other people as well. Remember, you're not someone's personal bank.

2. **Get comfortable with saying "no."** Try saying: "I really wish I could help, but right now, I'm not in a position to help. If that changes, I will let you know." *Or* "I can help; however, I'm able to offer only [insert amount]."

Here's a chance for you to set up your annual "Sharing" budget. After determining the amount (15%) of your annual income that will be placed into it, it's time to set the allocations. If you are a person of faith and already have an established commitment to your religious institution, designate that annual contribution. The remaining balance is what you have left to donate to charities and offer to loved ones in need. We suggest setting either a monthly budget for giving or a specific amount per situation/circumstance. This will ensure that you have additional resources to share throughout the year. Remember, your annual "Sharing" budget is the one from which you offer assistance, *not* from your "Spending" or "Saving" budget.

Investing

A minimum of 20% of your annual income should go toward your annual "Investing" budget. So if you're making $75,000 after taxes, you will have $15,000 to invest over the course of the year.

Investing can be scary, and many people believe that there's entirely too much risk involved. We know. At the same time, you're going to have to be willing to take risks and make big leaps if you truly want a life of financial freedom. The key to releasing your fear will be finding the right suite of investments for you and your goals.

A myth among many people is that there's only one kind of investment: stocks. That's not the only road to wealth there is. Some people do extremely well with real estate, ETFs, crypto, and other investment vehicles that come with different levels of risk and return. We break down the various types of investments in the next section of the book, but right now, it's important to us that you establish that you have room in your budget to make investments.

Now it's your turn to establish your annual investing budget. You'll come back and flesh out this budget later, once you've determined which investment types and strategies work best for you. In the meantime, consider that 20% of your annual income that you're setting aside is for the procurement of your financial freedom.

Tackling Credit Card Debt

So many people carry shame when it comes to credit cards. Either they're embarrassed that their credit is too shot for them to be approved for a better one, or they're frustrated about the balances they're carrying on the ones they do have. Currently, the national average per capita credit card debt hovers around $6,800. Studies have found that while fewer members of Black and Brown communities have personal credit cards, they are more likely to have the lowest credit scores and pay the highest interest rates. Wherever you find yourself in these stats, this can be a recipe for disaster if it's not handled now.

Carrying excessive debt means that an unexpected emergency has the potential to send you into a financial tailspin. And even if you're paying them in full, having too many monthly credit card payments can set you back when it comes to achieving your other financial goals. When it comes to creating a solid budget, tackling any credit card debt you may have will be essential. If you find yourself in a tough spot, here are some ways to address it before building your budget:

1. **List all of your credit card debt.** Before you pay anything off, take a moment to list how much credit card debt you have. Make a list with this information for each card: name, type of credit card (general/store/airline/gas), current balance, credit limit, interest rate, payment terms, minimum monthly payment.

2. **Determine the maximum amount you can pay each month.** If you don't pay your credit card balance in full each month, paying the minimum amount is not a strategy that will help you eliminate your credit card debt anytime soon. Take a look at the areas you've previously identified as unnecessary spending and determine how

much of that you can add to your minimum payment every month to pay down your debt quickly and with less interest.

3. **Use one of these strategies to pay your credit card debt.** When it comes to paying off credit card debt, these three strategies have proven to be the most effective:

- **Option one:** Focus on paying off all high-interest debt (10% rate or higher) first before moving on to the next credit card.

- **Option two:** Employ the "snowball method," which means paying off the credit card with the smallest balance first and then taking the payment from that credit card and adding it to the monthly payment of the next smallest credit card debt to begin eliminating that.

- **Option three:** Consolidate your credit card debt by using balance transfers or accessing the equity in your home. While a balance transfer often has an associated fee of 3% to 5% of the amount, it's a great way to move high-interest credit card debt to a card with lower interest. Also, while a home equity line of credit will most likely have associated closing costs, the interest rate is likely to be much lower than your credit card's.

4. **Use unexpected financial wins to pay down debt.** If eliminating credit card debt is your focus, this is an opportunity to put everything—from a bonus to the first few months of a raise to the $5 your grandma still slips into your hand for "gas money"—toward it. Using these

wins to pay off your credit card debt won't last forever, especially since it's one of the fastest ways to eliminate it.

5. **Buy with cash.** There's nothing like putting yourself on a "credit card time-out" and making purchases in cash to evaluate if you truly need them or not. Putting the credit card away and swiping the debit card can help you avoid too much emotional spending and overspending, as well as the interest that accrues with making credit card purchases that you don't pay off each month.

Also, don't forget that you have the power to change your situation, simply by picking up the phone. Taking an hour or two out of your day to get on the phone to discuss potential options, such as renegotiating your interest rate, can go a long way. While creditors still want their money and will hold you accountable for paying, they are more willing to work with you if you're honest and up front about what you need and why. Credit card debt will always seem overwhelming unless you have a strategic plan to address it.

The Power of Automation

Our EYL community member Jackie couldn't stop laughing when her friend suggested that she begin automating her financial life. "That's for rich people," Jackie said before she even realized what she was saying.

She's not alone. So many people think that putting your financial tasks, such as paying bills and making account transfers, on autopilot is something you can do only once you know you have more than enough money to cover the transactions. In truth, only part of Jackie's concern was her financial reality; the bigger issue was the fear she had that was associated with a lack of control and the idea that one mistake could set her back.

Jackie's right in that automating your finances is giving up control and deciding to be less hands-on in a literal sense. When you automate your bill payments, you might not actually review your bills because you're sort of in "set it and forget it" mode. Automating balance transfers might mean that you don't take the time to review and make any adjustments to account for changes in your income or financial goals. These are valid concerns for anyone who wants to cultivate healthier financial habits and is afraid that they might be making a bad decision. However, the cons of automation don't outweigh the pros.

Automating bill paying is a wealth-building strategy that saves us not only time but money. Automation enables you to take the time you would spend paying bills and focus on other more important things. Additionally, many companies offer an incentive, such as a percentage off your monthly bill, if you sign up for autopay. And signing up for autopay means that you're less likely to miss a payment and incur a late fee or additional interest. For those who are worried about autopay, when you couple it with your budget review sessions, you are less likely to fall into the trap of not reviewing bills or making adjustments to transfers.

Before diving headfirst into automation, here are some things you need to do:

1. **Review your money movements.** Studying your cash flow before setting up automatic payments is the first key to success. This means that you will track when money comes in and when it goes out every month. You'll make a note of the dates of each deposit and withdrawal.

2. **Match deposits and withdrawals to your monthly expenses.** This doesn't necessarily mean that you pay

your bills the exact same day that you receive your deposits. However, you need to track how close your paydays are to your due dates. With this done, you can begin crafting an automation system that will cluster certain bills together.

3. **Start with your fixed expenses.** Beginning your automation journey with your fixed expenses—such as your car payment, mortgage or rent, phone and cable bills, and insurance payments—is the easiest way to get started. Additionally, being late with those payments tends to accrue significant late fees.

4. **Wait four to six months before automating your variable payments.** Using autopay requires discipline. For some, building the capacity to automate variable payments will mean establishing more financial breathing room in their budget.

5. **Automate retirement contributions and transfers into a savings account from your paycheck.** When you set up the automatic withdrawal of retirement contributions and savings, you are best able to structure your finances around the EYL Money Principle. Not only does it give you the opportunity to build wealth through your paycheck, it gives you a clearer picture of how much money you have to work with.

Anybody can automate their payments, and everyone should. If you're afraid to do so, start small with one or two of your smallest fixed expense bills and commit to adding a bill to your automation schedule every other month until all your bill payments are automated. Take some time during your budget review session to assess your autopay schedule. How is it going? Would it create more breathing room in your budget and less stress if you adjusted your autopay schedule to deduct certain payments later, by requesting a new payment date? These are questions you need to ask and answer as you begin to develop strategies that will give you more control over your financial future.

Start Somewhere

We believe our EYL Money Principle Equation of 15% + 55% + 10% + 20% = 100% is the best way to structure your income. At the same time, we recognize that not everyone is there yet. Even if you have to start small, we want you to start somewhere. More than anything, we want you to stop putting the overwhelming majority of your money into your "Spending" budget. If this is happening, either your expenses are too high or you don't have enough income to do anything else. In either case, it's going to be important for you to take a serious inventory of how much is coming in, what's going out, and why so that you can make some serious changes.

If you're trying to prioritize your money movements, we recommend that you build your emergency savings fund first. Anything can happen, and in a postpandemic world, we understand that in ways we never thought we would. Having adequate resources should an emergency or immediate need arise brings its own sense of peace and security. Your emergency savings fund needs to be established, and it needs to be able to sustain you. Have a plan to ensure that it becomes what you need it to be.

After your emergency savings fund, we recommend that you establish your investment budget. This may sound a little harsh, so we apologize in advance: Even if you don't give away another dollar this year, people are going to be okay. They really are. Aside from the agencies and organizations that have been established to help people in need, people will find a way when their backs are against the wall. We talk about this more in chapter 9, but some of you are going to have to seriously ask why people have made *you* their financial plan. They know that you'll give them the money, and there is something in you that needs to do that. But why are you giving it to them at the expense of your future? A strong, dynamic investment portfolio is the key to building generational wealth and earning your leisure. You can't deprive yourself of the very thing that you want because you're too busy helping everyone else. In the end, it's irresponsible and helps no one—especially you.

Some of you are in a position to meet or exceed the standard minimums in our EYL Money Principle Equation. This is a good thing and suggests that you have the income you need to make your money begin to produce the kind of financial future you want to see.

When it comes to additional resources to allocate, we suggest designating them in your "Investing" and "Saving" budgets first. Ideally, the more money you have at your disposal, the more you should invest. This is the best way to see your money come back to you. A second option is your general savings fund. You can stash your money there until you decide what you want to do with it. Don't let it sit for more than three months without developing a solid plan for how it will work for you. Either way, the point is to get out of the habit of immediately spending first or saving with no purpose (once you've established your emergency savings fund).

Congratulations! You just established your first budget based on the EYL Money Principle! Here's what we can guarantee: Once you've gotten the hang of how to craft your budget based on your needs, you will never go without one again.

Reorienting your relationship with money is key to establishing the kind of financial freedom you desire. The truth is that many people simply don't want to do this work—and it is work. You're going to have to set some serious time aside to get your finances into order. And that's truth whether you're a millionaire or you're just trying your best to make ends meet. Establishing a personal economic system for ourselves should be one of the most important and intensive things we do.

Now that you have the bones and the structure for how to categorize your money and put it to work, it's time to learn how to make more of it. By now we hope you're recognizing just how possible financial freedom is for you to achieve. Without question, you're going to have to work for it, but nothing worth having ever comes easy.

B Side

Building Wealth

You've shifted your mindset and reassessed your relationship with money. You've addressed your financial traumas and realized that a budget can be your best friend. Now it's time to start making money!

There are a lot of misconceptions when it comes to building wealth. Some people think you must have a lot of money to start making more money. Others think all wealth-building strategies are scams and get-rich-quick schemes. In this section, we're going to spend time on the myths and false narratives that we hear the most. We'll also keep it real and be honest about the risky business that is wealth building. Then we'll break down examples of short-term and long-term investments.

To do this, we're going to help you assess your current financial situation and risk tolerance to determine which investment strategy makes the most sense for you. We'll break down key asset classes and show you how to select the ones that will create a diversified portfolio that reflects not only your financial goals but also your tastes and interests. Then we'll go into the specifics you'll need to execute your strategy—from opening a brokerage account to placing trades to monitoring your investments over time.

Wealth building sounds much more intimidating than it actually is. In its simplest form, it means taking advantage of avenues and opportunities that yield the economic benefits to secure your financial future. What that system will look like is entirely up to you. Here's where, with the proper education and information, you can be creative. Let's get started!

◆ ◆ ◆

CHAPTER FOUR

The Keys to the Kingdom

Bashir, another one of our community members, is a fifty-year-old high school math teacher living on the outskirts of Houston, Texas. As much as he knew he always wanted to be a teacher, he also knew he was choosing a career in which he would be underpaid. It has taken him twenty years in the field to get to an annual salary of $65,000— a feat many of his fraternity brothers surpassed years ago. And while Bashir is proud to shape the minds of the next generation, he wishes he could do it with a little more in his bank account.

At fifty, Bashir has become more financially responsible. During the initial years, when he was fresh out of college and well into his early thirties, he spent more than he made. Due to weekends he spent hanging out with his friends and trying to date beyond his means, his bank account was often overdrawn. But as he got tired of renting and wanted a more stable lifestyle, he made a commitment to achieving economic stability. He cleaned up his credit, created a sustainable budget, and is able to provide for his longtime companion and their seven-year-old son.

One of Bashir's fraternity brothers came to him with an investment opportunity. A local restaurateur had been extremely successful with one food truck. While many thought his success was a fluke, due only to the COVID-19 pandemic, the business had been extremely steady, making over $2 million annually in revenue over the past three years. Though many would have taken this success as a sign to open a brick-and-mortar establishment, the restaurateur preferred to add a second food truck and was looking for investors. He created a proposal, offering 25% equity for a $125,000 investment.

Before that opportunity was presented to him, Bashir had never considered investing in a business. On some level, he didn't think anything like that was possible on a teacher's salary. Yet as he had elevated his own financial profile, he'd placed himself in a position to be a solid investor. While the restaurateur was asking for an investment to cover the full cost of a food truck, which wasn't cheap, Bashir wouldn't have to make the investment alone; it would be split among him and four others, giving them each 5% of the 25% equity. If the profit projections were correct, Bashir would clear a minimum of $75,000 after the first year, making his $25,000 investment right back. After having an attorney and financial adviser look over the offer, Bashir joined his fraternity brothers in the investment.

Maybe you don't have an attorney or financial adviser as Bashir does. Even without them, you can still be able to identify a good investment opportunity when it's presented to you. **The first—and probably most important—aspect of a good investment opportunity is that it has clearly defined the way it will make money.** For Bashir, the investment proposal detailed the price of each item, the costs of production, and a schedule that positioned the truck in areas with high foot traffic during peak sales hours. The proposal included projections of potential revenue and broke down the expected profit that could be made off each item, paying special attention to fan favorites. Like Bashir, you need to understand how an investment will generate overall revenue.

Another sign of a good investment opportunity is that the investment is in a growing market. The failure rate for food trucks can be high, with many closing in the first year due to low customer turnout. But the pandemic had left many people working from home looking for convenient, socially distanced food options—and a thriving new food truck scene had emerged around the parks in town. The first truck's exceptional earnings were more akin to a bustling small restaurant, signaling that a second food truck made sense.

When evaluating a potential investment opportunity, you want to make sure it's in a solid and/or growing market. A large and growing market means more revenue, potential customers, and opportunities to scale up. Making money is, after all, the ultimate goal. We'll talk about key indicators of success, like expanding customer bases, steady revenue growth, and alignment with new social, technological, or economic trends.

While we don't want to deter you from investing in emerging markets, if you want to do so, taking time to do the research would be a wise idea. Though risk is inherent in every investment opportunity, an emerging market may not provide enough data to determine if the risk will be worth the potential reward.

At its most basic level, an investment is a type of trade. You are providing financial resources so that the business can continue operations or the investment can make you money. In turn, you're being offered a percentage or full ownership of the business. And while the numbers will depend on the size of the investment and its projected performance in the market, how much you invest should remain proportionate to what you're being offered. Here's a tip from us: Never be afraid to negotiate for more equity. An infusion of money makes things move and shake for a business. Your investment is making that happen.

A $25,000 investment was difficult to raise. Bashir had only

$35,000 saved, and dipping into his 401(k) was out of the question. The idea of making the investment worried his partner. If the investment were to turn out bad, it would set their small family back for quite some time. Even after making the investment, Bashir needed to be reassured that he had done the right thing. His attorney assured him that the numbers made sense. The projection of $1.25 million in revenue was aligned with the restaurateur's game plan and vision for his business.

Two years after making the investment, Bashir and his fraternity brothers had made more than their initial investments back. Due to great sales, Bashir's return was $175,000. That allowed him to put the $25,000 he had invested back into his savings account, propose to his partner, and put a down payment on the house they'd been eyeing. Additionally, he met with a financial adviser to craft a plan to diversify his investment portfolio. Based on the success and stability of the food truck, he has an opportunity to make new investments and take even bigger chances.

Why Invest?

Are you looking to supplement your income or fund your living expenses so you can add more to your monthly budget? Are you trying to generate enough income for a down payment on a home, as Bashir was? Or are you seeking to build a nest egg over the next couple of years because the idea of your Social Security running out doesn't align with the future you envision? Or is it (D) all of the above?

Determining why you want to invest will, in the long run, enable you to decide upon the most effective investment strategies and approaches.

1. **Short-term goals:** Whether it's a car, vacation, or wedding, this goal can be accomplished in two years or

less. Investment strategies with a quick turnaround are optimal.

2. **Medium-term goals:** Saving for a down payment or enough to send your child to college, even storing up enough to start a small business, will take time. Depending on your financial situation and the price of what you're saving up for, you may be looking at three to six years. When considering investments, you don't want anything that will tie your money up beyond that time.

3. **Long-term goals:** When it comes to saving for retirement, building generational wealth, or achieving financial freedom and independence, slow and steady wins the race. Investments that will take seven years or longer to fully mature and turn significant profits are what should interest you most.

Aisha, a thirty-eight-year-old earning $45,000 a year, wanted to go to ESSENCE Festival with her girls for her fortieth birthday. To make it the ultimate girls' trip and birthday weekend, she was hoping for floor seats to all the concerts, VIP passes, and a suite in one of New Orleans' luxury hotels. With its price tag of close to $6,000, Aisha needed a serious strategy. To make it happen, she cut back on eating out and began working for DoorDash and Instacart. That created an additional $500 per month. She set up automatic transfers to invest $300 a month in a brokerage account split between an S&P 500 index fund and a travel stock fund. The other $200 went into a high-yield savings account for spending money on the trip. By starting with $2,000 and staying disciplined, she saw her investments grow to $10,000 by the time she needed to book her travel. That was more than enough for "Aisha Takes ESSENCE Festival," and with the remainder, she established a travel fund and began planning to take a major trip every two years.

Even though Bashir's decision to invest in the food truck happened sooner than he had expected, it was in alignment with his medium-term goals. Whether he decides to reinvest in the food truck or take advantage of another investment opportunity, he accomplished his initial goal. That gave him the data and information he needs to reevaluate other opportunities based on his previous performance and what he is and isn't willing to risk the next time around.

When it comes to saving for the long haul, one person might start by automatically investing 10% of their salary into a diversified retirement fund, watching it grow over decades through employer matches and market gains, eventually allowing for an early retirement. Another family might invest in a balanced mix of stocks and real estate, inching closer to financial freedom every year as their financial cushion grows.

There are optimal scenarios that will make investing a much more comfortable risk than others—number one being money. Yet investing can be done without it. Now with as little as $1, people are able to enter the market and can begin building their portfolio. So the question of whether you are ready to invest doesn't come down solely to your available resources and the financial runway you need to make it happen. Ultimately, it boils down to whether you are ready to do what it takes to get started. So much has changed in recent years. At one time, investors could go only to a traditional brokerage firm to buy stocks. Now you can use robo-advisers, online financial planning tools powered by algorithms, and various investment apps such as Robinhood, E*Trade, Acorns, Stash, and Coinbase. These apps provide the best of traditional investing strategies and marry them with the technology and convenience that all of us have come to enjoy, making building wealth much easier than before.

In addition to deciding what kind of investor you want to be, you'll need to take some time to decide how you will establish your investment portfolio. **This process, which is known as asset allocation, is crucial because it is the most strategic and effective way to reach your financial goals.** This is where you will look at your goals and the time frame in which you want to meet them and match that with the asset class that works best. Creating the "right" formula for you will take some effort. Financial advisers say that there's no "perfect" asset allocation strategy. And while that may be true, in the next chapter we outline an asset allocation model that's worked well for members of the EYL community.

Depending on your goals and what you have to work with, your investing timeline to achievement will differ. And there are a number of factors to be considered.

In her work as a financial therapist and coach, Barbara Hudson offers that wealth has four stages: survival, stability, wealth, affluence. Using our EYL players, we'll work through Hudson's definition of each.

Survival: Financial survival mode includes living paycheck to paycheck, the chronic inability to pay bills on time, and a consistent lack of enough money to cover your basic necessities and desires. Survival mode is also marked by financial trauma, insecurity, and inferior thinking. Tracy, Dre, and Edwin would be considered as living in financial survival mode. None of them have enough money to cover their current needs, and they often find themselves either scrambling at the end of the month or accepting that they won't have enough to pay their bills.

Stability: Financial stability is marked by steady income, healthy credit, and the ability to pay your bills in full and on time. Whether you're paying rent or a mortgage, you can comfortably afford it. Your savings are robust and can cover emergency and infrequent expenses without throwing your budget into a tailspin. Corey and the Williams family fall into this category. If this is your situation, you're likely financially stable enough to begin investing if you can meet these basic criteria:

1. You've established your emergency fund or are 85% to 90% there.

2. You have a solid retirement plan.

3. You're able to fully reconcile your monthly budget and have money left over at the end of each month.

Wealth: At this stage, you've outgrown suffering from constant fear or worry over your account balances and are in a position to spend your time focused on the things and people that matter most. Currently, none of our EYL players is in the wealth stage, but that's why they *and you* are here.

Affluence: An affluent person has the ability to leverage their wealth for things beyond money—like influence and power. This doesn't necessarily mean you're a billionaire with an absurd amount of money. In Black and Brown communities, people who would be considered simply "wealthy" elsewhere can be deemed to be affluent, depending on how they use and express their wealth.

Aisha would be considered to be in survival mode, while Bashir is squarely in the financial stability stage. The food truck investment opportunity opened up a world of possibilities for him, and he began to explore what other wealth-building strategies were available. With this investment, Bashir's financial portfolio wasn't just his teacher's salary and pension anymore; he had a chance to create the kind of economic stability and streams of income he had thought were available only to other people. And as he surveyed the wealth-building landscape, he quickly learned what was and wasn't for him.

What About Debt?

Having debt can make it difficult to invest, but it is not impossible to do so. What matters is the kind of debt you have.

High-interest debt: Anything with an interest rate above 10% falls into this category, which typically includes credit cards and installment payments on things like furniture. In most instances, you'll want to pay this down as much as possible before investing.

Low-interest debt: Personal loans, car loans, and lines of credit are considered low interest. Investing while having these outstanding balances is much more ideal, as with proper budgeting, you have more disposable income than those with high-interest debt do.

Tax-deductible debt: Think student loans, business and investment loans, and mortgages. This is the "best" kind of debt to have. As it's generally also low interest, you can easily build an investment portfolio while you chip away at it. One possible strategy as you pay the debt down is to use the money you save on interest to begin investing.

Most people assume that they have to completely eliminate their debt before they can start. But doing that takes time and money that might be better directed toward your investing efforts. Think of it this way: you want to give your money as much time as possible to mature and make more of itself. As long as you're not carrying high-interest debt and you're making on-time payments and paying down as much as you can, you can work the plan.

A common initial strategy is to tackle debt with the steepest interest rates first and then start directing that same monthly payment amount into investments. When Peter and Yolanda got married, their joint credit rating was horrible. Neither of them believed they had enough breathing room to dream and create long-term goals. All they knew was that they wanted to start a family eventually and couldn't do it with all their debt. The couple gave themselves five years to eliminate their high-interest debt—which was the bulk of what they owed—and make a significant dent in their student loans. Though both of them had jobs, their checks were already stretched to the max and there was no wiggle room.

They took a huge risk, dipping into their 401(k)s and taking out just enough to place into a high-yield savings account, a CD, and a credit-rebuilding savings account that reported their monthly payments to the credit bureaus. Between the two of them, they invested $10,000 across those three options and agreed not to touch any of the money for the first four years. With interest rates at 5% and 6%, their investments garnered them an additional $2,000 and a higher credit score. That put them into a better position to refinance loans and turn the tide on their financial future. They were even able to take some of that $2,000 and invest it in the stock market, thus taking another step toward creating the kind of freedom and generational wealth that will make life easier for the children they were growing more confident that they would be able to afford.

You've Got Options

Now let's cover the basics of the various investment classes and the risks associated with each. Below are some of the more standard and proven types.

Stocks

When you purchase a stock, you are investing in a company. Through that stock, you are buying a share, or a predetermined portion, of the company's profits and assets. A stock can pay an investor in two ways: Its value can rise and the investor can sell it for a profit, or it can pay dividends, which are periodic distributions of the company's earnings. Whether through profit taking or dividend payments, stocks can be used for long-term wealth building or generating income to add to your current budget. Investing in the stock market is especially helpful if you have a goal such as retiring comfortably or funding a major purchase—something that requires long-term rather than short-term investing.

There are eleven market sectors:

- **Communications services:** companies, like Disney and Meta, that are entertainment, telecommunications, and media companies that produce content and provide social media platforms

- **Consumer discretionary:** companies, like Amazon and Ford, that produce goods, cars, and clothing, and include restaurants and hotels

- **Consumer staples:** companies, like Walmart and Procter & Gamble, that produce and sell food, drinks, and household items

- **Energy:** companies, like Chevron and ExxonMobil, that are engaged in the production of oil and gas

- **Financials:** companies, like Bank of America and JPMorganChase, that are banks, investment and brokerage firms, and insurance companies

- **Health:** companies, like Johnson & Johnson and Pfizer, that create and provide healthcare equipment, services, and technology, and engage in biotech and pharmaceutical research and development

- **Industrials:** companies, like Delta and 3M, that manufacture construction and electrical equipment and aerospace and defense equipment and include security, employment, and professional services companies

- **Information technology:** companies, like Apple and Microsoft, that produce and manufacture software, IT products, communications equipment, phones, and computers

- **Materials:** companies, like Sherwin-Williams and Dow, that produce glass, paper, metals, and steel

- **Real estate:** companies, like Simon Property Group and Public Storage, that develop and sell real estate properties and REITs

- **Utilities:** companies, like Duke Energy and PSEG, that provide electricity, gas, and water

It's important to note that stocks often have the highest risk of any investment. A company can lose value or go out of business, leaving its investors with little to no return on their investment. The unpredictability of the market can create the potential for high returns, but there's a greater risk of losing money, especially in the short term. For beginners, an effective and inexpensive way to enter the stock market is to invest in a low-cost index fund that tracks the broader market before beginning to pick individual stocks. For example, an S&P 500 index fund tracks the movements of the top five hundred businesses in the country. While you can start investing with a small amount of money, investing between $500 and $1,000 can help you diversify properly.

Equities

An equity is a stake in a company, whether a stock or purchase option from the company itself. While some use the word *equity* interchangeably with *stock*, they're not necessarily the same. Every share in a stock is a kind of equity, but not all equities are shares. Depending on how it is structured, equity in a company can offer the investor more than just profit shares. Equity could also give an investor a voice and voting power within the company. As the value of the company increases, the investor is able to either make more money through profit shares or sell the equities at a higher price. There are two kinds of company equity; public equity investing refers to purchasing shares of a company that is listed on a stock exchange, whereas private equity investing means investing in a company that isn't listed.

While private equity investing may seem more appealing because of its exclusivity, it often requires being an accredited investor with a high net worth. The exclusive nature of private equity investments makes them available to only a select group of investors. Private equity investing often requires tying up capital for several years. Overall, private equity investments create the opportunity for outsize returns if the company grows rapidly or goes public. Essentially, an outsize return occurs when you invest in a company for less than what it's worth and the company experiences a financial boom. But there is also the risk that the company will fail and all of your investment will be lost. When it comes to equity investments, you should focus on building wealth through public equities first before exploring private equities.

Bonds

Purchasing a bond from a government or a company means that it has your permission to borrow your money and pay you back with interest. A bond is a fixed-income investment, with interest being paid periodically and the principal paid back when the bond reaches maturity. Though there are several types of bonds, here are four of the most common types.

- **Corporate bonds:** These help fund a corporation's operations and expenses, and the investor receives regular interest payments. An investor's risk ultimately depends on the corporation's creditworthiness, the rate of inflation, and the overall state of the economy. Corporate bonds are more stable than stocks, as bondholders are more likely to receive a portion of their initial investment back if a corporation is liquidated or goes bankrupt.

- **Municipal bonds:** These are sold by city governments to improve the city's infrastructure. Because municipal bonds are an investment in the public's well-being, they are considered to be a safe investment and receive a tax break (no federal tax and various state and local exemptions) on the earned interest. Municipal bonds start at a minimum of $5,000, yielding much higher returns—and carrying a greater risk—than government bonds.

- **Government bonds:** These are sold to carry out government functions such as printing money, funding budgets, and paying down debt. U.S. government and agency bonds are considered one of the safest investments, carrying the "full faith and credit" assurance of the government. This means that regardless of the country's condition (including war and economic stability), the government will always pay its bondholders. Of the various bond types, government bonds carry the lowest risk.

◆ **International bonds:** These enable you to invest in countries other than the United States. Much like corporate bonds, international bonds have varying interest rates and maturity dates and depend on the creditworthiness of the country. Due to a lack of international bond regulation, these bonds are significantly riskier than other types of bonds. You are more likely not to have the full scope of information available to make an informed decision. The political and economic instability of a country affects the risk levels of that country's bonds and the likelihood of the country to default.

Bonds provide a steady income and can stabilize an investment portfolio, making them a good fit for conservative investors. Additionally, for those in the EYL community who are older and nearing retirement, bonds are a wise investment choice. For those who are interested in bonds, consider using mutual funds or ETFs for easy diversification. For those with a short-term goal such as purchasing a home within five to ten years, bonds are an optimal way to preserve capital.

Mutual Funds

Mutual funds enable you to purchase multiple investments at one time and are a great place for beginners to start. This is a group of investments that you can buy into, allowing a fund manager to make your investment. After paying an annual fee to invest, you're paid either through dividends or interest, depending on the type of investment. If you don't have a lot of money to play with or are still leery of investing, you might want to consider purchasing a fractional share of a stock or mutual fund. This will give you the opportunity to begin building a diverse portfolio without sinking everything you have into one investment. In the past, people had to wait until they saved enough money to buy a full share. That not only took a lot of time but decreased the number of people who could access this wealth-building resource.

There are several types of mutual funds.

- **Equity mutual funds:** These purchase stocks from various publicly traded companies. These funds have a higher potential for growth but greater risk as the fund grows. Equity mutual funds are optimal for younger investors, as they have more time to navigate instability in the market.

- **Bond funds:** These pay investors a fixed amount back on their initial investment. These funds invest in government and corporate debt and have less potential for growth than equity funds. Investors who are closer to retirement should have more bond funds than equity funds in their portfolio. This will allow them to protect their earnings while accruing more interest than a bank savings account pays.

- **Money market mutual funds:** These invest in high-quality, short-term debt of governments, banks, or corporations. They are optimal for short-term goals and are especially beneficial for those who are looking to fund their emergency savings. Money market mutual funds, which pay out monthly, are considered one of the safest overall investments and constitute 15% of the mutual fund market.

+ **Balanced funds:** These are a combination of equity and fixed-income funds with a set ratio of investments. The most common division is 60% stocks and 40% bonds. These funds reallocate the ratio of investments from equities to bonds when the investor is closer to retirement.

Mutual funds are categorized as index or actively managed. Index funds are mutual funds whose holdings track a specific market index, such as the S&P 500. These funds have become increasingly popular, as they typically yield better returns than other funds do. Actively managed funds use managers and finance professionals to try to out-perform the market. While actively managed funds have higher fees than index funds do, their managers and professionals work extremely hard with the funds to ensure that they cover their fees and expenses. Speaking of fees, pay close attention to them, as they can eat into your profits and returns. Mutual funds are for people who might be nervous about which stocks and bonds to invest in. And they are optimal for saving for goals such as college or retirement, when you want to "set it and forget it."

ETFs

Exchange-traded funds (ETFs) are combined investment securities that are bought and sold like individual stocks. ETFs can be structured to track everything from commodity prices to other securities and in-vestment strategies. The oldest ETF, the SPDR S&P 500, tracks the S&P 500 Index.

There are several kinds of ETFs:

- **Actively managed ETFs** utilize portfolio managers to make decisions about the securities that will comprise the portfolio.

- **Bond ETFs** provide income to investors, based on the performance of those bonds. Unlike bonds themselves, bond ETFs have no maturity date.

- **Commodity ETFs** invest in commodities and are cheaper than physically owning various commodities.

- **Currency ETFs** track the performance of domestic and foreign currencies. These ETFs are often used to consider the stability of a country's currency based on political and economic developments in a country.

- **Passive ETFs** replicate the performance of indexes like the S&P 500 or more targeted sectors.

- **Sector ETFs** concentrate on specific market sectors and industries.

- **Stock ETFs** are a combination of stocks that track specific industries or sectors, including high performers and emerging stocks with growth potential. Unlike stock mutual funds, these ETFs cost significantly less and don't require security ownership.

ETFs are great for beginning investors and those who don't have a lot of money to invest or a lot of time to research different investments. If you've been in the investment game for a while, an ETF is also a great way to become exposed to another sector at a lower cost, also meaning lower risk.

Fixed Deposits

A fixed deposit occurs when an investor deposits a set amount of money into a bank or corporate entity for a set time, with the expectation of a certain return. Banks and companies differ on whether they invest your fixed deposit in a secondary market in order to yield a higher return, but the investor who makes the deposit agrees to receive a set interest rate. The maturity is set by the institution and can range from seven to ten years. When it comes to this type of investment, it's important for the investor to be committed for the long haul. Early withdrawal from most corporate fixed deposits isn't possible. Banks allow early withdrawal with a significant penalty fee, which can often defeat the purpose of the investment.

Real Estate

Many people look to investing in real estate as one of the most popular and profitable opportunities. It creates the potential for steady income and long-term asset appreciation. While Teddy and Briana were planning their wedding, they were also deciding where they planned to live. Both of them had purchased their homes long before they met and weren't necessarily interested in selling. They decided to use one of their homes as a rental property to generate additional income and create the sustainable wealth that would help them start a family. Because their homes were approximately the same size, it boiled down to their doing the research to find out whose neighborhood would yield a more positive return. This meant that as they were selecting flowers and wedding cake flavors, they were also learning about current housing market value rates and other essential factors. They wanted to live happily ever after with as much money in their pockets as possible.

There are several ways to invest in real estate, including:

- **Real estate investment trusts (REITs):** These enable you to invest in real estate without purchasing physical real estate. REITs are companies that own commercial real estate and pay dividends to investors. Some REITs trade on a stock exchange, while others do not. Nontraded REITs tend to be harder to value than publicly traded REITs are.

- **Online real estate investment platforms:** These bring developers and investors together. Investors interested in financing projects through debt or equity receive monthly or quarterly distributions in exchange for taking on the risks and paying a fee to the platform. Investments made on online real estate investment platforms can't be sold as easily as stocks and are often open only to investors who have earned more than $200,000 in each of the last two years or have a net worth of at least $1 million.

- **Rental properties:** These create additional income by enabling investors to purchase a property that either isn't their primary residence or is their primary residence in which they rent out rooms. When purchasing a rental property, you need to look for one that has expenses less than your expected rent. And while having a rental property will officially make you a landlord, it's up to you to decide how much work you're willing to do. If you're not interested in doing the work yourself, consider getting a property manager.

- **House flipping:** This may seem easy: You purchase a property, renovate it as inexpensively as possible, and sell it for a profit. But with the rising cost of building materials and higher mortgage interest rates, many people find that this investment strategy is very expensive and eats into their potential profit. An additional risk of flipping is that the longer you hold a property, the less the profit. If you're interested in flipping, consider getting an investment partner to share the cost.

It's important to note that real estate investments have high up-front costs associated with purchasing physical properties (including down payment, closing costs, and repairs). If you're interested in venturing into real estate investment waters, consider starting with a REIT to gain exposure to the asset class with less money and hassle.

Commodities and Luxury Goods

Commodities include metals, oil, livestock, art, and other vintage, historical, and cultural items that have significant value. The return on investment will depend on the type of commodity. Oil and livestock generate revenue based on their demand. Metals, art, and other artifacts will continue to appreciate over time, thus increasing their value for years to come. It's worth noting that some commodity investments will yield a return that you will never see because they may not mature in your lifetime. In this way, these investments are investments in the generational wealth many of us seek to create.

Luxury goods as investments include high-end jewelry, watches, handbags and purses, and limited-edition clothing items and shoes. People underestimate and dismiss luxury items as investment options because of their exclusivity or purchase price. The assumption is that they are frivolous purchases that will never appreciate in value. That may or may not be the case. While the price may be steep relative to your financial situation, certain brands will yield a higher return and price over time.

One of the greatest benefits of commodities and luxury goods is that they provide diversification opportunities and a hedge against inflation. However, they are incredibly risky and volatile investments, considering the costs associated with them depend largely on the supply and demand of the market. Additionally, most commodity investing is done via futures contracts that are highly complex. Many luxury goods aren't recommended for pure investment purposes, but they can protect wealth in the long term.

If you're overwhelmed by the number of investment classes to choose from and wonder where you should start, you're not alone. Those big financial dreams of yours aren't going away. And you've pushed them off for as long as you could—or for as long as you need to. You're going to put a plan into place to start or build your investment portfolio, and we're going to help you.

Risk Tolerance

A key to effective investing is understanding the relationship between risk and return. The easiest way to remember the relationship is: **The higher the risk, the higher the return; the lower the risk, the lower the return.** Each asset class—or type of investment—has its own risk/return profile, and examining them as you consider your investment strategy will put you into the best position to create a portfolio that will be effective in meeting your current goals and aligning with your future goals.

A great deal of your preferred risk/return outlook will come down to preference. Risk tolerance metrics exist to tell you what you financially can handle, but at the end of the day, it's going to be up to your own level of comfort. We've seen people who have a lot of bandwidth for risk choose not to invest in something because the return wasn't on par with what they were willing to lose. And we get it; that's your choice. Part of it, though, is that many people's expectations of the relationship between risk and return aren't realistic. There's no investment that will have a minimum risk with a maximum return. If you're looking for this, we suggest that you invest more time in exploring any possible trauma connected to the way you view spending and losing money.

Risk tolerance quizzes and measurement tools are available online and if you consult a financial adviser. We strongly advise you not to skip this step. This is the best way to begin, and it ensures that you're more likely to remain invested and committed. If you can't afford to hire a professional or want to do a quick assessment of your tolerance level, here are some questions to ask yourself.

1. Why do I want to invest?

2. How close am I to retirement?

3. How quickly do I need my investment funds?

4. How long do I need the funds to last once I access them?

5. How would I rate my investment knowledge?
   a. Low
   b. Moderate
   c. High
   d. What is an investment?

6. Which statement best represents my overall position on investing?
   a. The less risk, the better—even if it means I won't make much money.
   b. I'm okay playing it safe with just enough risk and the returns to match.

    c. You can't make the big plays if you're not willing
       to take big swings.

7. Thanks to market shifts and the economy, my investment
   portfolio takes a 25% hit. What am I going to do?
    a. Restrategize and invest in more conservative assets
       to minimize any more losses.
    b. Nothing. This is what investing is all about.
    c. Wait six months before making a decision.
    d. Run me what money I have left! I don't have time
       to lose any more.

8. For a five-year investment opportunity, which risk/reward
   outlook best aligns with my investment vision to meet
   my medium-term goals?
    a. Gain of 28%/loss of 16%
    b. Gain of 20%/loss of 5%
    c. Gain of 40%/loss of 32%
    d. Gain of 35%/loss of 22%

9. Which is more important to me?
    a. Growing a diversified investment portfolio
    b. Growing a diversified investment portfolio and
       generating income at the same time
    c. Generating income from my investments

10. What worries me the most?
    a. Missing an investment window
    b. An underperforming investment that can devalue
       my entire portfolio
    c. Selling an investment too early
    d. Losing money in any way, shape, or form

How you answer these questions will better help you decide which
asset classes—and the risks associated with them—best align with your
vision for investing and capacity for risk-taking.

- **A conservative risk tolerance level is for those who are interested mainly in experiencing no loss with their investment.** Investors at this level sacrifice higher yields and returns if it means taking little to no risk. Bonds and CDs are the most common investments at this level. A conservative investment portfolio would most likely consist of 20% stocks, 50% bonds, and 30% cash.

- **An aggressive risk tolerance level is for those who are willing to make precarious investments.** While these investments have the ability to yield a higher return over time, they are more likely to lose value and money in the meantime. Stocks and real estate are the most common investments at this level. An aggressive investment portfolio would most likely consist of 50% stocks and 50% real estate.

- **A moderate risk tolerance level has its feet squarely in the conservative and aggressive camps.** Investors at this level want the opportunity to experience the benefit of high-yield investments while also including low-risk ones. Stocks and bonds are the most common investments at this level. A moderate-risk investment portfolio would most likely consist of 35% stocks, 35% bonds, 15% cash, and 15% real estate or business equity.

Having a low risk tolerance doesn't mean that you're not a serious investor; it simply means that your current conditions make it more favorable for you to enter into the investment waters as slowly as possible, with smaller investments. At the end of the day, it's best to operate at a level that's fully aligned with your investment vision and capacity. If you don't, you will be cutting off your portfolio's maximum earning potential. If you're okay with that, fine. But truthfully, we don't want you to be okay with it; we want you to generate wealth.

You also need to know the expenses associated with each potential investment. This is much different from determining your risk tolerance. Expenses can include registration, transaction, and management fees, maintenance costs, commissions, and spreads. You will also need to know the tax liabilities and implications associated with your potential investments, including income, withholding, and capital gains taxes. An optimal investment will minimize your costs and taxes and maximize your after-tax return.

If you're already investing and are considering enlarging your investment portfolio, we recommend sitting down with your financial adviser to reassess your risk tolerance. Just because you're currently faring well doesn't mean that increasing your investments, without strategic guidance, is wise. For instance, it's less likely that Gary and Morgan Williams would be considered to have a higher risk tolerance right now, given that they've got a kid about to head off to college. Their investment strategy will be aggressive, considering their current financial situation, but it will reflect the fact that their capacity to take on higher risk is mitigated by other, more important factors.

Or take Henry, who's sixty years old and nearing retirement. What he's put into the system will barely cover his expenses, and he needs to work pretty fast to make things shake. His investment portfolio should be more conservative leaning, focusing on bonds, dividend stocks, and annuities for guaranteed income. His investment portfolio looks completely different from that of his twenty-five-year-old granddaughter, Jada, a law school student with a higher risk tolerance. Jada's investments rely heavily on equities and growth-focused ETFs, and she's been saving her stipends to purchase her first investment property. Henry and Jada have different goals and different circumstances. Their investment portfolios reflect what their ultimate goals are and what's necessary to meet them.

The Next Steps

Now that we've explained what investments are and how you can examine your current financial situation to get started investing or make some adjustments to the way you're investing now, we're going to dive more into the risks associated with investing and offer you our EYL Investment Blueprint: our take on an asset allocation strategy that's worked well for members in our community. We know we just gave you a lot of information, and if you need to take time to process it all, take it. If you need to read this chapter again before moving ahead, feel free to do so. It's your book, and it's your future. For so long, we haven't had access to this information in a way that will make investing possible for all of us. We want you to do whatever you need to do to understand investing, because, once you do so, wealth-building strategies will become your best friends.

◆ ◆ ◆

CHAPTER FIVE

The EYL Investment Blueprint

Financial professionals and advisers believe that there's no one-size-fits-all formula for asset allocation. Because of this, many people don't really know how to begin building their wealth portfolios, and others don't know what to add to their existing strategies. However, we've seen a combination of formulas work extremely well in our EYL community. As you consider which wealth-building strategies are best for you, consider our EYL Investment Blueprint, which is a combination of **real estate, stocks, and business**.

The EYL Investment Blueprint involves strategizing across three tiers: base, median, and initial/smaller investments. Your base investment is the cornerstone of your portfolio, and it could be anything from a business to stocks or real estate. It's not necessarily your biggest financial commitment, but it's the one that generates the most steady, stable returns. Your median investment represents growth; it's more fluid and may include assets like a rental property that is just starting to generate steady income after renovations. Your smaller or initial investments are the ones that haven't had time to mature and develop yet. They might have the potential to grow into major players in your portfolio, or they may need rethinking as you watch their performance over time.

EYL Investment Blueprint

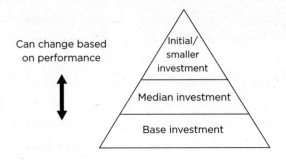

Real Estate

For many in the EYL community, investing in real estate and becoming successful occurred while they were still working their main job. Full-time employment doesn't have to be a deterrent to building an expansive real estate portfolio.

For years, Yolanda wanted to get into the real estate investment game because she heard it was a great way to build wealth. She spent three years focused on strengthening her credit, following one of the strictest budgets possible. In fact, she met with a financial planner and told him that whatever she needed to do to get her credit together, she would do. After three years, Yolanda's score had risen from 500 to 820. That put her into a better position to secure the best mortgage loan rates.

While looking, she found an affordable Nashville property, a duplex, that needed some rehabbing before it would be "rent ready." Each unit was a 2-bedroom, 1.5-bathroom town house. The price was $250,000 and Yolanda worked with a financial adviser to perform a real estate profit-and-loss analysis. Additionally, Yolanda was able to secure a grant to use for the down payment.

After putting $50,000 down on the duplex, Yolanda secured a thirty-year fixed-rate loan for $200,000. While exploring her tenant options, she decided that she wanted to offer exclusively to Section 8 tenants. That would guarantee that she'd receive rent on time every month without having to worry about collecting it. Another reason was that Yolanda's family lived off vouchers, and she wanted to pay it forward. Because of the renovations and upgrades she made, she was able to receive the top voucher allotment of $2,750.

Monthly, Yolanda's duplex brings in $5,500, with her expenses averaging $3,000. Those expenses include her monthly mortgage payment, property management fees, and $250 that goes back into her savings account each month to replace what she took out of it to complete the renovations. This creates $2,500 per month in additional income. And even though it would normally be taxable income, Yolanda doesn't have to pay taxes on it because of the depreciation deduction she gets on the investment property. Because of the city's rapid growth and community investments, Yolanda's duplex is on target to appreciate, giving her an asset in her portfolio that is potentially worth $750,000 in the next ten years.

With the additional $2,500 income per month, Yolanda had options. She was not yet ready to leave her job and really wanted to add another property to her portfolio. Each month, she moved $500 to her budget for investing in stocks. The remaining $2,000 stayed in an account, and she intended to secure another real estate property in the next year. She remained committed to its being another Section 8 property, but this time, she wanted it to be a single-family home with a big backyard, the kind of home she always had wanted when she was growing up.

Selecting the Right Investment Property

An investment property is a great addition to any portfolio. Not only is it a long-term asset that can generate wealth and provide stability for your family for generations, it can also protect you against the market volatility when it comes to your other investments. When your stocks are not as steady, your investment property won't lose much value, and if it does, you'll likely recoup it over time.

Here are the types of investment properties we want you to seriously consider for maximum gains and yields.

Land

Land is the one resource that can't be reproduced. Whatever is left is literally all there is. And two things are happening right now: Developers are rushing to acquire what's left, and there's a movement among many people to "return to the land" in a sense: living more simplistically, eating farm to table, and searching for a better life than the busyness of the one they're living now. In addition to residential land, here are other land investments we think you should consider.

- **Commercial:** These include care facilities for children and seniors, hotels, industrial spaces, multifamily residential buildings, office buildings, retail spaces, and self-storage units. When it comes to investing in retail spaces, consider investing in emerging and newly established cities and communities. Also, mixed-use communities are on the rise, as people enjoy the ability to "live, work, and play" in close proximity to one another, so these are also good arenas for investment. Speaking of work, coworking spaces, salon/barbershop suites, short-term office rentals, and spaces where creatives can do their thing are no-brainers in a time when we won't see a return to the traditional office again and rising costs are making it impossible for service providers and creators to maintain their own spaces and make a profit.

- **Farmland (for livestock and vegetables):** At the time we were writing this book, the average cost of U.S. farmland per acre was around $5,000 and investors were seeing an average annual return rate of 12%, higher than the S&P's average of 10%. While you buy land to farm yourself or rent it out to agricultural businesses—or even establish your own co-op—an investment in farmland has proven to be a game changer for many people. Add to that the immense sense of pride you will feel in owning the very land that our ancestors worked so hard to cultivate.

- **Vineyards:** Can you imagine going to your own vineyards for your next girls' trips? Well, it actually doesn't have to be a dream. The prices of California vineyards now start at around $50,000 an acre. One acre can produce close to eight hundred bottles of wine. The average annual profit on the lowest-priced acre is around $15,000. You'll need to do a lot of research and make a lot of connections for this to be an optimal long-term investment.

If the idea of owning land really interests you but you don't see yourself investing at a moderate or large scale, consider researching and investing in commercial, farm, or agricultural ETFs. They give you the ability to live your *Green Acres* dreams without swallowing all your investment resources and time.

If you decide that you want to own land, you have to be willing to educate yourself about everything that comes along with it. You don't own just a plot of grass and dirt; that acre or acreage has land use restrictions that you must follow or you risk being hit with serious fines or losing the land. And if your property is zoned for a specific use, you need to become aware of all the costs and fees associated with getting that land up to and remaining at code to do the things you want to do with it. That involves more than paying the annual property tax; land is a major investment with serious up-front and ongoing development costs. Keep this in mind as you calculate and consider your return on investment.

Rental Properties

When it comes to real estate investment, rental properties are what most people think of. Owning a home, town house, or condo and renting it out to someone else makes a lot of sense. You get to own an asset that you're essentially not paying for, and at the end of the day, everybody needs a roof over their heads. It's a no-brainer. But while it's a solid and wise investment—and one we wholeheartedly encourage— we've seen it go left for a lot of people and become more of a burden than the financial asset it should be.

When considering an investment property as a rental property, here are the questions you need to ask yourself.

- **How much can I afford to pay toward another mortgage?** This is the most important question, because regardless of the amount a bank or credit union may approve you for, only you know what your financial situation and budget look like. And while the ideal is that someone else will be paying all (or the bulk) of the mortgage via their rental payment, it will always ultimately be your responsibility.

- **How long can I pay this mortgage before it becomes a financial strain?** Things happen. In 2020, thanks to the pandemic, many landlords weren't able to collect rent from their tenants because the tenants weren't working and didn't have it. And then there's always the reality that there may be a time when you won't have a tenant occupying your property. Knowing how long you can make mortgage payments without detriment to yourself and putting a plan into place for what to do should you not have a renter for an extended period of time are crucial before you buy a property.

- **Do I want to manage this property myself?** Your dream of being a landlord may extend to wanting to be involved in every aspect of property management. That's cool. However, we strongly advise that you enlist the services of a property management company or hire someone you trust to manage it for you. The idea of a rental property as an investment is to make money. Most people want to make as much money as possible with as little expense as possible. That's wise. At the same time, sometimes spending the money to have someone else do the grunt work will save you a lot of headaches in the long run.

There are several factors to consider when choosing a property to buy, including location, crime statistics, and average property taxes. But within our EYL community, we've found that proximity to high-quality schools really matters. As you look at potential properties, recognize that proximity to good schools will be a great selling point. Also, if your rental property is accessible by a transit line, that may increase the number of potential renters. Additionally, if you're interested in a home in an established community, make sure you check all the rules. Some homeowners' associations (HOAs) have a limit on the number of renters in the neighborhood. Purchasing a home to rent and then finding out that the neighborhood is at its rental cap would defeat the entire purpose.

Unlike investing in the stock market, which you can do with as little as $1, you're going to need some money if you want to invest in real estate. When it comes to buying an investment property, you may have saved enough money to buy it with cash, leaving you with no mortgage and able to focus on the money you will make from rental payments. Even though we wouldn't advise this (because debt can be a good thing from a tax standpoint), we salute it if it's you. But if you're like most people, you're going to need a solid credit rating and a loan to buy the property.

- **Conventional loan:** Typically, the down payment on a conventional loan can be around 5% of the purchase price, with the lender financing the remainder. However, when it comes to investment properties, many lenders can require a 30% down payment with no adjustments for credit and income, which they would take into consideration when deciding on the down payment on your primary residence. It's also important to keep in mind that lenders won't use anticipated rent to calculate your debt-to-income ratio, and many will require proof of cash reserves to cover six to nine months of the mortgage.

- **Hard-money loan:** This short-term loan is used to purchase an investment property, more than likely one you plan to flip; you then pay off the loan with another kind of loan or the return made when you sold the property. Typically, hard-money loans are easier to obtain for properties that you plan to flip than conventional loans are. And unlike conventional loans, which don't use anticipated rent to determine your qualification status, hard-money loans factor in the anticipated value of the home after renovations and repair to determine your eligibility. And whereas it could take weeks to get a decision on a conventional loan, you can be approved for a hard-money loan in days. However, the costs, fees, and interest rates on hard-money loans are significantly higher than they are on conventional loans, and typically, such loans are expected to be paid back in a year or less.

◆ **Home equity loan:** If you have equity in your primary residence, you can use it to purchase your investment property. Whether you take out a home equity loan, get a home equity line of credit, or refinance, you have the potential to borrow or access between 75% and 80% of your home's equity. Many people access their home equity to purchase an investment property, and it makes sense to do so. However, you need to understand how it will impact your primary residence—reducing your equity, requiring refinancing, or extending the amount of repayment time on your current loan.

When it comes to getting the money to purchase an investment property, we're of the mindset that if we've done what we need to do to establish a strong case for approval, we're going to get the money. This doesn't ignore the ways in which Black and Brown people have systematically been denied home loans and opportunities to pursue real estate investing. It's unfortunate that these injustices still exist, and we will continue to use our platform to speak out against them and rally for the marginalized investor. While we're doing that, we want you to have the confidence that you're going to be approved and be able to purchase the property.

LET AI WORK FOR YOU

We know, we know. But you're not getting away from it. AI isn't going anywhere.

And here's the truth: Though AI has been all the craze recently, it's been around for a while and has already been an integral part of our daily lives. Here's an opportunity for you to be intentional about your use of AI, especially when it comes to your personal finances and your business. This book has given you all the tools you need. Allow AI to streamline your processes.

Personal Finances

After creating your EYL Baseline and using the EYL Money Principle, you can use an AI-budgeting app to create a detailed spending budget and track spending habits. Linking those apps to your bank accounts or cards and creating alerts will notify you when you're reaching your spending threshold. Additionally, you can use chat-based AI programs, like ChatGPT or Claude, to create a customized debt repayment strategy. For instance, if you have $25,000 in high-interest credit card debt and you want to decrease it by at least 35% in the next eighteen months, you would create a prompt asking the platform to provide you with at least three different repayment strategies that fit your timeline.

You can utilize the same strategy and principle to create a plan to increase your credit score, though many banks and credit monitoring services can already do this for you using AI. And, as we've outlined in our investment chapters, you can utilize robo-advisers to build and manage your portfolios. Additionally, if you're worried about how to calculate your risk tolerance and pursue investment opportunities based on that,

AI can help. After answering the assessment questions in the next chapter, create a prompt requesting investment options based on your responses.

Business

When it comes to implementing AI into your business practices, the opportunities are endless. Here are four ways that AI is a game changer for entrepreneurs:

1. **Automation:** As an entrepreneur, you need to spend the bulk of your professional time generating income. Automating many of your processes—like emails, appointment setting, invoicing, and payroll—saves you money and time.

2. **Content creation:** Using platforms like ChatGPT can help you to generate content for posts, newsletters, and potential product offerings. For those interested in increasing social media followers and engagement, consider creating a prompt that asks for an eight-week content calendar based on your specific interests and the needs of your platform.

3. **Marketing and sales:** AI tools and algorithms can help you to analyze customer trends and create specific marketing campaigns that appeal to your core base and will attract new consumers. Consider using AI platforms to create a marketing strategy that will increase the number of people who will interact with and support your business by 35% in six weeks.

4. **Processes and procedures:** This is especially important for small businesses and solopreneurs who can't afford to

pay for outsourced assistance. Every aspect of a business's infrastructure can be accessed through AI tools. Whether it's using AI to handle customer service needs or using AI prompts to get professional advice if you currently can't pay a consultant, everything is literally at your fingertips.

The key to using technology is to not be afraid of it. For so long, AI has been seen as the boogeyman that's going to take everyone's jobs and take over the world. Hear us when we say that there are some legitimate concerns about the possible overreach, and we've been grateful to be invited into many of those rooms to be a part of those conversations. At the same time, it's also important to not let this tech revolution pass us by. The time is over for playing catch-up. We need to be at the starting line.

House Flipping

Many people want to flip houses, and if you do it correctly, you can make a lot of money. But before we get into all the ways to maximize your investment, we want to tell you the truth: Flipping houses involves more than what you see on television and social media. Hit TV shows and social media personalities have found a way to sell a curated dream of what the experience is. And though it can be rewarding, we're here to tell you that it can test you severely before all is said and done.

When it comes to flipping a house, remember this: **Buy low and sell high with a fast goodbye.** Buying an investment property for the smallest amount possible and making the necessary repairs and good-quality renovations to sell it at or above market value quickly is your goal. Regarding time frame, it usually takes four to six months to flip a house. As soon as you're done with it, you should put it on the market. This means working with a Realtor and others who are knowledgeable about the area to make key changes and upgrades to the property so it will be most appealing. You do not buy and hold an investment property that you want to flip. The longer you keep it, the less of a return on your investment there will be.

You'll also need to make sure that you've scouted the right location for a house flip. While a general mantra in real estate investment is that everyone needs a roof over their heads, you don't want to go into the first neighborhood you see, buy a house, and flip it. Distressed properties are everywhere, but not everyone wants to *live* everywhere. You will find many homes that you could flip in less-than-desirable neighborhoods. They're going to be priced extremely low, and that will entice you. Before taking the leap, consider doing a bit more research about the neighborhood itself, taking into consideration what's happening in and around it. This will determine if the house is a potential rental property or a solid flip. Again, neither alternative is a bad one. However, if you're solely looking to flip a house, you shouldn't buy a home in a neighborhood with mostly renters or one that is even a few short years away from a boom.

That being said, success in flipping a house is all about location. You want a city that's experiencing significant growth through various offices and industries coming and making their home there; capitalizing on that growth, paying close attention to where businesses are heading and establishing new locations, will give you a number of potential options, as their incoming employees will need good-quality homes and may often be arriving with healthy relocation allowances provided by their employers. Additionally, we recommend looking at solid, established neighborhoods. Homebuyers tend to desire homes in communities where other families have thrived and continue to do so. The homes are well kept, and property taxes are moderate. Such properties aren't hard to find, especially in cities such as Atlanta, Charlotte, El Paso, Hartford, Nashville, and Jacksonville—cities where industries are booming and growth is exponential.

Doing all the necessary repairs and upgrades after purchasing a property is when many people get frustrated and lose a lot of money.

That's because they didn't do their due diligence before purchasing the property to make sure that it was actually worth it. You may have found the perfect property, but if it's not priced right or if the repairs and upgrades are not within your budget, it's actually *not* the perfect property. You're not going to maximize your return, and the entire process will more than likely drive you mad. Typically, those who have been through this experience are the ones who have nothing positive to say about flipping a house and will give you ten thousand reasons why you shouldn't do it when you tell them you're interested.

The 70% rule in flipping says that an investor shouldn't pay more than 70% of the anticipated value of the home after all repairs and renovations are completed. This is also known as the after-repair value (ARV). The ARV lets you know how much the house will be worth once all the work is done. To apply the 70% percent rule, we suggest working backward to get to the ideal purchase price:

For example, you've found a property in Atlanta that has a potential ARV of $350,000. If you consider the cost of materials, repairs, and upgrades, renovations will cost around $30,000. Applying the 70% rule, you shouldn't pay more than $215,000 for the home.

If your budget requires that you look for a flipping experience with a smaller price tag, of course you will be able to find one. Just remember that it's highly unlikely that you'll be able to buy low (lower than six figures) in a good neighborhood and sell high (in the mid-six-figure range). Where you buy will often dictate how much you will ultimately make.

As we said, we've seen some people get into some huge messes trying to flip a house. While any investment strategy involves risk, it doesn't need to rise to the level of catastrophic loss. Here's how you can sidestep a few of the most common mistakes we've seen people make when flipping houses.

- **Not being knowledgeable enough about the process:**
  We've seen entirely too many people make assumptions

about how much they could sell a house for that went tens of thousands of dollars over budget before they were done. Before you make a purchase, you need to take time to map out a strategy. This includes developing a solid budget for repairs and upgrades, pricing contractors, knowing all the tax and zoning laws associated with the property, and identifying the best Realtors and real estate agencies that will move the property fast once it's ready.

- **Not having enough money to do the job:** If you don't adequately budget to flip a house, you will spend more money than you need or even have. Unless you got your house at a major steal (which, again, is possible but not common), the heftiest price tag should be the acquisition cost. The same loan and financing options will apply to you as if it were a rental property, keeping in mind that hard-money loans are more favorable for flips. Additionally, you'll need to adjust your profit margins to account for capital gains taxes, which will be higher because this is a short-term investment. Here's an important tip: Do not skimp on renovations and upgrades. We know that the price of materials and the overall cost of doing business is rising. However, potential buyers are growing weary of purchasing homes with stock upgrades. While such upgrades may be cheaper for you, they provide no character to the home and look like a potential upgrading expense for the buyer sooner rather than later. If you're spending money to buy a recently renovated home, the last thing you want to do is spend money renovating it once you've bought it. For you as the investor, spending a little extra on upgrades will go a long way.

◆ **Lacking time and patience:** We've already told you that it's best to set four to six months aside to flip a house. While that's a fairly conservative estimate, understand that it will change depending on the time of year, the weather, and the availability (or lack thereof) of contractors. The worst thing you can do is go into this kind of project thinking that you'll get it done in three months. That's when you'll start to cut corners and make cheap decisions that will ultimately be costly. Additionally, unless you're doing the renovations and repairs yourself, you've hired professionals who know what they're doing and are more than capable of doing it. Second-guessing and rushing them simply because you've put yourself on the clock to sell won't work out for you and will cost more money in the long run.

◆ **Not understanding that you are not Bob the Builder:** You're laughing, but we're serious. Do you know how many people think they can flip a house simply because they've watched a season of a show on HGTV? While sweat equity is important and admirable—and sometimes the most celebrated part of the process—if you don't know what you're doing, you're only costing yourself more money and losing it by not maximizing on the potential gains. There are professionals—builders, plumbers, carpenters, and real estate agents—who are more than capable of doing their part to ensure that you make the most when it's time to sell. Many of them may even be reading this book right now and thinking of ways to grow their business. You will make a great team. The bottom line is that there's no reason to spend hours in Lowe's or Home Depot buying tools and materials when you have absolutely no idea what to do with them.

When it's done correctly, we've seen people make millions of dollars and fund their financial futures by flipping homes. But it didn't happen overnight. The key is to start small, with one property. After that experience, take some time to assess the process: What would you have done differently? What could you have done better? Who did you love working with? In what areas do you need stronger assistance? What did you like most about the process and why? Once you've answered these questions and establish a blueprint for projects going forward, you can determine how feasible it would be to do one flip each year. Who knows, you could take this experience and create a new business, complete with your own team of employees and divisions. Anything is possible.

Real Estate Investment Trusts (REITs)

If you're seriously interested in getting into real estate development but don't want to buy physical real estate, REITs are perfect for you. Also, if you see real estate investment as your desired path but you don't have much money, you can invest in a REIT with as little as $1,000. With REITs, companies and trusts use your money to buy and operate investment properties. The greatest advantage is that in order to maintain REIT status, these organizations must pay investors 90% of their taxable profits. The monthly or quarterly dividend payouts then become income that can supplement or replace traditional employment income.

Investing in a REIT starts with setting up a brokerage account, which we'll discuss in the next section. REITs typically fall into one of two categories: equity or mortgage. Equity REITs own actual buildings and focus on ownership, while mortgage REITs provide loans and financing, focusing on the money made from financing real estate deals. The high-yield returns that come from REITs make them a great opportunity for older investors and those with bad credit or other financial concerns that make larger-scale real estate investments unwise or undesirable.

Stocks

The base of your stock portfolio should include a 401(k) plan and your retirement account whether you're employed or not. Your employer's matching contribution is key to maximizing your company retirement fund. We encourage you to create a budget that doesn't include the amount of that matching percentage so that you can begin to adjust your current spending habits accordingly. Because the stock market is the cornerstone of our EYL Investment Blueprint, we receive questions daily about the best stocks and ways to trade them. *Market Mondays,* our live YouTube show, is the way we most frequently discuss stocks with our EYL community.

Getting involved in the stock market and investing in trusts and funds require a brokerage account. This account will allow you to purchase stocks, bonds, and mutual funds. As with your bank accounts, you can add money to your brokerage accounts by depositing funds yourself or setting up electronic transfers. You can set up a brokerage account online in less than twenty minutes, and **you should never have to pay a fee to open one**. But you'll need to have money in your brokerage account before you can make your first investment.

There are several kinds of brokerage firms to consider.

- **Full service:** In full-service brokerage firms, financial advisers are paid to help clients develop investment plans, execute transactions, monitor their investments and the markets, and more. A full-service brokerage firm can charge adviser fees or a commission on trades. A commission account generates a fee anytime an investment is bought or sold, whether the recommendation came from the client or the adviser and whether or not the trade is profitable.

- **Discount brokerage firms:** Charging lower fees than full-service firms, discount brokerage firms are optimal for investors who want to keep their costs low by using online trading platforms. This account type is largely for investors who want to handle most trading themselves and are looking only for a trading platform.

- **Robo-advisers:** With these accounts, algorithms are used to select investments, usually limited to mutual funds and ETFs. Robo-advisers appeal to new investors who want to enter the world of trading but either still don't understand it or want to engage in selecting stocks as little as possible; they're also for more experienced investors who are looking to scale up their investing experience and take a more hands-off approach.

- **Financial advisers:** Investors who desire a more personal relationship with their broker and boutique investment experience should consider brokerage firms led by financial advisers. Because these firms are independent, they can require a larger minimum investment and may cater exclusively to wealthier and high-profile investors.

- **Online investment firms:** These firms are for investors who want to select their own investments and make trades solely through a website or mobile app.

In addition to deciding on a brokerage firm, you also need to decide what type of brokerage account to establish. A cash brokerage account requires that you deposit money before you can begin trading.

This type of account is limited to purchasing stocks. A margin account allows you to borrow money to start trading. Brokers act as lenders, and the borrowed funds allow for larger and more advanced trades, including stock short sells. If you are new to investing, we suggest you begin with a cash account.

Many people have categorized the various brokerage firms out there. We want you to do your own research to determine which firm is optimal for your type of investing. Here are some of the top brokerage firms that are considered the best platform for beginners and offer great advantages and options for more advanced traders.

- Charles Schwab

- E*Trade

- Fidelity

- J. P. Morgan

- Robinhood

- Vanguard

There is no limit on the number of accounts you can have or a maximum amount of money you can put into a taxable brokerage account each year. Because your investments are subject to capital gains taxes, brokerage accounts are considered taxable accounts. They don't follow the same tax and withdrawal rules as retirement accounts, including IRAs.

In order to take advantage of your brokerage account's tax benefits, here are some things to remember.

1. You will more than likely have to pay capital gains taxes on stocks that you purchase and sell for a profit.

2. Short-term capital gains taxes are applied to any stocks sold a year or less after purchase. While the short-term

capital gains tax rate is typically equal to the standard income tax rate, it is often higher than the long-term capital gains tax rate.

3. If you sell an investment for a loss, you can use that loss to reduce your capital gains tax.

4. If you are paid dividends from stocks and funds purchased through your brokerage account, your brokerage firm will send you a DIV-1099, the amount of which you will include in your tax return.

We tell our community that investing in stocks will do two things: It will allow you to gain ownership in companies you know and love, and it will make your money grow. Typically, many people invest in what's known as the "Magnificent Seven": Apple, Microsoft, Alphabet (Google's parent company), Amazon, Nvidia, Meta, and Tesla. These seven stocks have consistently held and exceeded their value, making them lucrative for those who have the ability to make significant investments. Each of the Magnificent Seven has an average five-year return of around 300%.

However, instead of investing in specific stocks and companies, we encourage you to invest in specific market sectors. These are the sectors in which we see the most trends and consider to yield significant gains to investors. We introduce you to EYL's "Big Six":

- Communications services

- Consumer discretionary

- Financials

- Healthcare

- Industrials

- Information technology

Another strategy for selecting stocks is to invest in what you use and enjoy. If Pepsi is your drink of choice or your kids are always asking for Cool Ranch Doritos, why wouldn't you invest in PepsiCo? Everyone uses toilet paper, which would make investing in Procter & Gamble a win-win. And if you can't stay out of Target, why not invest in it so you can make some of your money back?

Business

Business as a part of your investment portfolio can take one of two forms: equity or entrepreneurship. Investors can purchase equity in one or more businesses, or they can own their own business. Again, this is not an easy investment decision to make. It will depend on your desire and availability of resources—primarily time. A general rule of thumb, though, is not to start a business if you really don't want to start a business.

Here are four businesses that can be incredibly lucrative.

- Cleaning services (including laundromats)

- Staffing agencies

- Vending machines

- Trucking industries

EYL community members have been able to pursue these businesses successfully without leaving their nine-to-fives. If you're considering starting a business and maintaining your full-time employment, consider these opportunities.

Christopher invested $2,500 in a vending machine. After researching, he contracted to place one in a local business with high foot traffic. To make his vending machine different from others, he wanted to stock premium snack items that people would find difficult to refuse. During a slow month, Christopher's vending machine generates a profit of $300. In nine months, he made his investment back and purchased another vending machine. His aim is to have vending machines as the foundation of his investment portfolio, planning to eventually own ten.

We focus on entrepreneurship much more fully in chapter 7 and provide you with resources that will assist you as you embark on that journey. For now, we want you to know that owning a business isn't the only way members of the EYL community are generating wealth. Investing in a business to gain a considerable amount of equity and ownership is a good idea for anyone who desires to have their hands in business without having to run one. Also, having equity in a business and receiving dividends free you to invest in even more businesses by either reinvesting those dividends elsewhere or having the time to pursue other entrepreneurial interests.

Investing in the Future

The gift of time and market predictions is that we're able to use both of them to make informed decisions about future investments and capitalize on things coming down the pipeline. Again, you can catch us on *Market Mondays* or our *EYL After Dark* show discussing many of these trends and how you can get in on them now before the market boom hits. When it comes to upcoming investments, here are the top sectors to watch.

- AI and cybersecurity

- Emerging international markets (specifically the booming economies of Africa, India, and the Middle East)

- Green energy

- Healthcare services, technology, biotech, and pharmaceuticals

- Residential real estate and land

To get prepared and begin investing in these sectors, not only do we want you to start watching the news and doing research, you also need to talk to your financial adviser and broker about the best opportunities for you. Preparing and adjusting for potential risks will better position you to maximize your gains and profits. Ultimately, it feels good to be in a position where we have information about emerging industries that allows us to make informed, proactive decisions. Too often, we get information late and have to make reactionary moves. Now we're leveling the playing field.

Go back to the EYL Investment Blueprint. **Your base investment will be the most stable one in your portfolio.** Depending on which of the three (stocks, real estate, or business) that you select from, your investments here will be the most solid and stable. **The median investment of your blueprint is where you're beginning some maturation.** It's not as solid as your base investment, but you can tell that it's progressing. **The initial or smaller investment in your blueprint is just that.** It's the investment either that's in the early stages and hasn't had time to play out yet or that takes up the least space in your overall investment budget.

Your EYL Blueprint is the cornerstone of your wealth building system. As you explore which asset classes work best for you and which formula of our three you're going to apply, remember that it doesn't have to become overwhelming and unattainable. Find what works for you, and then make it work. You'll be surprised where your blueprint can take you in five years!

◆ ◆ ◆

CHAPTER SIX

Risky Business

Veronica has a moderate risk tolerance level. At forty-four, she enjoys the investment portfolio she's built—one that's equally spread over stocks, bonds, and an investment that gave her a 15% stake in her best friend's nail salon—and she doesn't miss the opportunity to meet with her financial adviser quarterly and remain updated on the performance of all of her investments. While she understands that investing requires some risk, she's determined that her return rate should never dip toward a 30% loss.

Veronica's dedication to evaluating her investments is a characteristic that you will have to develop to ensure that your money works as well for you as it possibly can. Think of it this way: You've done the work to set your investment goals and determine how much risk you can assume; you've researched asset classes, decided which ones are the best for you, and created a formula to build an investment portfolio that reflects your tastes and preferences—and then you actually made the investment. There's no reason to stop now!

Spending the time to evaluate the performance of your investments is crucial because it will help you measure the success of your investments and create a metric that will assist you in further evaluating your financial decisions. Several factors can impact the performance of your investments, including your investment strategies, market conditions, economic trends, and portfolio management. You may not have a working knowledge of all these factors, but you should be able to access this information at any time as well as have someone on your team whose job it is to break it down for you. How these factors impact your investments will ultimately impact the amount of money you make.

Evaluating the performance of your investments enables you to determine whether each investment is making money or not. Some people get into investing just for the fun—or rush—of it. Thrill-seeking investing is its own thing, and often investors who do this don't necessarily care about the shifts in their investments' value. For EYL, investing is about generating wealth and attaining financial freedom. So yeah, the money matters. As you evaluate your investments, here are the things to consider.

Return on investment (ROI): This measures an investment's return in relationship to the initial purchase cost (including all the fees and costs associated with buying the investment). This is the most common and popular metric used to evaluate an investment.

Compound annual growth rate (CAGR): This measures the average growth rate of an investment over a specific time frame. This metric works best when you are evaluating long-term investments; coupled with ROI it gives investors a complete picture of the overall health and long-term potential of an investment.

In addition to these calculations, there are more sophisticated metrics that financial advisers and fund managers will use to assess your investments' performance. These evaluate the quality of your investment's "excess," which is the word used to describe the return of an investment after all purchase costs and associated fees have been accounted for. They are:

Information ratio: The excess adjusted for the risk taken to make the investment. The higher the information ratio, the more stable the return and its potential to continue.

Jensen's alpha: The excess compared to the expected return. If the Jensen's alpha value is positive, it means that an investment has outperformed expectations and is a solid addition to your portfolio.

Sharpe ratio: The excess measured against each unit of risk taken. A higher Sharpe ratio means that an investment, based on its risk level, has adjusted well to its risk factors and will continue to perform solidly.

Sortino ratio: The excess measured against the negative risk. Unlike the Sharpe ratio, the Sortino ratio focuses on potential losses. Remember, not all risk is bad; this measurement evaluates how an investment performs against harmful factors.

Treynor ratio: The excess measured against each unit of systematic risk. This ratio explores the excess based on the risk/reward profile of the investment. The higher the Treynor ratio, the more solid the investment.

Now, look: We know we've empowered you to take your financial destiny into your own hands and do much of the work to build wealth yourself. We want you to do that! But when it comes to fully understanding these metrics and ratios, don't hesitate to consult a professional.

Another way your investment can be evaluated is how it has met established benchmarks. The following measurements will give you tools to compare and contrast various investments and provide you with the information you need to determine whether your investments are meeting your goals. The most common benchmarks are:

Active/passive investment performance: Active portfolio management is a more hands-on approach to actively managing an investment or portfolio to generate returns that exceed those possible in the broader market and reduce the overall risk of investment losses. In a passively managed fund, the fund manager cannot determine the movements of the underlying assets. Comparing active and passive investment fund performance helps investors understand the benefits and drawbacks of each approach and make informed decisions.

Market indexes: Market indexes are hypothetical portfolios of investment holdings that investors use as an indicator of market movements. There are many different types of market indexes. They are also used to create index funds, allowing investors to buy a basket of securities rather than picking individual stocks. As a hypothetical portfolio of holdings, indexes act as benchmark comparisons for a variety of purposes across the financial markets. As mentioned, the Dow Jones Industrial Average, S&P 500, and Nasdaq Composite are three popular indexes. They include the thirty largest-cap U.S. stocks, the five hundred largest-cap U.S. stocks, and all of the stocks on the Nasdaq exchange, respectively.

Peer group comparison: Peer group comparison involves comparing the performance of an investment against that of a group of similar investments or funds. This allows investors to evaluate the relative performances of their investments within a specific category against those with the same investment characteristics.

A financial adviser can help you tailor benchmarks to your specific investment goals, risk tolerance, and overall outlook. This will be quite helpful in providing you with a personalized analysis of your investments' performance. You can then take that information and continue building a much more solid investment portfolio.

As you begin to understand the performance of your investments, you will learn that there are many factors that impact it—including the overall state of the market. To best understand what your investment is doing and can do, it's important to know the four cycles of the market:

Market bottom: The market has reached a low point and may stay there for a while.

Bull market: The market rallies from the bottom to reach the top and regain economic stability.

Market top: The market flattens out from a bull market and begins to trend downward again.

Bear market: This signals the beginning of the next market bottom.

Typically, the markets can predict the state of the overall economy between three and six months in advance. As the market indexes are ahead of the economy, paying attention to them will give you as an investor an edge in making investment decisions.

Depending on the cycle, you can participate in an investment strategy known as sector rotation. This involves moving the money invested in certain stocks to those in another sector in anticipation of a pending economic cycle. Sector rotation can be sparked by changing economic conditions, new innovations or inventions, new developments in global politics, or new moves in other financial markets. Sector rotation extends the life of your portfolio, even if you have to change the asset class. Then there will be times when you will want to sell an investment altogether. Any of a number of reasons may make you decide to sell an investment, including:

+ Freeing capital for another investment/needing money for a purchase or emergency

+ A major life event

+ Investment portfolio diversification and adjustment

+ The investment's having reached your target goal or price

+ Shifts in a company's or business's ownership and structure

+ Greater investment opportunities elsewhere

+ Tax implications and strategies

If any or all of these factors are your reason to sell, it's important to note that selling a particular investment is okay. Typically in our communities, selling an investment is seen either as a failure or as a greedy, capitalistic move to gain more money. Neither perspective is true and shouldn't factor into how or why you want to sell. If you see investing as the wealth-building strategy that it is, building wealth—not owning any particular investment—is the overall goal.

It's impossible to take investing seriously without realizing that there are risks involved. There are times when you will lose money, and when that happens, it's nothing to laugh at. Unfortunately, we see shady posts and comments all the time when we discuss dips and losses in the market. People literally make fun of people who lose money.

What part of the game is that? First, none of us has money to lose or waste, no matter how rich we may be or seem to be. We all work hard for what we have, and our ability to multiply it comes from a strong desire to create a better life than the one we have now.

To be fair, we don't think people who laugh at investment losses should be immediately written off as haters. While there will be some people who will be jealous of you and your ability to make different choices for yourself and your family, we've found that most people respond to others' financial wins and losses out of sheer fear and ignorance. It's not that they don't want the additional income that comes from investing; they either don't know how to go about it or are afraid to take the first step. And instead of learning what they need to know and overcoming their fears, they project their doubts and lack of self-confidence onto others.

Their projection costs them money. If you see yourself in them, it's costing you money, too. When you look at your EYL Baseline and evaluate what you really want and what it will take to provide you and your family with the financial freedom you desire, you'll understand that it's not going to happen without making some investments and taking a few risks. Think about it: There are only twenty-four hours in a day, and you need to spend a certain number of them resting and spending time with the family you're working so hard for. Investments are essential to building wealth, and there's really no way around it.

BITCOIN AND THE FUTURE OF DIGITAL CURRENCY

Not a week goes by that someone doesn't ask us about Bitcoin. They want to know what we think about it, whether it's a solid investment, and if it's safe. The idea of owning digital currency—which is what Bitcoin is—scares most people. At any moment, you can go to the bank, withdraw all of your money, and put it back either into your account or underneath your mattress. And while we wouldn't recommend doing any of that, we understand what it means in relationship to Bitcoin. You can see, feel, touch, and smell the money you have in the bank. With Bitcoin, that's impossible.

At the same time, it's important to understand that digital currency isn't going away. And with many people losing faith in the strength of the U.S. dollar, Bitcoin is becoming increasingly popular and making many people extremely wealthy. We absolutely recommend it as a financial product for those who are interested in creating a fully diverse investment portfolio. But before we try to sell you on an investment strategy, we need to tell you what Bitcoin is.

Bitcoin was created in response to the financial crisis of 2008–2009. It is a form of decentralized cryptocurrency, meaning that it is not controlled by any bank or government. However, that doesn't stop it from functioning like traditional money. You can use Bitcoin to purchase goods and services worldwide. More and more companies and businesses are accepting Bitcoin. All transactions are held in a public ledger, known as the blockchain. Because of its sophistication, it is impossible to duplicate Bitcoin. It's also why there is never expected to be more than 21 million Bitcoin ever created. At the time we're writing this, there are currently over 19.5 million Bitcoin in existence, with around 900 being created every day.

There are many investors who got in on the Bitcoin wave when cryptocurrency was emerging, back when the masses of people said that it was a fad. Those folks are millionaires now. And even though Bitcoin is a digital currency, they're millionaires with real money. There are web-based banking platforms that allow you to buy, sell, and trade your Bitcoin, cashing out your conversions into your bank account.

Currently, one U.S. dollar is worth 0.000015 in Bitcoin, but one Bitcoin is worth over $66,000.

Now do you see why folks are riding the Bitcoin wave? For those of you who are still leery, let us put your mind at ease. Decentralized currency isn't going anywhere. Just as technology continues to advance, there are ways our money is going to continue advancing with it. There are entirely too many people who have become wealthy from it for it just one day to no longer exist. If anything, governments will try to find a way to centralize it before that happens.

While we recommend investing in Bitcoin, it requires a strategy and we do not recommend putting your entire investing budget into your Bitcoin trading account. You can start small; $100 a month or week is manageable; even less works, too. We also recommend learning as much about digital currency as possible as you're investing—and even before. It's a leap, for sure. But it's potentially lucrative, and the right kind of investment into it can yield a solid payoff.

Navigating the Ups and Downs in the Market

Losses are inevitable. Their severity will depend on several factors. Many of them will be completely out of your control. For example, so much of the stock market's recent volatility and the current economic instability is due to a convergence of factors, including slow GDP growth, rising interest rates, and inflation. How you handle your losses will determine the overall success you will experience.

April makes $80,000 a year, and because she lives in a small town in Alabama, her money goes further than it could in a large city. She's done great work to put herself into a prime position to invest. And she needs to; her 401(k) and savings won't be enough to sustain her life post retirement. She's attended several investment seminars, read a number of books, and listened to many podcasts to prepare herself for investing. But unfortunately, she just hasn't been able to start. Even after she met with a financial adviser and was presented with various possibilities for creating a solid investment portfolio, she decided that the potential loss wasn't worth the investment.

Kyle has been trading on the stock market for quite some time but hasn't made much money. He's been following new and trending stocks. Many times, he's doubled his investment within a quarter. By then turning around and reinvesting the bulk of his profit in those same stock types, he's lost a significant amount of his investment. This has unfortunately set him back in the pursuit of his financial goals. It's been impossible for him to use his investment portfolio to save for a down payment on a home so he can stop renting.

April's attitude can be classified as loss aversion, which is an overwhelming fear of loss that causes investors and potential investors to act irrationally. This can include refusing to invest, holding on to a stock or other investment too long, or letting it go too early. Kyle's pursuit of hot stocks makes it clear that he doesn't understand the market. Entering and exiting the market at a high rate also reveal a fear of investing. Both April and Kyle, as well as other people like them, ultimately want to keep as much of their money as possible without taking real risks to grow it.

When it comes to trying to stay the course during market volatility and attempting to mitigate your fears about investing, the most important thing to do is remain calm. A market downturn will not last forever, and playing the long game will serve you well. The next step is to stay put: Don't sell or unload your investments based on current market trends. Ultimately, you will create an even greater risk for yourself. Having a diversified portfolio that includes defensive assets such as cash, bonds, and gold is an optimal way to navigate the market's volatility. Rebalancing your portfolio and adjusting your investments will also create economic health and stability in turbulent times.

Optimizing Your Taxes and Protecting Your Wealth

Creating a successful tax strategy for your investments is the best way to maximize your yields and returns. One of the best ways to achieve this is through asset allocation. Using this strategy, an investor determines which investments should be held in tax-deferred accounts and which should be put into taxable accounts to maximize after-tax returns. The best location for an asset depends on several factors, including the investment's financial profile, current tax laws, holding periods, and the investment's profitability.

Stocks, which are tax-friendly, should be held in taxable accounts because of their lower tax rates and the ability to defer gains. Riskier investments also belong in taxable accounts because of both their ability to defer taxes and their ability to mitigate losses on slowly or poorly performing investments. Index funds, mutual funds, bonds, and REITs belong in tax-deferred accounts because they generate high returns and distributions.

Just as it's important to have a diversified investment portfolio, the best way to benefit from asset allocation is to have investments in both taxable and tax-deferred accounts. A portfolio consisting of equity and fixed-income investments receives the maximum benefit from this strategy. Since most equity investments yield returns from dividends and capital gains, investors pay lower taxes when their investments are held within a taxable account. If an investor withdraws funds from a tax-deferred retirement account or will be doing so soon, the benefit of asset allocation is greater than for younger investors with many years left before they need to start withdrawing funds.

Another strategy is tax-loss harvesting. This occurs when an investor sells nonprofitable investments at a loss to offset the capital gains taxes incurred by the sale of investments for a profit. Tax-loss harvesting helps you reduce taxes by offsetting the amount you have to claim as gains or income, allowing you to sell investments at a loss, then use that loss to lower or eliminate the taxes you are required to pay. Essentially, if an investment creates a loss for you, you can reap a tax benefit.

Through tax-loss harvesting, investors can replace an asset sold at a loss with a comparable asset, assuming that certain rules and requirements are met. First, tax-loss harvesting can be applied only to investments held in a taxable account. Also, this strategy is best employed by investors in higher tax brackets and can be applied only to harvesting done within that calendar year. Certain types of investments are most optimal for tax-loss harvesting, including stocks, actively managed funds, and mutual funds.

Avoiding Scams and Staying Safe

The fear many people have concerning the risk of investing is warranted. And it's largely due to the rise of investment scams and tactics that seek to defraud people of their investments, retirement funds, and savings. Many people think they can spot a scam and would never be the victim of one. Yet as scams increase in sophistication, it's important to be able to spot their most common characteristics.

1. **One of the first things scammers will do is try to convince a mark that they don't have enough time to provide the specifics of the alleged deal in writing.** This is different from when you receive a letter or brochure in the mail. Every investment deal should be detailed in writing; if a written document can't be provided, there is a great likelihood that the investment isn't real.

2. **Scammers will sometimes say that your banking information is required to process an investment deal.** It will also be suggested that you'll need to provide

your financial information as a sign of good faith to initiate negotiations. Once you provide scammers with your financial information, they can use it to drain your bank accounts.

3. **Any promise of a free gift or trip or having "won" something is an indication of a potential scam.** Typically when an investment contract suggests that an investor has won something, it likely indicates that the investor will be making additional purchases throughout or on the back end of the investment.

4. **When investment partners are rude and engage in unprofessional conduct with potential investors, it's likely a scam.** It should go without saying that professionals should never be rude or refuse to return phone calls, answer correspondence, or give out their phone number. If someone always wants to meet somewhere other than in an office, this is also a red flag that can't be ignored.

5. **Investment partners and professionals who promise "inside information" are more than likely scammers.** As we've already told you, investments don't have a science that can ensure success. Investment professionals who say they know what others don't and can give you that information so your investment can thrive are lying. There's no other way around it.

Common investment scams include:

- **Affinity group fraud:** When scammers use a mutually shared ethnic or religious identity to gain the trust of a potential investor, it exploits our instinctual desire to trust people and believe the best of them. These scams include targeted advertising, employment offers, vocational training, and financial advice.

- **Annuity scams:** While annuities are legitimate services provided by life insurance companies, potential investors are often coerced into purchasing annuities that are not suitable for them and their situation. Because annuities can be a vital form of financial protection for seniors, seniors are the most vulnerable to these scams.

- **Business franchise scams:** Potential investors are approached with promises of becoming their own boss through a franchise or business opportunity. The fraudulent offer promises a high return to an investor who invests enough to cover all start-up costs. The only people who make money are the "business owners" who receive the investment money. These scams appeal to potential investors who have few job skills or prospects and are in desperate need of money.

- **Individual Retirement Account (IRA) scams:** In recent years, some IRA custodians have offered to hold unlawful and fraudulent securities in IRA accounts. When these securities are discovered, investors may not only lose their entire investments but also face IRS and administrative penalties.

- **Internet fraud:** Internet scams are numerous because the internet is far-reaching and expansive and provides scammers with anonymity. Internet scams include

pyramid schemes, online investment seminars, chain
letters, and prime bank investments. The level of
sophistication of the various scams means that anyone is
vulnerable to falling for them.

- **Fraudulent investment seminars and financial
  planning activities:** Scammers pose as financial planners
  and use investment seminars to offer unrealistic and
  ineffective investment advice that sounds appealing and
  attainable. Often these seminars are led by speakers and
  "experts" who are not licensed or registered financial
  advisers and who may fail to disclose conflicts of interest,
  as well as hidden fees and commissions.

- **Ponzi schemes:** Ponzi schemes pay a significantly large
  rate of return to their initial investors out of funds
  secured from later investors. The last investors lose all of
  their money when the scheme is upended.

- **Predatory lending scams:** These consist of various
  mortgage lending practices in which predatory lenders
  pressure consumers into signing loans that they can't
  afford. First-time homebuyers and individuals with bad
  credit are most vulnerable to predatory lending scams.

- **Promissory note scams:** Sold by independent insurance
  agents, fraudulent promissory notes offer investors a
  promise of high returns—up to 15% a month—at little
  to no risk. Many of the notes are short-term debt
  investments issued on behalf of companies and
  institutions that don't exist. First-time investors are
  typically the most vulnerable and susceptible to these
  scams.

- **"Pump-and-dump" stock schemes:** Scammers typically purchase a stock at a cheap price, then falsely claim that the company has made a groundbreaking development or is about to make a major announcement that will cause its stock price to double or triple in value. This results in an immediate increase in the price of the stock, followed by an equally immediate downturn when the scammers who purchased the stock early sell it at the peak price, gaining a huge profit. The remaining shares can then become worthless.

- **Pyramid schemes:** A pyramid scheme occurs when new investors are recruited to pay the initial investors at the top of the pyramid. The reality is that there is no actual product or service; the scheme's sole purpose is to recruit new investors to continue paying the initial investors.

- **Viatical investment scams:** The perpetrators of these scams buy an interest in the death benefits available through the life insurance policies of terminally ill patients. The insured receives a discounted percentage of the death benefits in cash to "improve" their quality of life in their final days. Investors receive their share of the death benefit when the insured dies minus a brokerage fee for the viatical investment broker. These investments are extremely high risk and predatory for seniors.

To protect yourself against scams and frauds, the first thing you should do when considering an investment is to verify the license of the investment professional. Additionally, you should verify the registration of the investment itself. Doing these two things in the beginning will keep you from a world of frustration and potential loss. Also remember that you don't have to rush making an investment. Take your time, request an investment prospectus and consult with qualified professionals, perform a risk tolerance analysis, and seriously consider the investment from every angle. And trust yourself; if you feel that something is off, there's a strong possibility that it is.

Risk is a tool of empowerment. Once you learn what is and is not optimal for you, you'll be able to make more informed and productive choices. And those choices can be incredibly lucrative. As you move forward with creating your financial future, you will revisit your risk capacity from time to time. And it will change. Let it ebb and flow as you grow and evolve and as your investment interests change. The ability of all your risk factors to be malleable will serve you well as you continue to pursue your financial freedom.

The Top Two Reasons People Don't Build Wealth

Fear of Losing Capital

When it comes to wealth building and investments, there is one main reason people steer clear of it: **the risk of losing money**. The housing crisis of 2020 was a prime example. Many people found great success in real estate, renting out several of their properties. However, according to the Joint Center for Housing Studies of Harvard University, only 62% of landlords collected at least 90% of their rent in 2020, down significantly from 89% in 2019. And when Realtor.com and the Urban Institute partnered to study independent landlords, they found that 62.7% of their respondents had been deemed ineligible to receive government-funded rental assistance in 2020. Many landlords in our EYL community took a hit during the pandemic. And when they shared their stories, there were people in the comments saying that what those landlords had experienced is exactly why they'll never get into real estate: They don't have money to waste.

None of us has money to waste, and the idea of losing capital scares people. We've all heard the horror stories of people losing their life savings, their college funds, and sometimes their homes after an investment goes awry. That kind of stress and agony fuels financial traumas and can lead to catastrophes in other areas of your life. Nobody wants to experience this. So instead of examining why losses may have happened to others, people would rather stay away from wealth building altogether. Essentially, this is counterproductive, because staying away might make you safer, but it won't give you what you need.

There are many reasons people lose money on investments, and the loss of capital can happen on a variety of levels. You can lose money on an investment simply because you weren't educated enough about what you were investing in. Now, this doesn't mean that the investment was inherently bad; it could potentially be a powerful and lucrative one. But if you don't know everything you need to know before investing, a great opportunity can become your biggest mistake. Rashad has been pretty honest about the times he's lost money on an investment. More times than not, he didn't know all he needed to before he took the risk. And while losing money is always frustrating and a possibility, he knows that he didn't set himself up for success by having all the information he needed. Now you'll find him asking a ton of questions and doing extensive research. There's always an inherent risk in investing, but it's also possible to mitigate that risk through education.

There are times when you can lose on an investment you were well educated about, simply because that investment just didn't go the way that you prepared for or expected. Unfortunately, this happens sometimes. Taking a risk means doing just that, and more often than not, you can't control for all factors. According to Experian, the investments with the greatest potential for financial loss are cryptocurrency and the stock market. In November 2021, Bitcoin saw a record high of $69,000. Two months later, the price had dropped by 37% to just under $43,000. In March 2024, its value soared again to over $75,000. At the end of April, *Forbes* reported that the price had fallen below

$60,000. And while the stock market is incredibly unpredictable, in March 2024, CNBC noted that investors who leave the market during a downturn miss an average of ten positive-trending days that consistently yield higher returns after the downturn.

The first thing we tell EYL participants is that they have to prepare mentally to lose money. No one likes to hear that, but preparing for losses is sign of wisdom. The key will always be to reduce the amount you lose, and later we'll go more into detail about how to do that. But understanding that loss is as much a part of investing as it is of life will go a long way toward your keeping a level head when things don't go the way you desire.

EXERCISE

If you are hesitant about investing because you're afraid of losing money, we want you to ask yourselves these questions.

1. **Can I achieve my EYL Baseline and earn my leisure without investing?**

   To answer this, you'll need to determine what your baseline is and how you can get there. Can you do it with an extra part-time job? Do you want to work another job? This is also a good opportunity to evaluate your time commitments and what you will have the capacity to do given your current schedule.

2. **Do I personally know anyone who made a bad investment? Did I talk to them about their experience, or did I make assumptions about what happened and project my fears onto their situation?**

   Information remains the most important asset we can have, and assumptions will mess all of us up. Here's an opportunity to reach out to the investors and entrepreneurs we know for guidance and wisdom. If they know you, they're going to give you the real, and that's exactly what you need.

3. **Looking at my current budget, what could I conceivably invest—and potentially lose—that would not place me in financial jeopardy?**

   No investment or commitment to your financial future should negatively impact your present circumstances. You should never have to worry about whether you can pay a bill because you're in the investment game. But you can and should see how much of your Starbucks or cigar budget can be moved over to your investment fund.

   Answering these questions will help you begin to analyze and release the fear you have of losing money when it comes to investing. This isn't to minimize the feeling of losing money but to push you to be honest about what's holding you back and why.

Lack of Confidence

We all know what it's like to be afraid of the unknown and to have a fear of failure. It shows up in other parts of our lives; we'd be foolish to not see that it can show up when it comes to investing our money. Confidence is one of the driving factors of a high quality of life, and we want people to have an "I can do it" attitude. When it comes to investing, we want to encourage you to develop and maintain an outlook that recognizes that failures in investing aren't a reflection of who you are. Yeah, your investments are not always going to work out. No matter how much research you do, no matter how much time you spend, they're not always going to go as planned. You can't lose your confidence simply because an investment didn't work out, but also, don't become overconfident because it did.

We saw that overconfidence arise during the 2020 pandemic. Despite the global pandemic and all the social and political tension in the country that year, the stock market did extremely well. Economists and strategists credited the strength of the Federal Reserve, congressional relief bills, the low risk of bonds, and the surge of tech companies for the boom. People made a lot of money in the stock market that year. It was one of the only investment arenas that endured the year. Unfortunately, people got a little overconfident and began to invest more than they could take on.

Two years later, the stock market had its worst year since 2008. Supply chain issues and the conflict between Russia and Ukraine were among the factors. People were shocked and disappointed. They had never experienced such a situation and were suffering more losses than gains. Overconfidence in the market can hurt because it gives the illusion that success and gains will be constant. Investments ebb and flow, and you have to be ready for that.

Too often, we see that the real issue behind the lack of confidence is embarrassment. If people lose money, they feel they should have known better. Before they even get into the investment game, they count themselves out because they're already blaming potential losses on themselves. Listen to us: You can't do that and be successful. When a loss happens, the only (positive) thing you can do is analyze your decisions and the context of the loss so you can apply the lessons to the next endeavor. There's absolutely no reason to be embarrassed or ashamed. No one gets to greatness without taking a loss somewhere. Those who are the most successful in business aren't worried about what anyone else thinks about their losses, nor do they second-guess themselves when a gain is nowhere in sight. They're off somewhere turning the *L* into a win somewhere else. Take a page from their book.

Investing Is Not Gambling

When it comes to investment risk mitigation, it's important to understand that you can't study and prepare enough to ensure that your risk index will be low. No matter what an investment is—it could be the "safest" in the world—there is still a possibility that it won't work out.

In this respect, investing is not gambling. While there is inherent risk in both, it's not the same thing. While there are professional gamblers who use mathematical equations to count cards and determine the probability of a slot machine paying off after a certain number of pulls, gambling is a game of chance for the most part. If you roll the dice, there's no skill involved. Literally, whatever happens *happens*. Investing is different. We don't consider it a game of chance; instead, it's a game of knowledge.

You can wake up, roll out of bed, and buy a lottery ticket or scratch-off at most gas stations in the country—and if you're lucky, you might win some money. Don't do this when it comes to your investments. You need to know everything you can possibly know about your desired venture. At the end of the day, an investment is just that: an investment. It involves a significant chunk of resources that you could be using to do something else. It is also something you desire to be lucrative and productive. You owe it to yourself—and your money—to put yourself into the best position for success.

Consider this: You have $100,000, and you just purchased a home even though you have no real understanding of the real estate market or what it takes to create a lucrative rental property. You're not sure what the market rate for the neighborhood is or the tenant turnover rate in the area. On average, how much does someone owning a property similar to yours expect to spend annually on maintenance and upkeep? What's the average amount of reserves a landlord needs to cover a potential late payment or nonpayment? If you don't have this information, then you are just *hoping* that you have a good investment. The truth is that you don't know. But when you are educated about real estate as an investment, you can investigate comparable properties and find out if there are even any renters living in the neighborhood. And you'll know the ins and outs of the appraisal and inspection processes. Once you're properly educated about the kind of investment you're pursuing, the probability of its working out in your favor increases. While the risk will always be there, **mitigating your risk through education is the key to success with investments**.

◆ ◆ ◆

CHAPTER SEVEN

Entrepreneurship
(A Beautiful Struggle)

As an executive in tech, Ibrahim was doing well. When COVID-19 hit, he was especially in demand as companies needed to create the infrastructure that would sustain them during the pandemic. Consequently, he made more that year than he had ever made in his life, his salary booming to over $300,000. Then the world opened back up and companies began to scale back on their hires. And Ibrahim found himself out of a job. As he looked for a job, he bemoaned to some of his friends that many of the companies still needed the services he provided. Just because the pandemic was "over" didn't mean that everyone would be going back to work as usual.

When Ibrahim's friends told him to consider starting his own business, he initially pooh-poohed the idea. In truth, he was scared. But considering the difficulty he was having finding a job, he decided he had nothing to lose by researching the idea of going into business for himself. Thanks to a few years at his previous salary, he had

$100,000 saved that he hadn't earmarked for anything in particular, and he was incredibly proud of that. All of his bills were paid, and until he found a new job, he cut many of his unnecessary expenses in half. By his estimates, he had a solid eight months before he would run out of money.

As many companies continued to offer work-from-home options for their employees, they needed to hire additional tech support to ensure that they wouldn't overwhelm their current divisions. Luckily, Ibrahim was offered a contract position with his old company. A friend encouraged him to establish everything he needed to create his own business and put himself into a position to secure other contracts.

The next day, Ibrahim went to the Apple Store to purchase a new computer and an additional monitor. He created an LLC and established a business account with Bank of America. He also updated his LinkedIn profile and paid someone to create a website and pitch deck for his services. After spending around $7,000, he was an entrepreneur with a legitimate business and one client. He set his sights on adding another client to his roster within five months. To achieve that, he began maximizing his connections and reaching out to his networks. Even though he was excited to be working again and working for himself, he had no idea what he was getting into.

Becoming an entrepreneur seems like the wave, but the truth is that there's a lot that goes into it and it's definitely not a decision to consider lightly. Not everyone is cut out for entrepreneurship. That's not hate; that's reality. In this chapter, we break down all the most important aspects of entrepreneurship and provide you with the tips we think can ensure your success. While being your own boss may not be easy, it can be rewarding for anyone who wants to put the work in to make it attainable.

We've encouraged many within our EYL community to take the various personality tests that are available online and through career coaching services to identify their particular strengths as they venture into entrepreneurship. This will help them begin narrowing their focus to businesses and entrepreneurial opportunities that would best align with their personality and overall pursuits.

So maybe the most important question to ask yourself is: How can I decide if entrepreneurship is right for me? Answering this question is crucial, and we'd suggest that you take some time to do so. To make the best decision for you, your family, and anyone else impacted by your choices, think about these important considerations.

1. **Why do you want to start a business?** There is a multitude of reasons you might choose the entrepreneurial journey, including the freedom to be your own boss, the flexibility of your schedule, and the opportunity to work from home or anywhere else you desire. Your reasons can also include making the kind of money that will create generational wealth. It could also be that you've been laid off, as Ibrahim was, and are having difficulty finding a job, so you decide to use your skills, gifts, and talents to go into business for yourself. Name your reasons and craft your why. Also, understand that the reasons have to be valid only to *you*. If you're looking to someone else to approve of your entrepreneurial decisions, you're already fighting a losing battle.

2. **Determining the right business model:** There are many types of businesses you can start. Each requires a different skill set and personality traits. Here are a few entrepreneurial models that we've seen work well within our community and what's needed to build and maintain them.

   • **A traditional brick-and-mortar business:** Such a business has a physical location where consumers and supporters go to shop and access goods and services. It can be a nightclub, restaurant, laundromat, car wash, nail salon or other aesthetic service, or daycare. Such a business requires an appealing location with high-quality amenities that will attract customers. Most important, it must also include a front-facing staff who are friendly and committed to good customer service. The ideal entrepreneur of a brick-and-mortar business is someone who is a people person and enjoys engaging with people.

- **A virtual goods and services business/ e-commerce:** This kind of business is conducted exclusively online. It may be a direct shipping T-shirt business, a dessert or candle company, or a virtual service such as human resources management, payroll, ghostwriting, or assistant for other small businesses or larger corporations. A business such as these requires a true self-starter, as it often involves having to follow leads and generate sales through online marketing and advertisements. This type of job can become all consuming, especially since there is often no physical location in which to do the work other than in the entrepreneur's home.

- **A franchise:** Instead of starting a business from the inception of the idea, an entrepreneur can pay a fee to open a new branch or location of an already established business. Franchises include restaurant chains and car washes. These businesses are ideal for entrepreneurs who want to start a business without the hassle of coming up with an idea or its structure. While franchise opportunities still require a lot of work, they come with their own set of rules and regulations that must be followed and not deviated from. However, in the end, a franchise can make an entrepreneur a great deal of profit based on the name recognition and success of the parent brand and company.

The best way to decide what type of business you'd like to open is to consider the specific demands of the business with regard to your strengths, personality traits, and interests. While work is still most definitely "work," the closer it is aligned to who you are and what you truly want to do, the more likely it is that you will love what you do. And when you love what you do, you are able to define success for yourself and thrive.

3. **Setting up a successful business:** Here is the opportunity to create success for your business. Do you want to have employees? A traditional brick-and-mortar business or a virtual business? Answering those questions will dictate the type of business model you'll pursue. Do you have product and profit goals? How will your entrepreneurial journey fit into the overall scheme of your life? The beauty of being at the beginning of this journey is that you get to decide. And if you're in the middle of your journey when you're reading this, you still get to decide. This is your road map. You get to craft it.

4. **Recognizing the demands of running your own business:** Being an entrepreneur is completely different

from being a traditional employee. Whereas when you work for someone else, your workday is set, there is no typical workday for an entrepreneur. Even if you have a brick-and-mortar business or a company with employees, your day as the boss will look much different from theirs. And while you can't necessarily prepare for unpredictable days, you can do what you need to in order to ensure your success. This includes making sure that your physical, mental, spiritual, and emotional health are always in good shape. A business is only as successful as its owner.

5. **Trusting yourself:** Some of you will go back and forth about your decision. Others will instantly be confident that they are making the right one. Ultimately, the most important thing you can do is trust yourself. Know that you will make the best decisions for yourself when it comes to your personal and professional life. When you've done the research to be as informed and educated as possible, you'll be able to be clear about your passion and purpose for your business. Knowing those is a major key to success.

6. **Ensuring there is a value add:** Your business just isn't for you; it's also to improve the conditions of your consumers and the community it serves. As you consider your potential business, make a list of all the ways it will enhance the lives of others. If you're providing a good or service, that's a value add—including providing jobs for others. If your business will employ only you, ask yourself how this business will help make someone's life easier. In its own way, this is also how you pay it forward.

In the EYL universe, we have a mantra: One income is too close to no income. This recognizes several factors. First, with the rising costs of *everything*, living off one income is becoming increasingly impossible. In addition to that, attempting to save your way into wealth won't likely happen with one income. The paycheck from your nine-to-five can go only so far. It will take care of your basic living expenses, and with some finesse, you'll likely be able to take one major vacation or a few small trips each year. But a single income doesn't leave much for investing or even being able to save aggressively in the hope of investing one day. For these reasons, we believe that every person has to have more than one income.

We never want to diminish the importance of or need for traditional employment. We've never been the kind of people to bash employees or buy into boss-versus-employee tropes. What we want you to understand is that you can work a job and still own a business. What would it mean for you to work from nine to five and dedicate seven to midnight to your business? Actually, that was exactly what Troy did.

Troy's Story

Looking back, Troy realized that he had always had an entrepreneurial mindset. His circle was filled with people who owned their own businesses, and many of his inspirations were entrepreneurs. Up close and personally, he saw their ethics and their grind. Even though he was a full-time schoolteacher, that same hustle was in him. Troy knew that his salary wouldn't support the dreams he had for his wife and two children. Simply put, he needed more money.

As he and Rashad continued to build the EYL brand, Troy continued teaching. What helped him greatly was applying the same kind of structure that he had established in the world of education to his new journey as an entrepreneur. As a teacher, he was required to prepare lesson plans and be consistent in his teaching and the flow of his workday. He applied that same technique to structuring his time as an entrepreneur. To build EYL, Troy and Rashad began filming and recording content and streaming. When Troy got off work in the afternoon, he spent time with his family and then devoted his evening hours to EYL. While it meant less sleep for Troy during the week, he had to do whatever was necessary to make sure that none of the three things that were important to him (his family, his main job, and EYL) suffered. If the new brand was going to work, Troy would have to be clear about his boundaries.

The year 2020 was a big one for EYL. The COVID-19 pandemic ensured that everyone was at home and on their phones. Added to that, people needed to know how to make more money with fewer resources, how to stay afloat in an unstable economy, and how to maximize what they had to get to what they wanted. EYL content was in demand more than ever. The company scaled up before their eyes, and it meant there was no more business as usual. For Troy, when it became clear that EYL was well on its way to becoming what he and Rashad knew it could be, he began the transition from being both a traditional employee and an entrepreneur to being a full-time entrepreneur. He knew it was time to leave when two things happened: spending time after his workday was over to work on EYL was no longer enough, and he was ready to focus exclusively on the brand. Financially, it was the biggest risk he had ever taken. Leaving the security of an assured monthly income to essentially "eating only what you kill" required serious planning and conversations with his wife. It wasn't just him taking the leap; his entire family was jumping with him.

Troy didn't make the transition into full-time entrepreneurship until he and his family had a solid financial plan. While

Ibrahim didn't necessarily have a choice because he hadn't yet found another job, full-time entrepreneurship was an easier transition because he had $100,000 in his savings. If you're considering making the shift to full-time entrepreneurship, it will be important to revisit your EYL Baseline and annual money principle budget, analyze the past six months of your business's revenue, and establish how much you need to generate—and save (that emergency savings account is going to come in real handy right now)—in order to shift into full-time entrepreneurship.

Understand that this is just the first financial step. How much you have saved and need will depend on what type of business you want to start. For instance, a brick-and-mortar business is going to require more start-up capital than a virtual business will. And if you're planning to franchise a business, you will need to pay a franchise fee in addition to all the other start-up costs. We suggest creating a checklist of all the costs and fees associated with your desired business venture. To get you started and help you determine how much you'll need to get your business off the ground, consider all these expenses.

Initial expenses and onetime fees:

- Business formation and incorporation costs

- Industry-specific licenses and permits

- Website design and production

- Business cards

- Business equipment and furniture

- Initial purchase of office supplies

- Down payment on location or office rental deposit

- Initial inventory or starter materials

- Signage

Recurring expenses:

- Rent/mortgage

- Utilities

- Business loan and/or credit card payments

- Insurance

- Business taxes

- Accounting and legal services

- Website maintenance and communications

- Marketing

- Your own salary and benefits

- Payroll and employee benefits

- Office supplies

- Inventory and business materials

Calculating the initial expenses and onetime fees is as simple as researching the costs and adding them up. Keep your calculation handy; you will need it. Recurring expenses will vary and will depend on the type of business you have; we advise having a minimum of four months' worth of these expenses available. Keep in mind that the greater your recurring expenses, the more income and revenue you will need. If you're just starting out, streamline your fees and expenses. What must you have now? What can you wait for? You know that you will need all the necessary licenses, permits, and insurance up front.

But waiting till later to purchase what you don't need right now will generate more profit that will lead to the financial freedom you're pursuing through entreprencurship.

So You Want to Be an Entrepreneur?

Semaj, a personal trainer, built his clientele working at LA Fitness, but now he was ready to expand and go into business for himself. He realized that many of his clients preferred personalized training sessions at more convenient locations—including at home, in the office, or in a local park. After creating online fitness content that had gone viral, he wanted to capitalize on having more than 300,000 followers to build a wellness brand that would be both practical and effective.

To do this, Semaj wanted to save a large chunk of his client fees to fund a future line of fitness products, including supplements and apparel. Through that, he hoped to ultimately become financially independent. He had big dreams, but he didn't have the equivalent resources. One of the early challenges was the initial investment in portable fitness equipment and a vehicle large enough to transport it. Leaving LA Fitness meant leaving all the equipment he had been using behind, and while he loved his Dodge Charger, it wasn't the best vehicle for a mobile fitness company. Balancing the initial costs with the uncertainty of client commitments was difficult.

Semaj chose to start small, with local marketing strategies, including social media campaigns and community event participation, to build a local client base. He quickly learned that a large social media following doesn't automatically translate into paying customers. He had to prove himself and what he could offer away from an established gym. To do so, he offered free sessions in the park to generate interest and relied heavily on word-of-mouth referrals. Within the first year, his business had a steady stream of clients, enabling him to purchase all the equipment he needed and to get a Ford Expedition, a purchase that qualified for a tax deduction because it weighed over 6,000 pounds. In the second year, he began to put a plan into place to hire additional trainers and began to consider a brick-and-mortar location.

In the beginning, not having much worked in Semaj's favor. It required that he be intentional and deliberate in his business-building strategy. Unlike others who might have had start-up capital available, Semaj had to offer free boot camp–style classes in the park to attract a faithful and more established clientele. Crafting workouts that focused on body weight, he didn't initially have to worry about not having any weights or equipment. Thankfully, for him, HIIT workouts had been trending and were incredibly appealing to potential clients. This is the first rule for any entrepreneur who doesn't have much but needs to start making money: **Work with what you have**. Your current laptop or computer is sufficient for what you need to start an online business. There's no need to incur debt when you don't have to.

Semaj's plan worked because in the grand scheme of things, he knew his market. Becoming an entrepreneur requires understanding what you will need to have and do in order for your business to be effective. To achieve this, we suggest conducting a few "test rounds" that will give you the information you need to make sure your efforts will be successful.

1. If you're considering opening a restaurant, a "pop-up" shop that features some of your signature dishes is a great way to gather feedback before opening the restaurant.

2. Scouting the potential location of a franchise to evaluate the foot traffic, the potential business, and safety is an essential strategy to ensure that the business will maximize profits and be a serious investment.

3. Scheduling meetings with members of your professional network to assess how effective your virtual assistant business could be is a free market analysis and will prove beneficial in the long run when it comes to establishing your infrastructure.

Everyone has a business idea, and what you'll quickly learn is that most people think their idea is the one that will make them a millionaire. This doesn't mean you won't be a millionaire, but it does mean that you should vet your idea properly to ensure that at the very least, it will make you money.

Do you know your market? This is the most crucial aspect of business that many people assume they can ignore. We can't tell you how many people have a great idea and jump into it without understanding how they will fit into that particular business's landscape. For many, this will mean exploring your niche and competitive edge. If you're opening a soul food restaurant, what will make people become patrons of yours as opposed to the soul food spots that are already in the city? What will set your direct shipping business apart from the others out there? The identity of your business, your brand's DNA, is its calling card. While you may have spent time crafting the idea itself, understanding how it will stand up in the market is key.

Determining your business's place in the market is only one part of what you need to do; it's equally as important to decide what its initial size will be. The notion of the side hustle has become increasingly popular in recent years. At its core, a side hustle provides secondary income, through either traditional employment or your business, that supplements your main revenue source. As we said earlier in the chapter, one income is too close to no income, so we are all for having additional income streams that will enable you to craft the life you want. Our issue is with the term *side hustle*. The impression it gives is that you're doing the job on the . . . well, side; it's not as important as your main revenue stream. Most people get a side hustle to make some extra bucks, and as long as they do that, they're good. But what if that's not good enough? When you are pursuing financial freedom, every step you take toward it matters. You have to be as intentional about your movements with a secondary stream of income as you are with your primary source.

If you start a business to generate additional income to supplement your main revenue stream, you don't have a side hustle; you're an entrepreneur with a business. It doesn't matter if you're open twenty hours a week or two. You have a reputable business that was created to meet a community need and advance your goal of financial freedom. For us, it's important that you shift your language around who you are and what you do. Because, when language shifts, so does your attitude and perception.

You can start a business while maintaining your traditional employment, as Troy did. That was Twana. A lifelong educator as well, she desired to create a business that would supplement her income. Add to that the fact that she and her husband had recently become empty nesters and she had a lot of free time. More money and flexibility would give her and her husband the opportunity to travel together and make some much needed renovations to their house. Looking for a fun and creative business venture, she started a T-shirt business that catered exclusively to Black women.

To set her business apart, Twana posted paid social media ads, created funny reels that highlighted her designs, and advertised that she'd launch a new design each Friday. Additionally, she used a newsletter to develop a community of women who believed in her vision and would buy her shirts and hoodies. In the beginning, she spent all of her time after school and on weekends building her business. Because her presence on social media drove sales, she used third-party apps to schedule content posts during school hours. Within the first two years, she made enough money in her business to leave education and become a full-time entrepreneur.

However, for close to a year, Twana's T-shirt sales dwindled to infrequent booms around homecoming season and holidays. The income she generated from the business was no longer enough to replace the income she made as an educator, and she found herself losing more money from her family's budget than she liked. As a result, she made the difficult decision to transition back to full-time traditional employment and work on her business after hours and on the weekends.

It took her a while not to see this decision as a failure because it wasn't. Transitioning back to traditional employment doesn't mean your business failed. In this and most instances we've seen with members of our community, the transition back has a lot to do with not understanding the cycles of particular businesses. Her business settled into a rhythm of increased sales around special occasions or whenever she had an exclusive design that coincided with a current trending pop culture moment. Owners of car wash franchises typically see high volumes of business in the spring, summer, and early fall months. Because of this, they budget and plan for the months when it's too cold for most folks to care about their cars.

Even though there will always be people who maintain a business and traditional employment simultaneously, there are also those who start a business with the intention of eventually leaving their jobs and going at their dream full time. The most common question they ask us is how they will know it's time to make that transition. Earlier in this chapter, we talked about the financial benchmarks Troy required EYL to meet before he left teaching. Those are crucial, but there are many other factors to consider before making the leap from traditional employment to full-time entrepreneurship.

1. **Do you have enough business to sustain full-time entrepreneurship?** Depending on the kind of business you are starting and your goals, the amount of business will vary. Take, for instance, a home bakery. If your current orders and potential customers aren't enough to

cover your monthly expenses, it may not be time to leave your current job to focus exclusively on that business. Twana's sales exceeded her monthly income at her teaching job for four months, and after talking with her husband, she made the transition because her business was stable enough to build upon.

2. **Have you established a replacement for your benefits?** Having enough business to sustain the transition isn't the only condition you'll need to meet. Traditional employment has its advantages, including health insurance and retirement plans. What have you done to maintain your coverage and protections once you leave your job? While we believe everyone should have medical insurance, it is essential for any entrepreneur with a family. We don't recommend leaving your traditional job until you have it in place.

3. **What is your plan?** A concrete plan for pivoting to full-time entrepreneurship is necessary. This includes a strategy for maintaining your current clients and gaining new ones. What might a workday look like? What are your quarterly goals and benchmarks? Moving to full-time entrepreneurship means that everything—profit and income—will be on you. This means that you have to recognize that responsibility for what it is.

If you are spending all of your free time working on your new business, you may think that it's time to pivot to doing so full time. And it might be. But you've got to be willing to do the work to prepare for everything that comes with it.

Our EYL player, Edwin, wants to open more businesses, but he also doesn't have the financial infrastructure to sustain his current lifestyle. We've already recommended that he scale down some of his expenses to establish a more realistic budget that creates the financial breathing room he needs. To be frank, though, Edwin also needs to bring in more money. An entrepreneur through and through, Edwin doesn't want to work for anybody else. You may be just like him. And, while we understand that, we also know what it means to need money ASAP.

Edwin is in a prime position, as his business is closed on Mondays and doesn't open until 4 P.M. This gives him the flexibility in his schedule to make more money, still working for himself. Edwin, and entrepreneurs like him, can pivot to contract and consulting work, within their fields or areas of interest, to generate significant income. Sites like Taskrabbit and Fiverr, where people can hire laborers and specialists for jobs, offer entrepreneurs the flexibility they're looking for, as they bring in additional funds. And if that isn't enough, there's nothing wrong with Edwin and other entrepreneurs getting full-time or part-time jobs to make ends meet. There's nothing wrong with entrepreneurs getting traditional employment when it's necessary. Remember, the goal is financial freedom, and you should be willing to do whatever's necessary to make that happen.

Entrepreneurship will look different for everyone, and its various stages may seem like a roller-coaster ride. **The key is to set realistic expectations for your business based on the industry and market.** While your nightclub may be a hit for the first few months, you have to understand that it may not be so consistently. Even if you haven't had an empty seat in your restaurant since it opened, you need to be prepared for the day when business will slow down. This involves understanding the difference between a business that is making money and one that is profitable. With grit and dedication in the beginning, you will make money. That doesn't mean you have a profitable business. Your start-up costs and overhead expenses have to be deducted from what you make. When you have more income than expenses, that is when your business has become profitable. Usually, it takes two to three years for a business to become profitable, but that depends on the industry.

We suggest you set the goal of making a profit within five years. This doesn't mean that your business can't and won't make a profit before year five. If it does, good job! It'll mean that you've got more breathing room. The beauty of a five-year profitability plan is that it gives you enough time to evaluate your business's viability, analyze trends you've established, and watch how your business responds to fluctuations in the market. With this information, you can make informed and empowered decisions about growing the business and possibly scaling up.

There will be some of you whose businesses will grow exponentially and need to scale up before year five. Not only did that happen with the EYL brand, we've seen it happen with others. DeShaun's tutoring business offered after-school tutoring and homework help for grades K–8. He started it in 2018 with only three clients. Then in 2020, COVID-19 changed everything. In less than two years, he went from three clients to seventy-five. To ensure that he was paid, DeShaun required new clients to sign a contract for the academic year with a cancellation fee should they decide they wanted to end the tutoring. Instead of using Zelle and PayPal to accept payment, as he'd done with his first three clients, he paid for a system that invoiced his clients every month or every quarter, depending on what they chose.

With the increased number of clients, DeShaun put students into groups to make it easier for him. Even after schools reopened, he didn't lose clients; he actually gained more. In 2021, he had clients in more than five states and a wait list. To accommodate the increase, he hired teachers and college students looking to make some extra money. Within three months of bringing them on board, he was able to transition out of tutoring and exclusively handle the business's logistics and infrastructure. In 2018, he made $3,000; in 2022, his business cleared $1.5 million.

As interest in his services grew, the major key to DeShaun's success was implementing a system that allowed him to maximize on that interest—namely, contracting for services for the academic year and instituting a cancellation fee. By doing this, he ensured that he would receive payment from each customer no matter how long they stayed with him. It was a system he hadn't thought he needed when he'd had only three clients. But having seventy-five clients and counting required him to level up his strategy and approach. Leveling up isn't just about thinking quickly on your feet; to be prepared to do so, you need to research the best practices and strategies within your industry. DeShaun didn't lose any income, because he created what he needed. Even if his business begins to decrease, he has an infrastructure that can assist him with a pivot. For instance, he may want to contract with school systems once his current clients either graduate out of his services or decide that these are no longer needed.

Pivoting is yet another aspect of entrepreneurship that every business owner must be prepared to do. There will come a time when your current strategies are no longer effective and your business will need a refresh. There may also come a time when you need to start a new business altogether. EYL community member Aja pursued entrepreneurship because it gave her the ability to be in charge of her schedule and spend more time with her two boys. As an HR professional, she started her journey into entrepreneurship as a contractor for corporate clients. Though it was good, steady work, each contract eventually ended and she had to look for a new one. When that got to be too taxing, she realized that the people who weren't always looking for contracts were the consultants who helped structure her departments for those corporate clients.

After establishing an LLC, Aja began to market her services as a consultant who could lead the divisions she had once worked in. That actually earned her more money and attracted more clients. Whereas she had been able to be a contractor for only one corporate client, she was able to be a consultant for several clients at once. Because logistics are her strength, it's nothing for her to have three corporate clients at once. To make it work, she needed structure and discipline. Recognizing that everything fell on her made having created both easy. Being organized helps Aja with structure. She has a general idea of how each day will go, and all her calendars are synced. Additionally, she has a separate phone for each client—something she includes in each contract and bills the client for.

There's No "Right Kind of Business"

We hope we haven't scared you away from wanting to become an entrepreneur, but we needed to paint the picture of all that the process entails. So you see where you are and where you want to go, and you're ready to pursue entrepreneurship. A question we're often asked (and the reason some of you probably purchased this book) is "What is the right business for me to start?" Usually, what we're actually being asked is "What business can I open that's going to make me a lot of money?" And while we get it, we're here to tell you that it's not that simple.

The truth is that there is no *right* business for any of us to start. There is only and always an opportunity. You must be willing to see it as such. Just look at our EYL players:

Edwin began as a party promoter and got an opportunity to take over a club. When he saw there was a need to pivot from a club-only business model, he added a restaurant component. Even if he's struggling right now, Edwin made all the "right" moves because he capitalized on all the opportunities that came his way as it related to elevating his business. This is the right mentality for entrepreneurs. We'll work on the other fundamentals he needs, but thankfully he's on the right track.

For years, Tracy has been toying with the idea of starting a virtual business providing college admissions consulting. She knows that overstretched counselors at most public schools rarely provide deep application essay editing or granular financial aid package comparisons. With traditional counseling services out of reach for many low-income families, she could help expand access. Yet without a completed bachelor's degree, she knows her credentials won't cut it. Every tuition payment she diverts to childcare represents lost potential—for both her business dreams and the students she hopes to help. The idea of earning her leisure seems more like a far-fetched dream to Tracy than a tangible reality.

Tracy's business idea is possible, even without the credentials she thinks she needs. She set up a website that tells the story of her passion to help students who aspire to go to college and provides an outline of her services. This will go a long way toward explaining her intentions and attracting business. By paying for social media ads and posting flyers at local high schools and recreation centers, as well as contacting youth ministry leaders at various churches, she got the word out and attracted clients. These small steps have enabled Tracy to take her idea from a passion and hope into a structured digital business that is ready to welcome its first client.

Lately, Gary Williams has been wondering if he and Morgan should take advantage of Atlanta's vibrant arts scene and purchase a high-end microphone and mixer to lease to local musicians and podcasters. The equipment would repay itself within two years if rented each week. But Morgan is worried about the unpredictability of artists and how that will affect their bottom line. They're in a good financial position now. Could going down this road potentially ruin it?

Gary presents Morgan with the market research he's done. They can spend $3,000 on high-end equipment and charge an equipment rental fee as well as a nominal fee for the required workshop to train people on the proper use of the equipment. They can also contact popular podcasts to purchase advertising space for a month to market their business to potential customers and clients. To calm Morgan's fears, Gary suggests a maximum investment of $5,000 for the business. He doesn't want to keep pouring money into the business at the risk of scaring Morgan, but at the same time, he really believes that the equipment quality and leveraging of the city's arts scene will translate to a booked calendar and generated income.

All these cases are examples of how to be innovative and recognize an income-generating opportunity. The ability to make money is all around you. It can start with monetizing your passions and hobbies. Or your starting point can come from seeing a need and coming up with a strategy to meet it. In this instance, the right business will always be the one that makes the most sense to you and that you're willing to put the work into to succeed.

We can't and won't glamorize it; everything about the entrepreneurial journey and process will test you. Every entrepreneur and business owner will tell you that they made some mistakes along the way. Some of those mistakes—most of them, actually—seem to be unavoidable. As we've reflected on our journey and what so many people have shared with us, we've narrowed them down to the top three most common mistakes and want to offer some suggestions to manage them.

1. **Not having enough start-up capital or cash reserves:** When it comes to starting a business, many entrepreneurs lack the start-up capital or reserves to successfully launch or sustain it. Even though they make do, they're starting without the resources that will place them on a level playing field with other entrepreneurs. As you consider your entrepreneurial journey, this is where benchmarks will matter. What do you need to transition from traditional employment to full-time entrepreneurship as seamlessly as possible? Have you established a monthly budget based on the past six months of income and expenses? Answering these questions will be key as you determine what you need financially to take the big leap. If you don't have or can't gather the necessary resources,

know that it's possible to begin your entrepreneurial journey as long as you develop a strong financial plan with the resources you have and strategies for capitalizing on it.

2. **Struggling with time management and work/life balance:** We'd love to tell you that you're going to be able to manage all aspects of your life as an entrepreneur, but that's simply not true. There will be some seasons when owning a business is all consuming, and there will be others when it will be less consuming. You can't avoid it. At best, you'll have to manage it. The most effective way to add boundaries to your work life is to create a schedule. Even if when you were working a traditional job, you always took work home with you; there's a reason traditional employment has established hours. You can't work every hour of every day. Consider utilizing your former work schedule as your new entrepreneurial work schedule. Take a lunch period, and take breaks. And when the day is done, go "home." This doesn't necessarily mean that you won't continue working after hours, but it does mean that you can shift your mindset from work to family and other aspects of your life. Additionally, don't forget to keep up your habits such as going to the gym and going out with friends. You previously had a routine outside work, and it's important to maintain it.

3. **Refusing or being unable to ask for help.** Contrary to popular belief, entrepreneurs aren't expected to be perfect or to understand every aspect of their business. No person in the history of this world has ever gotten it right; yet somehow there is the expectation that entrepreneurs will. If you own a business, let go of that

assumption right now. Freeing yourself from it will keep you from feeling an obligation to perform to perfection. The best way to free yourself is to ask for help when you need it. Being honest about what you don't know and seeking answers from more experienced and qualified resources will enable you to avoid a trap that catches entirely too many entrepreneurs. Each year businesses fail and have to close for a number of reasons. Many of those would have been avoidable had the business owners made different decisions with better information. Opening up and asking for help is the first step to ensuring that your business won't close because of mistakes that could have been prevented.

Making mistakes is common in business because we're human. Some of them are a result of structural and systemic inequalities. Not having the financial resources to fund your dream—or not coming from the kind of family that can give you a loan to start it—isn't the entrepreneur's fault. Other mistakes are on us. Refusing to ask for help is rooted in insecurity, pride, and ego—the three things that will break a business. Whether the issue at hand is your fault or the system's, making sure that your business doesn't suffer as a result is solely your responsibility.

Costly mistakes are, well, costly. Having a strategy to address whatever issue your business is facing is crucial. Do you have a "business bible"? This goes beyond the standard employee handbook that every business should have. **A business bible fully outlines the purpose of the business, its vision, and its strategic goals and plans and has an approach to every possible problem that could arise.** It should be an evergreen document that you update as you meet or miss targets and as you come across business issues. As always, we're going to suggest that you take some time to research your industry and meet with entrepreneurial colleagues to identify potential problems and the strategies to address them.

You Don't Have to Start a Business to Change the World, but . . .

Some people actually do want to change the world with the businesses they start, but we don't believe you have to start your business with some altruistic goal. At the same time, it's important to understand that your business does serve a purpose, whether you mean for it to or not. Your business does two things: It meets a community need, and it creates jobs and income for employees. Jobs change people's lives. Whether they are customers or employees, your business offers them something that they couldn't otherwise get.

When you understand this, you will recognize the importance of recirculating dollars within your community. More often than not, the people you employ will be members of your community. They'll be people who grew up in similar neighborhoods, attended similar schools, and have similar goals and aspirations. They are often people who need a single shot or opportunity to make a different decision that will change their lives. Your business can do that for them because it's done the same thing for you.

As you begin to think about the ways your business is changing the trajectory of your community—and ultimately the world—we want to talk about the ways the entrepreneurial landscape has changed through social and digital entrepreneurship. While many of you may have taken "traditional" entrepreneurial routes (opening brick-and-mortar businesses, providing goods and services), we all use and are impacted by social and digital media. These have opened up new ways of being an entrepreneur.

Social and digital entrepreneurship represents a new business eco-system. A wide variety of careers and positions allow people to tap into their natural talents and interests and be paid for doing so. They in-clude:

> **Content creators:** These are people who create content
> exclusively for digital and social media. Content creators

usually either keep their content on social media apps or use it to break into more traditional forms of journalism and entertainment.

Behind-the-scenes content creators: These innovators create content behind the scenes for various brands, influencers, and organizations. While they may not be as famous or well known as the entities they produce content for, these creators have the ability to make more than six figures annually.

Online businesses: Digital and social media have created an opportunity for businesses to exist solely online, eliminating significant overhead costs. Such businesses include retailers of clothing (especially T-shirts and athleisure), makeup, and other goods that can be purchased online and shipped directly to the consumer.

New Age media creators: Though they're being blamed for the decline in traditional media outlets, New Age media companies (consisting of podcasts, streamers, digital magazines and newsletters, and subscription-based media content) have created a faster way for news and information to travel around the world.

The team: As with traditional businesses, it's impossible for anyone to do everything. Digital and social entrepreneurship has created opportunities for careers including virtual assistants, attorneys, accountants, graphic designers, and project managers, as well as the ability and flexibility to create a team of people based anywhere in the world.

The new ecosystem created by digital and social entrepreneurship has brought power back to the people, giving everyday folks the opportunity to become icons. It has produced an opportunity for a high school teacher and a financial adviser to create content for the EYL brand. It allows a gym teacher to go on TikTok and create a routine that gets us moving in the morning. Someone who likes to try new things can create an account that reviews various products, receiving a percentage of viewers' purchases. A person who is good at organizational structure can start a business that helps entrepreneurs who are not. And someone who is great with makeup and beauty tips can create a YouTube channel that has a million subscribers. In the social and digital space, everyone is valuable and celebrated for their expertise and personality. Fame and notoriety aren't just for athletes and entertainers anymore.

While digital and social entrepreneurship has created amazing opportunities for people to start businesses and take their future into their own hands, there are some aspects of business that unfortunately tend to be overlooked. As we've worked with various influencers and entrepreneurs in this emerging space, we often find that their rate of success has overwhelmed them. Simply put: Some people started online businesses and ventures with no idea that they'd boom overnight. Consequently, they didn't have the business structures in place to accommodate such growth.

This is the complicated beauty of digital and social entrepreneurship. Everyone can do it, but if you're not prepared, it can be a disaster. Just as with traditional entrepreneurship, many people pursue it because they didn't want a life with the elements of traditional business. "I don't want to be corporate," they say. The reality is that the entrepreneurial and the corporate worlds need each other, especially when it comes to digital and social entrepreneurship. You may be a business owner in this space, but there are some "traditional" business items that must be on your checklist. They include:

1. **Separate accounting for business income and expenses:** It doesn't matter what kind of business you've

established in the digital and social entrepreneurial space, your business and personal finances must be kept separate. Even if you're using money services such as PayPal or Cash App to accept payments, the accounts need to be distinct from those you use for personal expenditures. In addition to separate accounting, you will need to maintain accurate accounting and bookkeeping records, as well as payroll services.

2. **A retirement plan:** If you're pursuing a career in the digital and social entrepreneurship space, you need a plan for retirement. This is where we emphasize the need to incorporate corporate structures and principles into your business. Here are some elements you can include in your retirement plan.

   ◆ **401(k) plan:** If you have a business, setting up a 401(k) plan is a great way to create a financial pathway to retirement. If you have employees, the traditional 401(k) plan gives them—and you—the opportunity to contribute toward their retirement as they would if they were in the corporate world. A solo 401(k) plan creates the opportunity for a business owner to establish an account and contribute as both the employer and employee. A solo 401(k) plan is especially beneficial for independent contractors and freelancers. Unlike the previous plans, a Roth 401(k) plan is an opportunity to make after-tax contributions, which is a great benefit during retirement. However, this does require a greater financial sacrifice as you're working, something that could leave digital and social entrepreneurs especially vulnerable financially.

◆ **Individual Retirement Account (IRA):** An IRA is a self-managed fund that can generate greater financial resources than many other retirement plans. With a traditional IRA, you will pay taxes once you start withdrawing the funds. When it comes to a Roth IRA, contributions aren't tax deductible; however, withdrawals are tax and penalty free after you turn 59½. If you are a small-business owner with employees, you have the option of establishing a Simplified Employee Pension (SEP) IRA or a Savings Incentive Match Plan for Employees (SIMPLE) IRA. Only employers can contribute to SEP IRAs and adjust their contributions according to how well their business is or is not doing. A business with fewer than one hundred employees can establish SIMPLE IRA accounts that will receive both employer and employee contributions. The employer can match either 3% of each employee's annual contribution or a nonelective 2% of each employee's salary.

◆ **Profit-sharing plan:** A profit-sharing plan is an opportunity for employers to contribute to their employees' retirement income while also driving employee performance and motivating company growth. There are two kinds of profit-sharing plans. A stand-alone profit-sharing plan allows only employer contributions and is especially beneficial for small businesses with limited resources. With a profit-sharing 401(k) plan, an employer can offer the combined benefits of profit sharing and 401(k) contributions.

    ◆ **Defined benefits plan:** While 401(k)s, IRAs, and
profit-sharing plans are considered to be defined
contribution plans, a defined benefits plan
guarantees a specific monthly income upon
retirement. However, it's important to note that
defined benefits plans have become less common as
they are extremely restrictive to employees. Only
employers are allowed to determine investments,
and employees aren't able to port the plan if they
change jobs.

Retirement plans are difficult to explain and tedious to establish. It
would take more space to fully explain all they entail than we could do
in this book. For that reason, we strongly encourage sitting down with
a financial adviser to discuss and set up the best plan for you and your
business. We do not recommend going at this alone. This is your financial future, and it deserves serious time and attention.

When it comes to your retirement plan, no matter which option
you choose, we recommend setting at least 10% of your annual income aside for retirement. For an entrepreneur, this means taking 10%
off the top of your earnings *before* you figure your EYL Money Principle Equation. This may mean becoming more creative and intentional
with your saving and spending plans, but it will also mean having
money available for the day you no longer wish to work. We also want
to make clear that there should be a difference between your retirement contributions and your investment fund.

Digital Marketing

Whether or not your business is in the digital or social entrepreneurial
space, its future depends on digital marketing. In our EYL community,
we have encountered business owners who are resistant to it. More ac-

customed to a traditional entrepreneurship model, they say that they're "not online people" and the social media space isn't for them. And while we understand that the climate and politics of digital and social spaces can be a deterrent for some, these days it is impossible to run a successful business without some sort of digital footprint.

As you seek to build or scale up your business, here are the aspects of digital marketing that we believe will be critical to your success.

1. **A website:** Regardless of what kind of business you have, you need an active and updated website (or blog) that is easily accessible and viewable on both computers and mobile devices. Consumers check to see if there is a website to determine if a business is legitimate and reputable. Maintaining an online presence that provides an overview of your business, products, and services is the minimum you need to do.

2. **Social media accounts:** In addition to your website, your business will need a social media presence. Currently, 60% of the world's population uses social media, spending an average of 2½ hours daily on various apps and sites. Among millennial and younger generations, the percentage increases to 80%. While Facebook and YouTube remain the most active and engaged social media platforms, it's best to find platforms that align with the character of your business. TikTok and Pinterest may not be for you, and that's okay. You don't have to be everywhere, but you need to be somewhere.

3. **Communication touch points:** Engaging with established and potential customers is a vital part of

business. Thanks to advancements in technology, there are numerous ways you can connect with your consumer base. While many businesses still opt for traditional email marketing through newsletters, texts and other phone-based marketing touch points have become increasingly popular. We live in a digitally connected world. Getting in touch with and remaining close to those who make your business thrive is key.

A healthy digital marketing strategy will go a long way toward helping you achieve success. Optimizing your business's search engine optimization (SEO) results and maximizing its social media algorithms can add thousands of dollars to your bottom line. The best part is that you don't have to be good at digital marketing—or even do it yourself—to use it. Looking into the new ecosystem for professionals to handle the job will not just free you to focus on the goods and services of your business, it will recirculate dollars into your community and sphere of influence, which goes back to the initial benefits of starting a business in the first place.

The existence of the new ecosystem gives you the opportunity to get creative about your business's marketing approach. Here are a few ideas.

1. **Affiliate marketing:** Creating an opportunity for customers to promote your business to their respective online communities is a great way to increase revenue and be introduced to a new group of potential customers.

2. **Community building:** For certain entrepreneurs, including public figures and thought leaders, continuously engaging with your social media followers and creating a presence and connection with them will

translate into future opportunities to market events and products, such as books and courses, effectively.

3. **Cross-promotion:** Businesses with smaller marketing budgets can collaborate to highlight each other's products and services, splitting marketing costs and creating opportunities to expand their businesses' reach into new markets and territories.

In addition to initially providing free boot camps in the local park, Semaj offered discounted monthly memberships to his clients who posted about their workouts and progress three times a week. As long as they made sure to tag him in each post, he let them be as creative with the content as possible. That created an opportunity for friends of his clients to watch their friends' progress, become inspired by it, and potentially become one of Semaj's new clients. It also created the ability for Semaj's clients to save money, leading them to remain his clients and feel an element of buy-in to his success. All of it was a win-win for Semaj. It was an epic marketing strategy that didn't cost him anything. What he "lost" by discounting membership fees, he made up for with new clients.

A Word About Tax Strategies

Remember when we told you that tax codes were created for entrepreneurs more than for employees? Now more than ever, it's time to meet with a tax attorney and establish a strategy that will benefit you and your business. Developing a tax strategy with a professional will help you identify the tricks and loopholes that are to a business owner's advantage—including not "paying" taxes. Ironically, many individuals frown upon businesses' not paying taxes and see it as a way to "get over." But when you work with tax strategists and attorneys, you recognize that the long game is the only game you and your business should play.

Entirely too many entrepreneurs make the mistake of not taking their taxes seriously. This includes not separating their business and personal expenses. The quickest way to head to an IRS audit is not to take the few seconds needed to reach for your business debit or credit card to make purchases pertinent to your business. We can't tell you how many people we've talked to who have adopted the "We'll sort it all out at the end of the month/quarter" strategy. We're here to tell you that "the end" never comes. When it comes to taking the deductions that each business can take advantage of, it's not possible to do so without proper accounting and categorizing of expenses. Trust us: Nobody wants to wade through a mountain of receipts and bank statements trying to decide which expenses were for the business and which ones weren't.

While it goes without saying that your tax returns should be filed on time, we need to stress it again. Filing your taxes on time keeps your business from having to pay penalties and interest. Additionally, you can't underestimate how much you should pay. One of our community members is a successful ghostwriter and copy editor. As a 1099 employee, she wasn't setting aside enough from each contract for taxes. At a max, she'd been setting aside 10% when she needed to allocate around 30%. When it was time to file her tax return, she didn't have enough saved to pay her $65,000 tax bill. She also didn't know that she needed to be paying them throughout the year to avoid penalties and interest. Establishing a payment plan to bring her tax payments current and to pay the penalties and interest set her back for the upcoming year. In addition to saving the 30% from her new contracts for the current tax year, she had to use a portion of those contracts to pay her back taxes. Her miscalculation cost her thousands of dollars and required that she take on extra work to cover her expenses and make up for what she was losing.

The flip side of undercalculating tax responsibility is not maximizing tax deductions. You've spent money to create your business, and you've worked hard to make it; you deserve to keep as much of it as possible. We can't stress this enough: as a business owner, you need a professional handling your taxes to maximize your deductions. And though you leave the taxes to the professionals, here's a list of deductions that every entrepreneur should be aware of.

- Initial start-up costs (including market research expenses, employee training, advertising, and fees paid to business professionals)

- Insurance premiums

- Bank fees and interest

- Rent, utilities, and auto expenses

- Office furniture and supplies

- Marketing expenses

- Inventory

- Travel expenses

- Business trips and meals

- Professional services and contractor fees

- Employee salaries and benefits

- Continuing education

- Charitable donations

Now do you see why we say that tax codes were created to benefit business owners and entrepreneurs? Literally, the cost of doing business is tax deductible! If ever there was a reason to keep clear, detailed business records and make sure you have a solid strategy in place to keep your money, this is it!

You Eat What You Kill

For all the freedom and benefits of entrepreneurship, we're not going to lie to you: This is hard work, probably some of the hardest you'll ever do. In the entrepreneurial world, there is the saying "You eat what you kill." It means that a business owner's monthly income and bottom line are dictated by the sales generated. Whether you own a restaurant, an apparel business, or a virtual HR company, you have to be motivated and committed to making money for your business.

When it comes to this entrepreneur's mantra, here are **EYL's Steps for a Full Plate**.

1. **Keep your composure.** Determining your monthly revenue goal requires keeping a level head. You can't look at how much you need and how much you have and get nervous. While it's said that desperate times call for desperate measures, you can't act that way. Even if there is an extreme deficit, you've got to be calm and strategic. Making moves based on desperation and fear can create more problems down the line.

2. **Act in real time.** Though you may have annual and strategic plans, you also need a plan to approach your monthly revenue goal. This can be created at the beginning of each fiscal year and be adapted as needed. The plan should take into consideration the needs of your business and recognize how long it may take to produce revenue. For instance, a business that makes money by selling products will generate income differently from one that relies on contracts. Your strategic plan will be unique to your business model and revenue stream.

3. **Execute your plan.** A plan is a plan only when it's executed; otherwise, it's wishful thinking. When you're trying to make payroll or hit a specific financial benchmark, wishing doesn't pay the bills. Generating potential income is as important as the work you do. Devoting the necessary time to executing that plan is the difference between making money or not. At the end of the day, you just have to do it.

4. **Identify and hire talented people.** You can't make money alone. Meeting your financial benchmarks will take the right team of people, and you will need to identify and tap into them as resources. Whether they are part of the new business ecosystem or from the "traditional" corporate world, getting the help you need can drastically improve your business's economic condition. This will mean releasing any insecurity or apprehension over needing help and admitting what you don't know. Think of it this way: Do you want to keep your prideful arrogance, or do you want to make money? You can't do both, and only one leads to financial freedom.

You can make money if you want to. Perhaps that's all you need to keep telling yourself to get it done: I can make money if I want to. Sometimes that's enough to get you started. When you are considering becoming an entrepreneur, know that owning your time and crafting your future will be two of the greatest benefits. If you want the freedom to do what you want with your career, having your own business is the only way to go. And though being your own boss is attractive in itself, starting a business also gives you something to pass down to your family.

Troy would often say that he could work thirty years in the school system, retire, and the building where he worked will never have his name on it. With EYL, he and Rashad have created something that their children will be able to benefit from—whether it's the lessons, the education, or the business itself. For members of marginalized communities or those with a history of financial insecurity, what greater gift can you give to the next generation than a vibrant business and the wisdom you gained from creating and running it?

CHAPTER EIGHT

◆ ◆ ◆

Love and Money

EYL players Gary and Morgan Williams are in a great financial place right now. But their early years together were a rocky road. Gary came from a single-parent home where his mother didn't have enough to provide adequately for him and his three brothers. The four sons often joke about how their childhood was a miracle, with their mama making a way out of no way to ensure that they had what they needed. Gary grew up seeing every penny accounted for and never spent on unnecessary purchases. And when you don't have much, any expense that doesn't cover your basic necessities is unnecessary.

Morgan's childhood was much different, filled with summer vacations on Martha's Vineyard, study abroad semesters, and a full-time nanny, and she quickly understood that she lived a different life from most people's. Both of her parents were doctors, and there wasn't much they wouldn't do for their only child. She was the center of their world, and she had the toys and experiences to prove it. When Gary and Morgan met in college, they were the Dwayne Wayne and Whitley Gilbert of their campus. They knew they were from different sides of the tracks, but they loved each other and were committed to making their relationship work.

To afford the kind of ring he felt Morgan deserved, Gary worked two jobs during his junior and senior years of college and three during the summer. And even that wasn't enough. It was years before Morgan learned that Gary had taken out a loan to buy her engagement ring. And when it came time to pay for the wedding, Gary had total sticker shock! It didn't matter that he wasn't paying for it. He just didn't understand why anyone needed to spend $15,000 on flowers. Morgan tried to explain that she was her parents' only child and they'd been dreaming about her wedding since she was a little girl. No matter how much she tried to convince him that the wedding was more for her parents than it was for her, Gary knew that Morgan wanted a big wedding just as much as they did.

What neither of them realized was how much their approach to finances would cause them to butt heads during the early years of their marriage. Gary was much more frugal, finding creative ways to make their money stretch, while Morgan had no problem spending money if she felt they needed something—and if they wanted it, that was enough of a reason for her, too. Many arguments and nights sleeping on the couch ensued before the two lovebirds made a commitment to each other that they would not let money and their refusal to understand each other's attitudes toward it keep them from living happily ever after.

Gary and Morgan sat down together and created a sensible budget that made Gary feel confident about saving for the future and gave Morgan the opportunity to enjoy some of the money they were working hard to make. Over time, they continued to adjust their budget to meet the financial goals they had as a couple. Now, on the cusp of being debt free, they sometimes can't believe they were the same couple who didn't speak to each other for two weeks after Morgan bought new towels and washcloths at Macy's.

When we enter any relationship, whether romantic or platonic, we do so with our upbringing and cultural and personal experiences informing us. They shape our emotions and behaviors regarding finances. We can find ourselves judging the ways the person we're in a relationship with spends money based on our own projections and fears. As we discussed earlier, financial trauma can impact every aspect of our lives, including our relationships with others. Some of the first work you can do to ensure that that doesn't happen is explore your own "money story." Taking the time to think about how money has shown up in your friendships and relationships and how you respond to it, as well as linking it all back to the work we outlined in the chapter on financial trauma, is a step in the right direction.

There will be people who will tell you that love and money don't mix. They'll say that the moment money enters into the equation, everything will change. We don't believe that. The truth is, you can't have a sustainable relationship or build a family without money. Try staring into each other's eyes and telling each other "I love you" over and over again. Does that keep the lights on? What about watching your kids while they sleep and being filled with such gratitude and pride that you could create such an amazing human being? Do those heartwarming emotions keep them clothed and fed?

Our relationships—all of them—need money. And no, money shouldn't be the root of our relationships, but it definitely impacts their success. We know that discussing financial matters in families and relationships is difficult. For whatever reason, we think that sweeping the conversation under the rug and pretending that money doesn't exist is the best approach, but it isn't. The key to financial freedom is the ability to access it in every area of your life. You can't be successful in your profession, making the kind of money you've always wanted to make, but walk on eggshells when it comes to money in your relationships. That is the opposite of financial freedom, and none of us is going backward.

In this chapter, we're going to break down the financial decisions you should be making and strategies you should be implementing at every stage of the relationship- and family-building process. Whether you're single and looking to date or you've been married for years, there are some tips and principles that will help you fortify any relationship. And if you're a single parent, a couple thinking about starting a family, or two parents trying to find the best way to co-parent, we offer you tools that will help lay the foundation for your child's financial freedom.

Financial Maturity

While we were writing this book, a story trended on social media that had people talking for days. A woman's brother went to her, asking if she'd cosign a car loan for him. He told her that all he needed was a cosigner and he'd be able to make the payments with no issue. When she talked to her husband about it, he didn't think it was a good idea. The brother had messed up his credit to the point that he needed a cosigner; the husband wasn't convinced that his wife's credit wouldn't be next.

The wife decided to help her brother anyway. She cosigned for the car, and sure enough, within a few months, her brother stopped paying the car note. The car was eventually repossessed, and of course, the sister's credit took a massive hit. Fast-forward to two years later; it was time for her to get a new car, and her credit hadn't fully rebounded from the repossession. While she was eligible to take out a car loan on her own, the kind of car she really wanted required a cosigner. Her husband refused. His reason was that his wife's decision to help her brother had put them into an extreme financial bind and her consequence for that would be not getting the car she wanted right now.

Social media was divided, with many commenters agreeing with the husband's decision and others calling him controlling and vindictive. Wherever people landed in the conversation, the couple's argument isn't uncommon. Situations and scenarios like this happen in so many relationships, and people walk away from each other as a result of them. Some of the most common financial disagreements in relationships and marriages are:

- **Different financial goals and investment strategies:** If one person wants to save for a house while the other desires to become debt free first, it can cause serious problems—even if both goals and strategies are admirable and attainable.

- **Different spending habits:** In the beginning, Gary and Morgan Williams had completely different spending habits, which threatened the future of their marriage.

- **Financial baggage:** Even the deepest love is tested when one partner has bad credit, high credit card and/or student loan debt, and mounting personal debt that impacts both people in the relationship.

- **Financially supporting family members:** As was true with the couple trending on social media, feeling obligated or pressured to help your family financially can lead to problems in your relationship and cause your partner to resent your family members who keep asking for money and needing help.

- **Joint accounts:** Couples can become frustrated by the lack of privacy that comes with a joint account and the distrust, judgments, and questions about purchases.

At the heart of all these disagreements is a failure to communicate effectively. In every area of our lives, good communication is key; as we said earlier, we've been taught to avoid money conversations in our relationships. But that leaves us moving backward.

When you are discussing finances in your relationships and family, you want to consider the concept of financial maturity. **We define financial maturity as the ability to have conversations about money and make sound financial and economic decisions.** Having financial maturity means you recognize that your financial freedom and that of the people you love are connected and interdependent. That means you will always be willing to have the hard conversations and will never shy away from making tough decisions when it comes to what's in the best interest of all parties involved.

We recognize that for some people, developing financial maturity will be exercising a new muscle. Here are a few steps that will help you begin to cultivate it.

- **Hold financial accountability meetings.** Just as some people incorrectly assume that everybody knows how to budget, there's an incorrect assumption that people are taking constant inventory of that budget and their spending habits. Holding a monthly financial accountability meeting enables a family to review the previous month's spending habits to evaluate if they're moving closer to or further away from their EYL Baseline and financial freedom. If you're single, consider partnering with a trusted friend or relative to meet monthly and hold each other accountable to your goals. If you have children, consider including them in the accountability meetings so they can discuss what they are doing with their allowance or their earnings from their job. This will also give them the opportunity to see you, an adult couple, discussing finances and allow them to normalize the experience. The point is to begin talking and communicating about your finances so that it is not a foreign concept when more serious financial concerns arise.

- **Assess your financial mistakes.** One of the greatest signs of achieving maturity is owning our mistakes. Sometimes things weren't our fault and circumstances were beyond our control. Other times, it was all on us, and the moment we can admit that, we've already grown from the experience. None of us is perfect, so it doesn't make sense to pretend to be. Everyone already knows that you're lying. If you've never made silly or ridiculous decisions regarding money, congratulations! But the majority of us have messed up and, thankfully, lived to tell the story. And we need to tell it. Being honest about what we did and what we learned is not only a sign of financial maturity but also proof that our mistakes do not have power over us. It's important to note that if you are in a marriage or relationship and make a significant financial mistake, you may need to take additional steps to repair what was broken and regain the other person's trust. We advise you to take those steps. While adverse financial circumstances end many relationships, a relationship can also be salvaged when people are willing to do the work.

- **Recognize that you don't know everything.** We know that some of you have already circled this section and are planning to meet your significant other with it at the door as soon as they come home! But hear us out. A relationship is between the people who are in it; a family is made up of the people who are in it. That means there are multiple perspectives and viewpoints that must be respected. Understand that there can and should be one common, shared vision for the direction of the relationship and family, but each person's idea of how you will get to that vision may be different. When it comes to financial decisions, everyone's voice matters. This is, of course, within reason, because if it were up to our children, we'd all be at Disneyland every weekend. But it does mean that you can find room to include your child or children in certain conversations about money. But obviously more than including your children, this is meant to recognize the value of hearing your spouse or partner when it comes to the financial direction of your relationship and family. If you are unilaterally making all the financial decisions, that's not a good thing, and chances are that it's showing up in other areas of your relationship. Everyone involved has a voice, and that voice matters.

As you develop financial maturity and seek to employ it in your relationships, you will also need to cultivate the skill of active listening. This doesn't mean that you hear what your partner says, take a minute, and then respond; it means that you hear both what they say and don't say by taking their words, emotions, and disposition into account. **Active listening involves knowing your partner and their intentions— even if they don't articulate it well.** Your understanding their current financial situation, goals, hopes, and fears gives them the benefit of the doubt. Through active listening, you will gain a greater understanding of your partner's financial outlook, including how it will impact what the two of you want to build together.

As you try to engage in active listening, you will want to be in a comfortable environment where you can talk. Before the two of you begin, commit to each other that the feelings and concerns of both of you will be heard and respected. During the conversation, put the phone down, turn off the television, and give the other person your full attention. Maintain eye contact, and use physical and verbal cues to show that you're actively engaged and listening. Avoid asking questions that can easily be answered "yes" or "no"; asking open-ended questions encourages your partner to be as expressive as possible. Last, take the time to paraphrase your partner's key points to ensure that you have understood them.

Next, we're going to go through the various relationship and family stages, addressing the financial issues that may arise in each and how you should handle them.

Dating

Today's dating scene is . . . different. This is not the same dating pool where our parents and grandparents found each other. At a time when—let social media tell it—$200 dates and conversations about who is or isn't high value reign supreme, it's hard to know if people really want to get to know you or are just looking to create viral content. The risk of getting their hopes up only to be let down has many people not even wanting to try. They think it's not worth it.

We'll never tell someone to abandon their hope of finding love. Just as you deserve to be rich, you deserve to find love if that's what you want. But understand this: **Dating is both an expense and an investment**. It's not something to be taken lightly, especially if you're looking for someone to spend the rest of your life with. If you're single and dating, here are some suggestions to ensure that your experiences will align with your financial goals and ultimately sustain your financial freedom.

Create a line item for dating in your budget.

If you want to date, you should be budgeting for it. This should come solely out of the "Spending" portion of your budget. When it comes to how much you spend on dates and courtship, only you can determine that. However, any dating experience should reflect your personality and character. If you can't afford to do that and pursuing high-quality relationship partners is important to you, we suggest looking at ways to increase that line item. It may sound counterintuitive to think about getting another job or starting a business to make extra money to date; the reality is that you *and* the person you're dating deserve a high-quality experience that could potentially be the start to your happily ever after.

Discuss your financial expectations.

When things have progressed to a point where you can see yourself becoming serious, it's time to have the conversation. The aspects of that conversation may vary, but one question that needs to be asked is: "What are your financial expectations in a relationship?" This matters more than people realize; how else can you be aligned? If the two of you have radically different financial expectations (for example, one of you wants to split bills 50/50 and the other would rather have an 80/20 split), that needs to be discussed. The good thing is that if you're both coming to the relationship with financial maturity or are developing it, these financial expectations won't be instant deal-breakers but opportunities for the two of you to create a financial structure that's in the best interest of your relationship.

Be aware of each other's financial situation.

When dating, we tend to want to put our best foot forward. Leading with our flaws doesn't make sense. And because many people see a less-than-desirable financial situation as a flaw, we tend to be less than forthcoming about it. But remember, you're working to make financial maturity the foundation of your relationships, so you're going to have to have conversations about the hard stuff. Does the person you're in a relationship with need to know your exact credit score? Not necessarily, but they do need to know that if it's a low one, you're actively working to improve it and are hitting benchmarks. Does the person you're in a relationship with need to know that you're unemployed? Yes, they absolutely do. Full stop. It doesn't have to be a deal-breaker, but your employment status and current financial situation are something the other person needs to be aware of before getting serious. Just because you like them and want to be with them doesn't mean you get to take away their ability to choose.

Long-Term Relationship/Marriage

Without question, two incomes are better than one. The additional resources enable you to approach and reach various benchmarks. When you move into the realm of long-term partnership and marriage, it's important to recognize that **everything has changed**. And when we say everything, we mean *everything*. Your expectations, family systems, norms, and customs have all changed, and the unit the two of you are building is the most important. When you're in this space, here are some things to consider that will keep you aligned with your financial goals.

Have a clear definition of what financial freedom looks like for the two of you as a unit.

The first thing the two of you want to do is get onto the same page financially. This includes going back to your EYL Baseline and establishing what a new baseline for your partnership and union will look like. Now do you see why having a conversation about your financial expectations during the dating phase matters? Whatever the two of you decide about those expectations will directly impact how you will move toward your EYL Baseline and earning your leisure. This will include discussing what additional employment, entrepreneurial, and investment opportunities might look like. It will also mean creating a solid household budget that takes the EYL Money Principle seriously and leaves more room for emergencies and less room for spur-of-the-moment financial impulses that can lead to not only financial problems but relationship woes.

Establish a banking structure early.

Deciding how the household finances will be handled and putting a system into place will save a lot of time and energy and cause less financial strain and resentment. Each relationship and household is different. Developing emotional maturity and communicating well with each other will be how you will determine what banking structure will work best for your family. However, if you're looking for examples, consider doing this:

- **Have a joint bank account for family expenses and personal bank accounts for individual expenses.**
  Whether you've decided to split all household bills 50/50 or have a different variation of the split, consider establishing a joint bank account for all family expenses. Using the EYL Money Principle, this will include all the income that goes toward the family's **saving, sharing, spending, and investing**. Even if you've decided that one person will be responsible for all the household bills, we still recommend having a joint bank account for full transparency. Our personal bank accounts, still structured around the EYL Money Principle, will be for

our personal expenses such as student loans, self-care and personal maintenance, and other expenses that are solely our responsibility. When starting a joint bank account, we suggest selecting a bank or credit union that neither of you is using—unless one of you is already a member of one you both deem has the best benefits.

Explore the benefits of filing your tax returns jointly and making combined purchases.

Remember when we told you that the tax code was built with business owners in mind? The same thing is true for couples. There are great tax benefits and incentives to filing jointly and making combined purchases. We strongly encourage taking the time to sit down with a representative at the bank or credit union where you have your joint bank account or with a financial adviser to go over what will provide the greatest financial benefits to your relationship. Meeting with that person will help create a plan for any purchases, giving you more buying power as you work to be strategic with your resources. Making financial moves, knowing the tax structures that will benefit your relationship and your family, will put you ahead of the game when it comes to the pursuit of financial freedom.

Have a strategy for lending money.

Nothing causes problems in a relationship quicker than lending money to a relative or agreeing to cosign on a purchase without your spouse or partner's knowledge or consent. This is where financial maturity—or immaturity, in some cases—is on full display. In a relationship, the two of you are the most important unit, and the family you're building together is your most important priority. Every financial decision you make should reflect that. While we lived full lives with our friends and loved ones before we began this chapter, we cannot exclude our significant others from having input into how we lend money. We suggest having a conversation about how you will be willing to financially assist your loved ones and creating a set annual budget for doing so that you don't exceed. This can be a line item in the family's overall "Sharing" budget.

Once you've exceeded the budgeted amount for the year, the answer to anyone who asks for a loan has to be "no"—unless the two of you sit down together and make a decision to help. Should this happen, we encourage you to tap into other line items in your "Sharing" budget first, then your "Spending" and "Investing" budgets. **Do not lend money out of your "Saving" budget unless it's an extreme emergency and you have a plan to replace it within the next two to three months.** Your savings are for you and whatever emergencies may arise within your household. Consistently dipping into them can set a dangerous precedent and create major problems down the line. We understand that some family and friendship dynamics are unique and circumstances may require that you make a decision to offer financial assistance against your partner's wishes. The financial assistance you offer should come out of your "Sharing" budget, and even then, you should communicate to your spouse or partner your plan, including how you will ensure that it will not impact your joint finances and budget.

If there's going to be a wedding, make a realistic budget.

Who doesn't love a good wedding? Weddings are beautiful moments in time, but they are also not cheap. If marriage is in the cards for the two of you, there needs to be a serious conversation about what celebrations you want to have and what you can afford. This is an opportunity to discuss what your immediate financial priorities are. If you want a house more than you want a luxe wedding, consider holding a smaller, more intimate gathering and placing the rest of your resources toward the down payment. A destination wedding is also a great way of having your wedding, going on a vacation with family and friends, and lowering the cost of your nuptials.

Now, there are some people who have dreamed of their wedding day for their entire lives, and they have a specific vision that they won't deviate from even if you pay them to do so. If you want your dream wedding at all costs, it would be best to employ all the strategies we've offered in this book to go make the money you need. **You should not borrow money or go into your "Saving" budget for your wedding (unless you have specifically been saving money for your big day).** How the two of you handle the finances and expenses of your wedding will set the tone for your marriage. Both of you must be fair to each other.

Create a prenuptial agreement.

There are so many misconceptions about prenuptial agreements. The first and most important one is that they are seen as necessary only for extremely wealthy people or for those with a family business to protect. The second most common misconception is that they are created because people don't trust their partners. Both couldn't be further from the truth. Nobody thinks they're going to get a divorce until they're getting one, and prenuptial agreements protect assets, future earnings, and retirement funds.

In 2019, a study found that there was a 62% increase in the request for prenups, with millennials and middle-class couples making up the majority of that increase. A prenuptial agreement helps you agree on what will be a fair and equitable split in case of a divorce. We recommend sitting down together to iron out the specifics before you consult an attorney. This will ensure that the process isn't adversarial and nobody is caught by surprise when legal counsel presents their client's requests. Remember, you can still love each other, live happily together, and have protections in place should the unthinkable happen. Divorce already costs money; you don't want to lose more than you have to.

Get onto the same page about kids.

You can both love children and recognize that becoming a parent or guardian will be the greatest financial expense of your life. Kids aren't cheap! A conversation about whether the two of you want children should already have happened by now. This is a more specific conversation about how you want to raise your children. Will you need a nanny? Will your children go to public or private school? Montessori daycare? Will they have a supplemental tutor? Do you want them to be consistently exposed to various cultural enrichment activities and sports throughout their childhood? How many vacations, domestic and international, a year would you like to take with them? Many people will dismiss these questions as superficial, but the worst thing that can happen is the two of you not being aligned regarding the upbringing of your children and not being financially prepared for them. There are some things you can begin to do as a couple to prepare for the kind of childhood you want for your kids. But you can't do them without having the conversation first.

A Note on Going into Business Together

There are many people who work with or for their spouses and significant others. And in the quest to build wealth through entrepreneurship and investments, many couples are considering making the move to becoming business partners. It's a situation that we don't think you should enter into lightly, and you should be aware that it can make or break your relationship. Keeping this in mind, here are some points of advice we'd like to offer.

- Set communication expectations, and agree on boundaries for work/life balance.

- Maintain your hustle. Don't slack just because you're working with your spouse or significant other.

- Establish business etiquette and protocols.

- Operate at the highest level of respect, and set the tone for how others will interact with your spouse or significant other in your business dealings.

Children

In 2024, *Newsweek* published a study showing that 47% of parents spend roughly $18,000 a year on childcare; 20% spend around $36,000. That's already a lot of money, but when you compare it to the average annual cost of in-state college tuition—$24,000—it makes your head hurt. And here's the wildest part: You're more than likely going to end up paying for both daycare *and* college. Kids are expensive.

Whether you're married or single, we don't want to deter you if parenthood is what you desire. If it's what you want, it's best to get your personal financial situation together before the kids arrive. Here's what you need to do.

- Pay off all or the majority of your debt.

- Build an emergency savings fund with the minimum of six months' worth of expenses, and create a baby fund in your "Saving" budget.

- Shore up your personal retirement portfolio and increase your investments.

Once you've welcomed children into your family, here's what you need to do.

- Have a will in place with someone you trust designated to be your child/ren's guardian should anything happen to you.

- Establish a line item in the "Spending" and "Saving" budgets specifically for the child/ren's needs.

- Take out life insurance policies: one for you with your child/ren as the beneficiary and one for your child/ren with you as the beneficiary.

- Establish a Roth IRA for your child/ren and strive to contribute the maximum allowable amount annually (currently $7,000).

- Establish a UGMA or UTMA account for your child.

UGMA and UTMA Accounts

As it relates to building your child's financial freedom, we strongly encourage parents to establish UGMA or UTMA accounts for their children. The Uniform Gifts to Minors Act (UGMA) and the Uniform Transfers to Minors Acts (UTMA) are custodial investment accounts that a parent or guardian is in charge of until the child comes of age. A UGMA account can hold financial assets such as cash, stocks, mutual and index funds, and insurance policies. A UTMA account can hold those financial assets, as well as physical assets including real estate, art, jewelry, and other commodities.

The best benefit of the UGMA and UTMA accounts is that there's no restriction on the use of their funds. Unlike with the 529 college savings plan, your child does not have to use the assets in a UGMA or UTMA account exclusively for their education. This provides parents with a great deal of flexibility, especially if their children decide they don't want to pursue higher education after high school. However, it's important to note that UGMA and UTMA accounts are held in the name of the child. So if your child does decide to go to college, having a UGMA or UTMA account will impact his or her financial eligibility. Still, these custodial accounts are the best way to build sustainable wealth for your children over the course of their childhood.

Child Support

When it comes to the ending of a relationship that includes children, child support is one of the most contentious topics. You can't scroll social media without seeing a noncustodial parent upset about how much they have to pay and a custodial parent upset that they're not receiving enough or anything at all. According to data published by the Census Bureau in 2020, here are the numbers.

- One in five children lives in a house that receives child support payments.

- The median amount of child support is $1,800 per month.

- Roughly 46% of custodial parents receive all of what is owed to them in child support.

- 30% of custodial parents who are owed child support receive nothing.

- Black children are less likely to live in a home where the child support that is owed is actually received.

Add to that the fact that there is no universal formula for calculating child support. Judges have the freedom to determine payments based solely on the noncustodial parent's income or include other factors such as the custodial parent's income and the amount of time spent with each parent. If we take all of this into consideration, it's understandable that everyone involved is frustrated.

The truth is that both not paying *and* not receiving child support can set you back financially. While it is frustrating and can severely impact the noncustodial parent's lifestyle, we understand why many custodial parents who are not receiving payments keep their child support order in place in the hope that the noncustodial parent will decide to pay their share on their own or be made to pay it. While there are horror stories about custodial parents using child support payments to do everything but care for the child/ren, the reality is that the rising costs of caring for children mean that it takes *both* parents doing their part to ensure that their child/ren have what they need to thrive.

If you are a noncustodial parent paying child support, here's what we suggest to ensure that you can provide for your child and stay on top of your financial goals.

- Include child support in your budget. The payment needs to be a line item in your annual "Spending" budget, and there needs to be an allocation of your general savings account dedicated to your child.

- If the income from your current job does not allow you to pay your child support obligation and continue to live comfortably, you may need to secure additional employment or pursue entrepreneurship.

- Keep all of your documentation current, and develop a tracking system of the expenses you incur and resources you provide in addition to your mandated obligation. Child support payments can always be readjusted and negotiated, but you must have documentation to support your claim.

- Keep an open line of communication with your co-parent. If that is impossible, utilize a mediator, neutral third party, or legal counsel.

- If you are in arrears, establish a plan to come current within three to six months.

Edwin pays $925 a month in child support. While he and his son's mother are on good terms, he really can't afford to pay that much and should consider requesting a reduction. His first step should be to talk about this with his son's mother, and be as transparent as he can about his financial situation. Hopefully, she will agree to a reduction, and they can present the request together. If she's hesitant or unwilling to agree, Edwin should consider formally requesting a reduction through the courts. It may make for some tense times temporarily, but at the end of the day, he's not avoiding his responsibilities. He's doing what he needs to do to put himself in a better financial situation. In the long run, that will only benefit his son—providing him with a positive image of his father modeling financial stability and security.

Many people have been calling for a reform to the child support system that is long overdue. It will provide greater transparency and fairness and ensure that payments are actually received. Until that day comes and even if it never does, every parent has a financial obligation to support the human being/s they brought into this world. If you are a noncustodial parent paying child support, it's up to you to utilize every resource at your disposal to ensure that you are contributing your rightful and equitable share. At the end of the day, there is a child who needs to be supported, and their needs come first. You can't secure financial freedom if you're unwilling to do what needs to be done for your child.

DINNER WITH JAY-Z OR $500K?

This hypothetical question makes its rounds across social media platforms seemingly every other month. The scenario is that you have the option of having dinner with Hov, arguably one of the greatest emcees in the history of rap and hip hop's first billionaire, or receiving a check for $500,000—free and clear, no strings attached. The premise, for those asking the question, is that your answer will reveal how serious you are about your financial future.

When you read the social media comments, people are divided. The proponents of dinner believe that the wealth of knowledge Jay-Z holds can't be quantified. You can leave your time with him and completely transform your life in a way that wouldn't necessarily be possible with a lump sum of money. Sure, money is great, but what happens when you run out of it? Those who would rather take the check laugh and say "Wait until the deposit clears, and I'll show you how to never run out of that money." For them, it's not about denying Hov's impact. It's about recognizing that for many of us, the only thing that stands between us and the future we want is the resources to create it.

This question can spawn days and weeks of conversation about who's right and who's wrong. Jay-Z himself finally weighed in when his music-streaming company, Tidal, posted on X (once known as Twitter) to "take the $500K" back in 2021. Of course, some people had a field day with that. It confirmed everything they were saying: At the end of the day, the money was the most important value-add.

At EYL, we don't think it's that black-and-white or cut-and-dried. Without question, there are many people who could take that $500,000 and shift the trajectory of their families for generations, just as there are people who would blow it all in a weekend. And because Black and Brown people have been systematically kept away from ever having that kind of money, we don't blame people for hypothetically taking the money and running. Choosing the $500,000 doesn't mean that you don't value yourself or your financial future.

But we're taking the dinner with Hov, and here's why. So much of what we have been able to accomplish with the EYL platform has been a result of relationship building and encounters like that dinner. Sitting down and articulating our vision to someone who had the resources to make things happen was a complete game changer. None of us should ever underestimate the value of relationships and mentoring as we look to build our financial future. An opportunity such as a dinner can provide us with the tools we need.

Additionally, there is an old saying that we are the sum total of our life's experiences and the people we choose to surround ourselves with. That's why our mamas told us to be mindful of the company we keep. If this is true, being gifted $500,000 wouldn't change us. But sharing a meal with an icon such as Hov would open the door to shifting our mindset toward becoming an icon ourselves. And as we've said so many times already, a shift in how you see yourself and your relationship with money is the key to earning your leisure.

What to Do When You've Made a Mistake

Whether you were afraid to share your credit score, have been hiding a great deal of debt, made a purchase you said you wouldn't, or lent money you agreed you wouldn't, there are times when a financial mistake can be the final straw. Your partner may love you, but now trust has been broken and the question of whether to continue the relationship is a genuine one. Too often, people don't realize that these aren't just instances of dishonesty; our financial circumstances impact each other's in our relationships. And while people may understand why you did what you did and were afraid to share what you had done, it doesn't change the fact that the issue is no longer just about you.

If you're the one who has been dishonest or less than forthcoming or done something that you weren't supposed to do financially and there is an opportunity to salvage the relationship, you should be willing to do whatever you can to reestablish trust between the two of you. More than that, if your actions put them into their own financial bind, you should do whatever is necessary to make them whole. Here are some things you should do.

- **Apologize and offer an explanation.** We owe it to our partners to be honest about our shortcomings and mistakes. A genuine apology is the first start. Look your partner or spouse in the eye and take full responsibility for whatever you did. When explaining yourself, be clear and fully transparent about your thought process. It doesn't have to be deep; it just needs to be the truth. If you're the partner receiving the apology, remember to engage in active listening and offer grace and empathy. You can hold the other person accountable without being mean.

- **Establish a repayment plan.** Once you've apologized and been honest about your reasons, showing your partner or spouse that you've researched or created a plan of financial restoration will go a long way in showing that you're invested in fixing what has been broken. Additionally, be willing to listen to your loved one's input in the creation of this plan. If you need help, don't be afraid to ask for and accept it. This is their problem now, too, and they may have some thoughts on how to handle it.

- **Commit to full transparency, and accept the consequences of your actions.** You may have to show the other person your monthly financial statements for a while. You may even have to relinquish control of the family budget and accounts for a few months. These can be some of the consequences following a financial breach of trust. When trust has been broken, steps must be taken to regain it. If you're the injured party, make sure that whatever actions are required reflect what actually happened and aren't a way for you to exact revenge.

- **Be patient.** Rebuilding trust takes time. Before everything is whole and well again, there will be tense moments. There may even be a few nights of sleeping on the couch. It will be a tough time. But it's not a time that you won't be able to atone for and bounce back from. Don't try to rush someone to forgive you and move on.

Love requires work and is hard enough without adding the pain of betrayal. And financial betrayal doesn't just hurt you; it can set you and your financial goals back and cause you to return to the starting point. The key is remaining humble and open to the process of repair. If you're willing to do the work, things will eventually get better.

A relationship can often take a sharp, unexpected turn when it comes to money. The truth is that money impacts the condition of all our relationships. While it doesn't buy happiness, it can definitely dictate whether happiness is present. The key is to remember that you have to be honest about your financial circumstances with the people you love and make financial decisions that have all of your best interests in mind. You're securing your financial freedom and earning your leisure so that you can enjoy it with the people you love. Don't let money and bad financial decisions get into the way of that.

◆ ◆ ◆

CHAPTER NINE

Legacy, Legacy, Legacy

Helen's children and adult grandchildren have finished settling her estate. Once they received the final life insurance payment, her sons were able to complete her final wish: the creation of a family scholarship. Helen always wanted to go to school and become a teacher. However, shortly after she graduated from high school, she got married and became a mother. Her dreams of becoming an educator gave way to her focus on her budding family. Still, when it came to her children, she prioritized education and wanted them to go far.

A hands-on grandmother, Helen watched as educational opportunities increased for African American children and the costs associated with them increased as well. She saw how much her older grandchildren took out in loans to attend college and how much debt they walked across the stage with at graduation. And she saw how hard it was for them to work full time, keep up with those payments, and make it from paycheck to paycheck. She didn't want that for her great-grandchildren.

Helen left a will that instructed her family to take the money from her accounts and life insurance policies and the payments they'll receive from renting her home and establish a family scholarship fund. Any child seeking to attend college will have all their expenses covered. Unlike the previous generation, they won't graduate with debt and will be able to start their lives with a true head start. This is the kind of creation of generational wealth, financial freedom, and legacy that Helen believed was possible.

When it comes to financial freedom, one of the most important aspects of it to many of us is the ability to create generational wealth. Moving into a place where the children in our families, and their children, don't have the same financial barriers as we did is the goal. When you've gotten to a point where you can see this freedom for yourself, it's equally as exciting to know that you've made it possible for loved ones you'll never know to see it, too.

Your financial freedom doesn't just create generational wealth for your family; it can also help shift the economic trajectory of people you will never personally know. For EYL, a component of your financial freedom has to be philanthropy. The entire basis of our platform is about providing our community with the financial tools that were hidden from us. While that is its own gift, we don't stop there. We've been incredibly blessed to be able to offer scholarships and grants to undergraduate students and to business owners looking to scale up. Paying it forward is not a suggestion; we see it as the responsibility of anyone who is in a position to help make someone's situation better than it is right now.

In this chapter, we'll walk you through the two pillars of **EYL Legacy Building**. They are estate planning and creating a philanthropic arm of your personal and entrepreneurial endeavors. Putting these two pieces into place will not only solidify your commitment to the future and your community but also institutionalize your wealth in a way that will validate all the work you've done to get here. Money is immortal; your imprint on this world can be, too.

Estate Planning

Loss is inevitable, and no matter how much we know that, it's still hard to think about living without the people we love. It's equally as tough to think about what will happen to our loved ones after we're gone. Will your children be okay without you? Is your significant other prepared to live without your input and direction? These frustrations and emotions are hard to navigate and can often keep people from doing the work they need to do to make sure their loved ones will be cared for after their death.

Long gone are the days of believing that estate planning is just for the rich. Actually, that has never been true. When a person dies, their estate must be settled. That means their house, their car, their *debt,* and their last paycheck have to go somewhere or to someone. These pieces can't be left lingering after their death. To put it plainly: If you have an asset (checking account, car, furniture, etc.), you have an estate.

Because you have assets (and an estate), you can determine what to do with them and who will be the recipient of them in the event of your death or incapacitation. When it comes to estate planning, there are three essential aspects.

Beneficiaries

Beneficiaries are the people you designate to have access to your assets in the event of your incapacitation or death. Specifically in regard to your bank accounts, life insurance policies, and employee retirement and investment accounts, selecting beneficiaries ensures that the people you want to receive access to them will do so and prevents that access from defaulting to your next of kin. The most important part of having beneficiaries is keeping them up-to-date on all necessary forms. It doesn't matter that you have other estate-planning aspects in place; the beneficiary form will always hold the most power.

When Rashad first started in the financial planning industry, senior financial planners offered the cautionary tale of a man who worked for thirty years, divorced his first wife, remarried, and had children with the second wife. After he passed, his current wife learned that he had never updated the beneficiary form for his pension. As a result, the pension was automatically paid to his first wife. Legally, she had no obligation to share any or all of it with his widow or their children—and she didn't. For his later family, it was a costly mistake.

Unfortunately, it's a mistake that happens often. People forget to update their beneficiary forms, and those to whom they would rather pass their assets on are excluded from them. We recommend reviewing all your beneficiary forms annually and updating them within thirty days of a major life event. While designating beneficiaries empowers you to choose what happens to your assets after you are gone, what good is that power if you don't use it correctly?

Wills

A will is a legally binding document that outlines your desires for your assets that don't have direct beneficiaries. It also makes clear your wishes for your minor children in the event of your death. We recommend a will for all parents and anyone who has assets totaling more than $100,000.

In the previous chapter, we stressed the importance of parents' making plans for their kids as soon as they have them. If you have children, you need to have a will. Who do you want to raise your children if you pass away or become unable to care for them? When considering who should become the guardian of their children, parents should consider the person who is most likely to raise their child as closely aligned to their values as possible. This question isn't one to take lightly, nor should parents allow guardianship to default to their next of kin.

Parents should take their time, make the right decision, and put it into writing.

If you're not a parent but have less than $100,000 in assets that don't have direct beneficiaries, you should also consider making a will. Whom do you want to have your car? Or your prized collection of books, art, or albums? Whom do you want to take care of your pet after you've passed? Establish a will to answer these questions and make your intentions clear. Remember, it doesn't matter how old you are or how much money you do or don't have. If there's something you value, put the proper documentation into place to ensure that it will go to someone you value.

Trusts

A trust is an entity established by a grantor that gives power to a trustee to hold assets for a beneficiary or beneficiaries. It separates the grantor's assets from the estate, shielding them from various taxes and probate fees. We recommend a trust for those with $100,000 or more in assets but believe it's necessary for those with $500,000 or more in assets. Unlike a will, which is public, a trust maintains the privacy of a person's assets, and the contents of that trust are available only to those whom the trust benefits.

When it comes to trusts, a great benefit is that they don't incur the same tax liabilities as inherited money does. However, if your assets are not significant, a trust might be too costly to establish and maintain. If you have assets in your trust, they can gain interest as long as they remain in the trust.

There are two types of trusts. A **revocable trust** is one that can be adjusted or modified by its creator at any time to add or remove beneficiaries, include or remove assets, or change designations. One of the most famous recent examples of a revocable trust was that of Kobe Bryant. During his lifetime, he had amended his trust to include each of his daughters as a beneficiary after her birth. However, when he and his daughter Gigi died tragically in a helicopter accident in 2020, his nine-month-old daughter, Capri, had not yet been added as a beneficiary. His widow, Vanessa Bryant, had to petition the court to add Capri as a beneficiary, saying that that was what Kobe would have wanted. Her petition was granted.

An **irrevocable trust** can't be amended, modified, or changed after being established by the grantor. The only way an irrevocable trust can be adjusted is if all the beneficiaries of the established trust are in agreement about doing so. Irrevocable trusts create more tax shelters and provisions than revocable trusts do. However, grantors of irrevocable trusts give up a great deal of control over their assets, and beneficiaries often have to wait for up to a year to receive their designated assets.

Life Insurance

A life insurance policy is another aspect of estate planning and a way to care for those you love. It's also an opportunity to assist your minor children to build their own wealth. When it comes to life insurance, the first thing to determine is how much you need. The minimum should be ten times your annual salary. If you wish to be aggressive in your provisions for your loved ones, twenty times your annual salary is generous.

As you begin to establish life insurance as part of your estate planning, there are various products to consider.

- **Group life insurance** is a product employers offer their employees through their company. We recommend that every employee take advantage of their company's group policy, as the premiums are offered at a reduced rate and the risk/reward ratio is in the employee's favor. There are, however, disadvantages to having group life insurance as your only policy. A group policy is not always portable after you leave the company, and there is a cap on how much the policy can be worth (usually one to two times your annual salary). When a group policy is portable, you can keep the policy, paying the entire premium yourself. While porting the policy should happen no more than two months after you leave your job, you should compare the policies available to you to make sure you're paying the lowest possible premium.

- **Term life insurance** provides coverage for a specific amount of time, usually ten to thirty years. If you take out a term life insurance policy, your beneficiaries are guaranteed a payout if you die within the specified term. The advantage of a term life policy is that the premiums are extremely affordable, allowing the insured party to obtain a high amount of coverage. The disadvantages, however, are major: A term life policy does not accrue cash value, and most insured parties outlive the term of their policy. When this happens, a beneficiary will receive the value of premiums paid. Some term life insurance policies are **renewable,** meaning they have a clause that allows for renewal without the need for new underwriting. The conditions for this should typically be met before the insured turns age seventy. Some term life insurance policies are **convertible,** which means that before the insured turns seventy, the policy can be converted to whole life coverage.

- **Whole/universal/permanent life insurance** policies require significantly higher premiums. However, the coverage lasts for the lifetime of the insured party and the policy gains cash value over time. The cash value of a whole/universal/permanent life insurance policy operates similarly to home equity: Money grows inside the policy, and down the line, you can borrow from it. You can use the money that has grown in the policy to pay for your children's education, buy a car, start a business, or make a down payment on a home. For all intents and purposes, you can consider it another kind of savings account. However, borrowing against the policy reduces the value of the benefit.

Here are more things to consider.

- **Universal life insurance** allows you to raise or lower your payments as needed. However, lowering your premium payments can reduce the cash value of the policy. This can result in your having to pay more money in later years to keep the same level of coverage or death benefit.

- **Indexed universal life insurance** connects the cash value growth of the policy to the performance of an index, such as the S&P 500, with a cap on the rate of return.

- **Guaranteed universal life insurance** doesn't focus on building cash value but instead provides permanent coverage with lower premiums than whole life insurance.

- **Variable life insurance** connects the cash value growth of the policy to a group of investments.

Life Insurance Trust

One option is to place your life insurance policy into a **life insurance trust**. This separates the policy from your estate. This is significant because it prevents the policy from being added to the estate, thus increasing its value and placing the trust at a higher taxable rate. Once the life insurance policy is placed in a trust, the insured person no longer owns it and it will be managed by the trustee on behalf of the policy's beneficiaries.

Another option is to place your life insurance policy into an **irrevocable life insurance trust** (ILIT). An ILIT has significant perks, including tax advantages, asset protection, and the confidence that the death benefit can be used only the way the insured person intended it to be. An ILIT can also minimize estate taxes for wealthier individuals by making the trust the owner of the policy. If you are the insured party and own the policy, the death benefit will be considered part of the value of your overall estate when you die. When you put the policy into an ILIT and the trust becomes the owner of the policy, the death benefit is no longer included in your estate and won't contribute to its value.

To terminate an ILIT, certain criteria must be met. The value of the life insurance policy inside the trust can be exchanged for the equivalent amount in cash. When this happens, the policy reverts to the individual owner and the ILIT reverts to a grantor trust. When you stop paying the policy's premiums, it will lapse and cause the ILIT to revert. If the insured is over sixty years old, he or she can set up a life settlement agreement, in which a buyer becomes the new policy owner and beneficiary and pays the trust a cash payment. If the beneficiaries consent, an ILIT can be terminated.

A death benefit is considered tax-free income for the beneficiaries. However, life insurance proceeds can increase an estate's value above the estate tax's threshold. When it's held in a trust, it's possible to increase only the value of the beneficiaries' estates.

Don't Sell Grandma's House

Many of us come from families where our parents and grandparents were adamant that we not sell the family home. Purchasing that house was a major accomplishment and the pathway to economic freedom. Now, with their deaths and the varied needs and interests of their descendants, we see the future of our family home up for grabs. And family members are often at cross-purposes as a result.

When it comes to what we want the future to look like when we are no longer here, we can learn a lot from our families' mistakes. Taking the time to establish an estate is essential. No matter how much you have in assets, you can't afford not to have an estate. It offers you peace of mind and ensures that your family members won't have to fight over what you want them to have anyway.

Philanthropy

When it comes to building a legacy, paying it forward must be part of your plan. Charitable and philanthropic endeavors are part of that. We incorporated this into the EYL Money Principle through "Sharing." This provides the opportunity to give back as an individual or a business entity.

The opportunities to give back include creating nonprofit organizations, establishing scholarships, and making grants. An increased benefit is that these ventures also provide tax relief and benefits. The more money you have and income you generate, the more you can keep by channeling some of it into philanthropic and charitable endeavors.

A giving strategy needs to be part of your plan for achieving financial freedom. As always, we recommend sitting down with a financial adviser to create philanthropic and charitable products that can protect your assets and help change the lives of people in your community. They can be as creative and innovative as you are and want them to be. Doing this also provides a blueprint and model for the way you desire future generations of your family and your beneficiaries to care for the world with the resources they've inherited.

What Kind of World Do You Want to See?

Creating financial freedom and building wealth allow you to do something incredibly profound: help shape the world as you want it to be. In school, we were taught about our civil rights leaders and global icons who fought for various freedoms and changed the face of the world in service of the oppressed and marginalized. What is often not taught or discussed is the rich and wealthy entertainers and business leaders who often funded and underwrote their causes. Their resources sustained the movements for freedom and justice, and their contributions were as important as those of the people on the front lines.

Maybe you aren't that kind of warrior, and that's okay. There's still a role for you in this fight. Activists and social justice leaders need resources to sustain them and their causes. And they need resources that aren't attached to political agendas that mandate their silence on other issues. This is why wealth generation is so vital to our community. We can provide the financial resources that will enable our established and emerging leaders to speak truth to power *freely*, with no fear of having their capital snatched away.

As we were writing this book, we thought about a concern that keeps coming up with many in our EYL community. It's also something that, when we interviewed wealthy minorities about their initial experiences with their wealth, they told us they had struggled with. It's the stress of being "the one" to "make it" and the responsibility that comes along with it. We call it paying the "other" tax. You created a plan and stuck with it. As the saying goes, heavy is the head that wears the crown.

It's important that you develop a focused mentality and strategies to deal with your newfound wealth *now*. And this isn't one of those "fake it till you make it" techniques. You need to develop a new posture now because you're developing a new mentality now. As you shift, you will see that the people around you will notice your evolution. They will do one of two things: support it or hate it. If they hate it, their hate can take many forms. It can take the form of downright jealousy, something we've all seen up close but can never really get used to. Or it can take the form of believing that you have to be the one to shoulder everyone else's financial burdens.

Justice for Terri

Do you remember the movie *Soul Food*? Do you remember how Terri, played by Vanessa Williams, was her family's personal bank—despite the fact that Big Mama was still alive and hiding tens of thousands of dollars in Uncle Pete's broken TV? The unfortunate truth is that Terri isn't an anomaly. Many families have a "Terri," someone who has more money than everyone else in the family and is financially responsible for the family as a result. Sometimes people don't even go to the bank anymore to try to get a loan; they go straight to the Terri in the family, tell a sad story, and pull their phones out to wait for the deposit notification.

And you know what the worst part is? They know that no matter what, Terri is going to give them what they ask for. More than likely, she's never going to see the money again, but she'd rather give it to them than hear anybody's mouth about the fact she didn't. It's just easier that way. But nobody ever checks to see if Terri is okay. It doesn't matter if she's actually in a positive economic situation. The only thing that matters is that she has a "good job" and she's got money.

Reading this, you might identify with Terri. You're the one in your family who made a couple of right decisions and found yourself in a pretty solid situation. Unfortunately, your family sees *your* situation as *their* situation. There's nothing wrong with recognizing that who you are wouldn't be possible without the people in your corner who have supported you. At the same time, you don't have to bankroll their life as a perpetual thank-you.

If you're the Terri in your family or friend circle, we want you to take some time to evaluate why. What is it in you that feels the need to always say "yes"? Are you doing it out of a sense of obligation or a sense of superiority? As you answer these questions, also spend time exploring what it has cost you to say "yes." Here's the truth: Being Terri comes at a great personal cost to you and your relationships. Remember, Terri could barely be around her family without their expecting her to pay for something, and the tension of that ate away at their real connections. You can't be everyone's bank and expect to see them as your loved ones. Everything they do will be seen through the lens of the fact that they owe you—and how much they owe you—and that's not fair to anyone.

It's important to recognize how and why you feel the need to bankroll everyone else, because that isn't a mentality that will secure your financial freedom. Feeling obligated to your family and loved ones limits your ability to take greater chances to invest in yourself and cultivate generational wealth. Think of it this way: If it matters more to you that you are someone whom people can continuously call for loans they will never repay, the chances aren't great that you will develop the keen insight and business sense to make sound investments.

If you set up an annual "Sharing" budget with a giving threshold, you know that when that budget is gone, so is the ability for anyone to get any more money from you until next year. While this may sound harsh, you have to keep your ultimate goal in mind. If financial freedom is your goal, you're going to have to have some hard conversations with yourself, and "no" is going to have to become your favorite word.

A Loan Is a Gift

Before we go any further, we want to offer you this nugget of wisdom that will make life so much simpler for you in the long run: **A loan is a gift.** We already see you shaking your head and ready to go back to Barnes & Noble and get a refund. But hear us out: A loan is a gift. We know it's not a gift when Navy Federal Credit Union, Bank of America, or Wells Fargo lends money to you. But here's the thing: If the person who is asking you for a loan could get it from a bank or a credit union, they would've gone there. They didn't, so they came to you—a place with extremely flexible terms and conditions.

A loan is a gift because no matter what people promise you about paying it back, you're giving it to them assuming the risk that it won't be returned by the time you need it again or at all. And this is hard because some people just don't have it. Not everybody is borrowing money from you to buy expensive gifts for themselves and take luxury vacations. Many people are borrowing money because they seriously need help making ends meet and there's a likelihood that they won't immediately rebound out of that situation within a single pay period. Even if you create a repayment plan and it's agreed upon by all parties, understanding that you may never see your money again is the first thing you need to do before saying "yes."

Recognizing that a loan is a gift should also help you stay within the parameters of what you can give. If someone needs $1,000 and it will be a strain to give them the whole amount, you don't need to give them the entire thousand dollars. Putting yourself at a greater financial risk to help someone isn't noble or commendable; it's just not smart. You should also apply this logic when it comes to being a guarantor or cosigner on a loan. Assume that at some point, the loan will become your sole responsibility. If you will not be able to manage that, the answer to the request has to be "no."

How Is This Benefiting Me?

Whether you say "no" or not, here's what we know: People are always going to ask for money. There's no shame in their game, and if they need it—and think you will give it to them—they're going to ask. But as they're asking you the question, you should be asking something of yourself as well: How is helping them going to help me?

In the past, when you've given people money, you've just given it to them. Can we let you in on a little secret? Most wealthy people don't do that. When they give money, it is intentional and has some direct benefit to them, namely a tax deduction. You may not be in their or your desired tax bracket right now, but you can still employ the same principle and mentality. Before loaning or giving any money, determine if there will be a benefit for yourself. Will there be a tax break you'll be able to use? Can you hire the person as an independent contractor to perform a service instead of simply giving them money? It's your money, and you worked for it; it should work for you. At the very least, there's nothing wrong with requiring that the other person work for it. These questions may apply only to specific people in your life, which, again, may also help you decide who's eligible to get money from you.

As you look to shift the dynamic in your relationships concerning money, another suggestion is to define how you plan to offer assistance. Instead of your family coming to you throughout the year whenever they want to, you can decide that you'll assist only with back-to-school shopping or emergencies. Placing boundaries around the allocation of your resources frees you from the obligation to be the personal solution to the financial woes of everyone else in your family.

Establish a Process

One thing you'll quickly gather as you read this book is that we're all about successful processes and procedures. Building an effective personal economic system takes a lot of moving parts. If you want to be successful with your money, you have to do what successful people with money do. This means that unless the situation is urgent and pressing, you can't stop what you're doing to send money via Cash App or Zelle. While you love the other person, their emergency is not yours.

When it comes to a request for a loan or any other financial assistance, we suggest that you create a quick form or Google Doc. It will have the amount that's needed, the amount being requested, and who the money can be paid/sent to. The first thing people are going to do is say that you're acting brand-new. You are. You're putting a system into place that will allow you to track all of your expenses, because when it's time to balance your budget in three months and you forgot where that $2,000 went, you'll be able to track it down.

This also eliminates those who are asking for money just to ask for it and think *you* think you're the newest branch of OneMain Financial. And when people ask, you can tell them the truth: "I'm working to keep better track of my finances and expenses. I want to help you, but I really need you to fill this out so I can stay on top of things." Those who get it and respect you will do it. Those who don't just helped you keep money in your pocket.

Unless it's an urgent need, never fulfill a request the same day. You can choose a weekly, biweekly, or monthly processing day, explaining that this is your process. If you don't do anything else, don't deviate from this. You have a life that is filled with other responsibilities and commitments; you're not sitting around waiting to give people money. Additionally, doing it this way requires that those requesting money from you operate with a certain standard of professionalism and respect for you and your time.

Even if you think of every loan as a gift, you still need to put policies into place to collect what you're owed on the agreed-upon timeline. The key phrase in that sentence is "agreed upon." Do not provide any loan without establishing a repayment plan. And, no, "I'll get it back to you when I can" isn't a date. On the request form that you create, you can also have a place where the other person states when he or she will be able to repay the loan. Using an invoice-tracking system, you can send out reminder emails a few days before the due dates. The system will keep sending emails until the other person repays using the invoice system or you discontinue it after he or she has paid you. We suggest this an option because it will allow you to maintain your professionalism and continue your relationship with the person without having to initiate the awkward "Where is my money?" conversation.

We know this feels different from anything you've ever done before when it comes to giving money to your family and friends. At the same time, obtaining financial freedom isn't something you've done before, either. Putting policies and procedures into place isn't a bad thing. Reestablishing your identity in your circles when it comes to money doesn't make you the enemy; it means that you're evolving in how you understand money and its function in your life. It means that you've been incredibly blessed to be in a position to help and you want to show respect to that position by putting structures into place to maintain it. When you think about the wealthy people and entrepreneurs whom you admire, they all have a similar organizational framework in place. They're just waiting for you to join them in the winner's circle.

"This Applies to Everybody but My Mama"

If we're being honest, there are some people in our lives who can get whatever they want from us. Whether it's our parents, an uncle, a mentor, or a best friend—these people have been here for us in ways that make pursuing financial freedom possible. To show our gratitude, we want to give them the world, and they deserve it. As you work to cultivate generational wealth, you may want to consider how to repay their investment in you.

In the budgeting section of this book, we walked you through how to create a line item for taking care of or "retiring" a loved one, but more than that, this kind of care takes planning. Sit down with your loved one, tell them your desire, and discuss their monthly expenses. We recommend that you speak with a financial planner to create a more detailed strategy that will help you set a target date of when you will realistically be able to provide consistent assistance.

We all want to help people, and we all recognize that without the contributions of many people, we wouldn't be where we are today. All of us have depended on someone else at some point. But there is a difference between being grateful, being an enabler, and being used. On our journey to financial freedom, we have to free ourselves of the "survivor's guilt" we may feel that things worked out for us in ways they didn't work out for others. The truth is that many of us grew up in the same house, in the same family, and in the same neighborhood, went to the same school, had the same opportunities, but made some very different decisions. Our lives should be proof that anything is possible, and the decisions we make about our financial resources should reinforce our gratitude for our circumstances. It's only through acknowledging that gratitude and making sound decisions that we can pass our new mindset and mentality on to future generations.

Many people resent the growing capitalistic nature of our nation and our world. They are frustrated by and with anyone who seems to justify it. Even we have some concerns about aspects of our overly capitalistic society. However, we do not believe that those issues and concerns need to be addressed at the expense of members of marginalized and often excluded communities attempting to get ahead—namely, because people from these communities often use their resources in significant ways to advance and improve the conditions of their people. But more than that, until the world changes, having money and adequate resources matters. We encourage you to make as much money as possible so that you can shape your own life and the lives of the people around you.

◆ ◆ ◆

CHAPTER TEN

What to Do with Your First Million

You applied all the principles, tools, and strategies, and you did it! You made your first million dollars! Congratulations! This is a major accomplishment, and it shouldn't be taken lightly. You're probably the first in your family or friend circle to do this. Don't dismiss the magnitude of the moment. You worked hard toward this goal, and you achieved it. You should be proud of yourself. We definitely are.

Can we be honest with you? If you can make $1 million once, it will be fairly easy to do it again. You've unlocked a new hustle within you. What you thought wasn't possible for you to do, you've actually done. Repeating it over and over again will be the easy part. You'll have more million-dollar moments to celebrate. We just want to make sure that you handle this *first* one the best way possible.

Below is our step-by-step process for what to do when you make your first million dollars (or insanely large sum of money that you'd never thought you could make). Before you make the first purchase or buy out the bar, read this carefully and follow these instructions.

1. Contact a financial adviser, and reevaluate your financial goals.

There are a lot of places in this book where we've given you the tools to generate wealth *without* a financial adviser. This isn't one of them. If you find yourself with the kind of money you've never had before, you need someone to help you make sense of it and allocate it properly.

When you work with a financial adviser, you'll also have an opportunity to establish a plan to meet your current financial goals and/or establish new ones. Some people assume that the first thing you need to do with a sudden influx of money is to pay off all your debt. That makes sense; we come from families and communities in which being debt free is the ultimate goal. But developing a strategy with your financial adviser will prioritize what you need to do to achieve your ultimate goals—and don't be surprised if keeping a little of that debt is part of it.

2. Create a financial plan.

While this money can change your life, structuring it to do just that is something you've already done. Before spending anything, you need to take some time to ensure that how you structure the money will align with the EYL Money Principle. But before you do that, we need to break something to you, and you might need to sit down to read it. Are you ready? Okay, here goes.

Technically, your $1 million isn't a full $1 million. Uncle Sam will most definitely get his cut, because you'll have to pay taxes on it. On $1 million, you will pay roughly 37%. For this exercise, we're going to say that you'll be able to keep around **$630,000** of that million. Yes, you've just made your first million dollars, but this is what you're working with. To refresh your memory, here's how we break down your first million using the EYL Money Principle:

Saving (15%): $94,500

Spending (55%): $346,500

Sharing (10%): $63,000

Investing (20%): $126,000

Total: $630,000

When you see a million dollars—or any other amount of money—broken down like this, it helps give you clarity and focus concerning what you actually have and where you have it. Now that you know what you should allocate to each budget, we suggest that you go back to chapters 4 and 5 so that you can dedicate some time to learning how to craft a complete budget for your million dollars.

Even as a millionaire, you will need emergency savings because emergencies will happen. Emergencies and crises don't care if you've got money, and there's the old wives' tale that once you finally get some money, trouble will find you. *Everything* in your house will fall apart and in a major way. The washing machine won't just conk out on you; it will leak, and you'll need a new floor. That tree that's been standing strong for centuries will bow to a thunderstorm, and you'll need a new roof. Maintaining emergency savings will act as a buffer that will prevent the need to liquidate investments hastily in a downturn or personal crisis.

3. Develop a tax strategy.

This million dollars may shift you into a higher tax bracket. You've already set $370,000 aside for taxes. If you've inherited the money, estate taxes may be on the table. Whatever investments you desire to make may also be subject to capital gains, property, and other taxes. If you don't already have a tax account, we strongly suggest that you set one up. If you're often paid as an independent contractor or are an entrepreneur, you need an account separate from your business checking, savings, and other accounts. Also, setting up quarterly tax payments is clutch and will keep you from having to pay penalties and interest, if you wait until the end of the year. It's also a good business practice to establish a tax account as you're thinking about what systems and procedures need to be in place to ensure your financial success.

When it comes to a tax strategy to maximize your tax benefits, consider these tips.

1. If you'll make either more or less than a million dollars in the next year, consider timing certain deductions or delaying some of your income to the following year in order to reduce this year's income and thus take advantage of more favorable tax rates.

2. Consider tax-loss harvesting with your stocks to reduce your taxable income and lower your tax liability.

3. Invest in an account such as an IRA or 401(k) to reduce the taxes you have to pay on the million dollars while your investments are in a tax-free account, building up and waiting for your retirement.

4. Invest in bonds, since the interest and income on them are often tax exempt.

5. Donate to 501(c)(3) charities to reduce your taxable income.

THE MONEY TEAM

Nobody obtains financial freedom alone. If it takes a village to raise a child, it's going to take a community to help you access the wealth and financial resources you desire. When it comes to building your own financial empowerment community, here are some of the members we recommend.

1. **Mentor:** Because you don't know everything, a mentor is important. This is someone whose journey and ascension into wealth creation can be proven and is well documented. They did it—and the right way. Meeting with them, whether monthly or annually, can help provide you with the advice and guidance you need to avoid making costly mistakes. If you don't have access to someone like this in your personal life, there are many you can follow on social media. By supporting their content and applying their suggestions, you can find yourself in an optimal position.

2. **Financial planner:** You can't go on the journey to financial freedom successfully without a financial planner. Just as you need a physician to be your best self, you need a financial adviser to help you get into the best financial shape of your life. This person will sit down with you and your finances to determine the products that best align with your vision of financial freedom. If you can't afford an independent financial planner, there is good news: Most banks and credit unions offer financial planning services for free or at reduced rates for their members.

3. **Accountant:** As you continue to grow your net worth and cultivate your financial freedom, an accountant will

be essential. While it will always be important for you to know your current economic condition at all times, an accountant can help you establish your budget and keep you on track to accomplishing your goals. As an entrepreneur, you will find that having this person on your team is clutch! Add to that the fact that preparing taxes and making sure you are compliant personally and/or professionally is tedious work. Why do it if you don't have to?

4. **Attorney:** When it comes to building a financial legacy, especially regarding estate planning, you're going to need an attorney. Some documents must be legally established and filed. Additionally, if you are in a co-parenting situation, having an attorney as part of your team is crucial. And when you are in your role as an entrepreneur, having legal representation for contract negotiations and other matters legitimizes you and your entrepreneurial pursuits. There are some levels of business that cannot be handled without or by anyone other than an attorney. If you currently can't afford to have an in-house attorney or keep one on retainer, there are many attorneys who will represent you on a case-by-case basis.

5. **Assistant:** Contrary to popular belief, you are not superhuman. You can do many things, but you can't do everything. When it comes to business, freeing yourself from having to complete your business's administrative tasks will make room for you to be even more creative and focused on expanding your wealth-building capacity. Even if you don't have a business, there are assistants who can help with your personal tasks, taking them off your

plate. You can actually hire someone to coordinate meetings with your money team! The opportunities are endless!

6. **Accountability partner:** Equally important is having someone on your squad who will motivate you to achieve your highest financial success. This isn't just someone who will help you celebrate the wins; it must also be someone you can be honest with about the losses. The two of you can be transparent about what went right, what went wrong, and how you both can make the best financial decisions possible. A financial accountability partner must be someone who can see your vision and won't be intimidated by your growth and success. At the same time, you can be that for them. How much faster can you run toward your financial future if you have someone running alongside you?

Mentality Shift

Things change when you start making the kind of money that changes lives. We've spent a great deal of time in this book discussing mindset in different ways because we truly want you to get the point. Achieving financial freedom and creating generational wealth mean that you can't operate business as usual and expect to see a different reality. Everything about your behavior and your mentality has to be upgraded. Here are some ways to do that.

1. **Keep your phone on "do not disturb."** There was a meme circulating on social media telling people to beware of anyone who always has their phone in "do not

disturb" (DND) mode because no one is that busy. You'd be surprised at how many people agreed with that. Too many people use DND mode only at night or when they're extremely busy. What we need you to understand is that when you begin generating the kind of wealth that will change your life, you will also begin to see your time differently. Time is one of the most nonrenewable resources you have; you can't get it back. You need to be spending your time creating new strategies for wealth generation, enjoying your family and the people you love, and resting. Being tied to your phone, easily accessible to everyone, isn't conducive to your goals.

2. **Evaluate your circle.** We live in a time where people idolize haters and jealousy. For some, it's fun to know that people around them envy what they have. We're not that kind of people, and we don't want you to be, either. While it's true that you can't help it if people get jealous of you, you can still protect your energy and peace. You don't have to stay around people who are resentful of your success out of some misguided sense of obligation. Remember, we said we weren't going to be the Terri of our family or friendship circle anymore. With greater resources and opportunities, you can gain greater insight and vision. This doesn't mean you should start to act brand-new and switch up on everyone in our life. It does mean that you get to take inventory of who we spend time around and ask yourself if you can push one another to be the best versions of ourselves. Some of the people in your life want this as much as you do. You can motivate one another.

3. **Be careful with generosity.** When people learn that you've made your first million dollars, expect them to ask

you for help. As the old truism says, if you build it, they will come. You built a dream. It wasn't necessarily for them, but they hope to benefit nonetheless. Understand this: You can't help everybody, and you shouldn't even try. According to your "Sharing" budget, you have $94,500 to assist people with, and we recommend that that's all you use. In EYL, we say "Give an opportunity instead of giving money." For us, that means hiring friends and loved ones as independent contractors instead of giving them money. An example of this would be purchasing a property to create an Airbnb revenue stream and hiring a loved one to manage the property. Not only is this a tax benefit to you, but it ties work equity to what you've offered. Remember, we don't believe you should be the only person working for your money when other people are asking for it.

4. **Develop and maintain a life of discipline.** After you make your first million dollars, things can't remain the same, and we're not just talking about your financial habits or your mentality. Your actions also need to evolve. You need to level up every area of your life. If you've been slacking in the health and physical fitness department, it's time to step it up. If your workspace is cluttered and messy, it's time to put this book down for a few minutes and clean up. Discipline must be present in every facet of your life for you to be able to optimize the advantages of financial freedom and wealth creation. Who wants to sit in a millionaire's nasty car? Or have a conversation with someone who isn't well versed in current events and the arts? It's not enough to take pictures with "important people" and be posted on Instagram. Your life, in every way possible, needs to reflect your leveling up.

Your First Million-Dollar Flex

Look, you're going to do it. We already know you are; we did! And why shouldn't you? Working hard and accomplishing your goal deserves to be rewarded. You deserve to stunt. Here are a few tips to ensure that your first big-money flex is as strategic and beneficial to you in the long run.

1. **Set an amount, and stick to it.** Hear us clearly: We don't care how well your business is doing. At no point should all or even the majority of the $346,500 in your "Spending" budget go toward your flex purchase. We know you're excited, but there's not that much excitement in the world! This is where wisdom and all the financial discipline you've displayed up to this point have to go into overdrive. Decide how much of your "Spending" budget will be used for your purchase, and don't exceed that. If the purchase costs more than what you've allotted, you should be able to pull from your savings—because, hopefully, you've already been saving toward it—to make up the difference.

2. **Purchase through your company/business entity.** The first thing many people want to do after they make their first million dollars is buy a house or a car. This is a great investment, especially if it's done right. Purchasing the house or car through your business will create less of a tax burden for you as an individual and an even greater tax benefit for you as an entrepreneur and business owner. Remember when we told you whom tax codes overwhelmingly benefit? This is an opportunity for you to take advantage of those tax codes.

3. **Make it a company trip.** If you've decided that your million-dollar flex is going to be a vacation, make it one that can be written off on your taxes. Again, all of the moves you make must be as strategic and as beneficial to you as possible. There are stipulations concerning what can and cannot be understood as a business trip, depending on your field. We encourage sitting down with your tax accountant or financial planner to get clear about what's possible for you and plan your trip accordingly.

4. **Buy the right things.** It may not be a house or a car that you're interested in for your million-dollar flex purchase. It could be a luxury watch or designer purse. Don't listen to people who tell you not to spend your money on "things." Commodities aren't bad purchases—if they're the right commodities. If you're a sneakerhead, buy shoes that will appreciate in value over time. If you want a watch, make sure it's a watch that is known to have a profitable vintage status. If you're interested in a handbag, it's important that the price of the brand will increase over time. And if you're looking to get into the art world, your million-dollar flex purchase is a great way to start. Whatever you purchase, remember to have it insured.

5. **Don't forget about the kids.** When we say, "Don't forget about the kids," we're not saying you have to buy them an equally expensive million-dollar flex gift. If you want to, that's up to you, and we're sure you'll probably be seen as "Parent of the Year" in their eyes. What we mean is that part of *your* flex should consist of ensuring *their* flex in the future. You can make some of those purchases and

add them to their UGMA or UTMA accounts. You
could increase your contribution into their Roth IRA.
You could plan for a business trip to be an opportunity to
expose them to another part of the world and culture
they wouldn't otherwise see. Building generational wealth
is a mindset, and how you celebrate your wins will reflect
yours.

One of the first things we told you in this chapter is that if you've
made a million dollars once, you can make it again. It was hard, and
it required that you take a lot of risk and bet on yourself. But it's not
rocket science. And part of what you need to do when you make
your first million dollars is create a strategy to make the second
million.

This moment is what separates the lucky from the legendary. Anybody can put some money into the stock market or Bitcoin and make
it big off a price increase. Anybody can buy a property, rent it out, and
create residual income. All these things are possible to everyone, but
not everyone has great longevity. When you look at reality shows and
stories that follow lottery winners and business owners who blew
through insane amounts of money and never recouped it, you see just
how important it is to make a plan for what you have and what you
want to do with it.

**Within the first ninety days of making your first million dol-
lars, you should create the general structure of the plan for your
second million dollars.** As you build your plan, here are some questions you should ask yourself and discuss with your team.

1. **What did I do, and how did I do it?** Evaluate just
   how you made your first million. What exactly did
   you do, and how long did it take? Write everything
   down. That was the blueprint of your first major win.
   Reflecting on every decision that brought you here will

create the framework to be able to do it stronger next time.

2. **What worked? What didn't?** Making your first million dollars means that you did something right, but it doesn't mean that you did *everything* right. You're going to stumble and fumble on your way to financial freedom. Mistakes will be made; mistakes were made. Identify the pros and cons of this particular journey; this will help you determine your approach to making the second million.

3. **What do I want to do this time?** There's a saying: "If it's not broken, don't try to fix it." When it comes to securing their second million dollars, some people use this approach. But just because you made your first million dollars one way doesn't mean that that's how you have to do it the second time around. This is an opportunity for you to decide what you want to do next. If you're interested in switching up your method, remember to revisit your EYL Money Principle budget to make the necessary allocations.

4. **Who will I need to help me succeed?** No one makes it alone. Every "self-made" millionaire had people in their corner. And when you evaluate how you were able to accomplish this goal, you'll acknowledge that you had people in your corner as well. This is an opportunity for you to reflect on this and identify whom you'll need this time around. In this book, we've given you suggestions for who should be on your "money team," but this is the time for you to identify those you will need to help you make your next million.

5. **What will be my benchmarks?** While it will be easy to continue making money, it's going to be important to measure if you're on the right track. You may not have had benchmarks the first time around, but this is the time to implement them. What kind of movement would you like to see in the first ninety days? Six months? How will you "check in" with yourself and your goals? You and your team will know what's best for you and what best aligns with your particular strategy and approach to making your second million. You will need to have measures in place; establish them.

As you're celebrating your first million and planning your attack on the second, it's important to realize that you're somebody's inspiration. Where many people come from, they don't see people like you. And they need to see people like you. Paying it forward matters. You may not be in a position to actively mentor someone right now, and that's okay. At the same time, it's necessary to recognize that you're providing information that they can use on their journey. Who you are is already inspirational. Who you have become has heightened that. People need to see models like you to visualize what is possible. Someone did it for you; it's only right that you do it for someone else.

There's nothing like making your first million dollars. We can't underscore just how much it will change your life. Not only does that transformation occur from a financial perspective, you become a completely different person. Understanding financial freedom and continuously generating wealth means that you will celebrate the major accomplishments as they become stepping-stones to bigger achievements at the same time.

Who you allow yourself to become after this milestone will set the pace for who you will be on your continued journey to financial freedom. You deserve to be rich, but you also deserve to be a person whom everyone still wants to be around. This money will change your circumstances, and it will change your behavior. But it doesn't have to fundamentally change the core of who you are. It's possible to be kind, considerate, *and* wealthy. We want you to enjoy the money, enjoy the journey to making it, and enjoy the person you've become at the same time as you enjoy the money itself.

◆ ◆ ◆

CHAPTER ELEVEN

EYL in a Year

Okay, maybe the title of this chapter is a bit misleading. So let's put our disclaimer up front: We are not saying that it's going to take you only a year to earn your leisure and build the kind of generational wealth that will sustain your family long after you're gone. What we are saying is that if you follow the blueprint we lay out for you in this chapter, you will be closer to financial freedom than you've ever been before.

Everybody loves a plan. The truth is that you probably bought this book because you were looking for a step-by-step plan for getting rich. We hope we haven't disappointed you—although if you've gotten this far in the book, we know you've picked up some gems. Here's our opportunity to give you what you're looking for. We genuinely believe that if you take the time to apply what we've outlined in this book, you will be able to unlock your economic potential at the highest levels.

In alignment with the new year and its associated resolutions, most people tackle a new approach to their finances in January. Others wait until they can use their tax refund to pay down debt and move into a greater space of financial ease. We don't know when you'll pick up this book, but whenever you do, we want you to start implementing the plan as soon as possible. That's why we're not creating our plan in the traditional calendar format beginning in January. For us, it's financial freedom *now* (whenever now is for you) or never.

Months One and Two: Mindset Work

In actuality, taking eight weeks to focus on your financial mindset may not be enough time. The truth is that it's a lifelong work. When you've experienced years of financial trauma and come from a family and community where economic empowerment was not a priority, there will be times throughout your life when those old tapes will resurface. The work you will do in these two months will establish a foundation that you will be able to rest on and refer back to when those times come.

Go back to the beginning of the book. In the introduction, we gave a definition for earning your leisure. It's "having the active and residual income that affords you the freedom to control your time and live a life on your terms." We also provided you with our EYL Thesis for Wealth: Increase your income. Lower your expenses. Invest the difference. We want you to go back to that and consider how you can do just that. Then go back to the principles we laid out in chapters 2, 3, and 4. These two months of mindset work are your opportunity to establish your EYL Baseline and decide whether your current financial situation has you on track to achieve it.

Consider these activities:

1. Go to one of your favorite restaurants, coffee shops, or
   places to think and create a list of five to ten ultimate
   financial goals. This is the time to dream. The world will

tell you that you need to be more realistic, and that's the problem. Too many of us have been told to be "realistic," which is always code for dreaming small. This isn't what you're going to do anymore. It's time to take the big swings.

2. Get out a notebook and a pencil, and calculate your EYL Baseline. If you're going to engage in goal setting, it's time to have *the* number in mind. Calculating what it will take to maintain you currently and what you will need to thrive in the future is its own strategy, and your financial goals will become even more attainable once you've established it.

3. Spend some time evaluating your relationship with money, exploring why you make the choices that you do and what lessons you have carried over from your childhood and the relationship your family had/has with money. Healing from financial trauma will take more than two months, but this is the time for you to begin this work.

4. Select another book, podcast, television show, or video series that focuses on a specific financial area that you want to work on. We know you've read this book (thanks again, by the way!), but the commitment to achieving financial freedom requires going beyond just this one. We've given you a solid overview of financial tools and strategies. Taking time to go more into depth with other resources will yield maximum returns.

5. Set up an appointment with a financial adviser. Whether you already have a financial adviser or not, this is a great

time to set an appointment so you can get some additional advice. If you don't already have a financial adviser and aren't sure of who to enlist, start with your bank or credit union. There's someone on staff who can assist you with advice and preliminary steps.

It would also be extremely beneficial to take inventory of how much time you spend surrounding yourself with wealth-building principles and like-minded people. Ask a core group of friends if they'd be willing to do "EYL in a Year" with you; the group can meet monthly to ensure that everyone stays on track. Curate your social media feeds in such a way that you'll see more economic empowerment content than celebrity gossip. Find a conference (such as InvestFest) or mastermind workshop that you'd like to attend. Pay the registration fee, put the dates on your calendar, and continue shifting your approach to achieving financial freedom.

If you've seen yourself in our EYL player Dre, you may have an inclination to think that you need to focus on making more money before you put a plan together. Some people think that they can't afford a plan. This is actually the opposite of what you need to do. For Dre and people like him, this is the best time to conceptualize your goals. It may be frustrating, but it will allow you to get a very clear picture of what you need to do in order to get out of your financial hole. How powerful would it be for Tracy to commit to "EYL in a Year" with other single mothers? Not only would it provide them with the community they need to remind them that they are not alone, but they could also share their tips and best practices (and the costs of resources and materials) to help one another achieve their financial goals.

For Gary and Morgan Williams, taking this time to plan is critical. As parents, they know that if you blink, your kids will go from babies to high school seniors in a moment. Before either of them realizes it, college will be on the doorstep. Yes, they want to take that luxury vacation, but more than that, they want to make sure that their kids will have what they need to be successful. This is a plan they can't waste any more time putting into place. Corey knows what he wants to do: He wants to get serious about investing. Taking this time to sit with the traumas and triggers that are keeping him from doing it and "investing" in more books, seminars, and other resources on investing is the best way to spend these first two months. And Edwin has to get serious about his budget and where he can cut or minimize spending. Until he figures out how to best manage his money and create the savings that his family needs, he can't focus on the plan to bring in the kind of money he desires.

During this time, we have only one rule: **No unnecessary spending**. Understand why we're saying this. First, you need to create a budget anyway. It is an essential tool for achieving financial freedom. If your goal is to be wealthy, recognize that rich people have budgets. Also, this rule is to assist you in taking control of your spending. During this time, you'll be evaluating your bank statements and spending trends for the last three months (at a minimum). There's no need to continue the unhealthy behaviors that you're identifying as counterproductive. So put a pause on the spending for these first two months. As a matter of fact, put the money you'd normally spend on unnecessary purchases into your savings account, and look at how much you have at the end of these two months. You'll be amazed.

Months Three and Four: Clean It Up and Figure It Out

In Months Three and Four, you're going to get to work. We call these months "Clean It Up and Figure It Out" because you're going to be doing two things. Let's start with the cleanup. During Months One and Two, you did the groundwork of evaluating your finances. You know what your weakest areas are. During Months Three and Four, we want you to attack them. If there's a bill that's become too high or gotten away from you, use the extra resources you have (if you cut your unnecessary spending in Months One and Two, you should have at least two months' worth available) to pay it down. If the issue is your credit, consider sitting down with a credit professional (you may have access to one through your bank or credit union) to create a plan to strengthen your score. You've done the work to create a clean slate; now you deserve to have one.

Here are some suggestions to clean up your finances.

1. Identify two to three paid subscriptions that you can eliminate, and cancel them. You probably thought you got rid of all of your unnecessary spending two months ago, but it's time to go through them again. Do you need all of those music-streaming subscriptions, or can you get away with one? Can you live with the free version, with commercials included, if it means you can save money? We'll save you some time: The answer is yes.

2. Pull your credit report, and analyze it for mistakes. Remember, if a credit agency can't prove that you "own" a debt, it can be removed from your report.

3. Identify your highest expenses, and research cheaper replacements. You can probably find a cheaper cellphone plan or internet service. There's a cheaper option for almost everything, and finding it will save you money. Ultimately, that's all that matters.

While everyone can clean up their budget, this is an opportunity for people like Dre and Tracy to spend a significant amount of time streamlining their budgets for additional ways to save money.

So you've cleaned up your budget; now is the time to figure it out. This is the time when we want you to do your research and identify potential investments you'd like to make—and you'll need to take this research time seriously, because you'll be making that investment before the end of the year! In chapter 5, we broke down the various types of investments and the EYL Investment Blueprint. Go back to that chapter, and familiarize yourself with the investment types that most interest you. This is important because it will help alleviate the fears you may have when it comes to investing, due to a lack of information and education. Take the time to learn what you can so that when the opportunity comes to invest, you'll be ready.

Consider these activities.

1. **Perform a risk tolerance assessment.** Before making any investment, it's important to know how much you can afford to invest.

2. **Explore the various asset classes and research how you might structure your investment portfolio.** Asset allocation is a prime opportunity to establish how you will build your investment blueprint.

During this time, Dre should research investing opportunities for folks with bad credit or fewer financial resources, such as a high-yield savings account or a real estate investment trust. Remember, these are among the options that require as little as $1 to $1,000 to start investing. This would also be a prime opportunity for him to open a brokerage account. It's likely that Tracy already has a brokerage account and is making minimal investments and contributions through her job. Now is the time to research how to scale up those contributions, create a 529 college savings plan for her daughter, and find out what she needs to do to begin her virtual business.

Gary and Morgan Williams will take this time to research the audio equipment business they want to start. They'll also meet with their financial adviser to explore what kinds of investments are optimal for maximizing the remaining time they have before their children will be ready to go to college. Corey knows that he wants to own several investment properties; he should meet with a financial adviser and Realtor to identify his first investment property and funding. Additionally, he will invest in REITs, though his investment level will be higher than Dre's. Right now, Edwin should be looking into short-term savings and investment opportunities that will help him pay off his $40,000 debt faster. He set a goal of eighteen months. While he's been able to cut some of his spending and keep making his payments on time, it's also going to take income specifically devoted to paying off the high-interest debt. Placing a lump sum in a high-yield savings account and CDs, for the set time period, and then using it to pay down his debt will help him become debt-free faster.

During Months Three and Four, we also want you to do something else: If you've established your EYL Baseline and it requires additional income, now's the time to secure a second job or a salary increase or explore a side hustle. Finding a second job will be as easy as getting on the internet, searching based on your criteria and desired career field, and applying. Seeking a raise or promotion at your current job will require more effort. We encourage you to put together a résumé of your professional highlights, including the ways you met and exceeded company benchmarks, so you can make a case for why you have earned and deserve what you're requesting.

If you've been wanting to start a side gig, chances are you've already looked into what it will take a thousand times already. If you haven't, we want you to look into it just once. If you've done your research and have just been putting it off, it's time to get it together. By the end of Month Four, you should either have begun to increase your income and lower your expenses or be well on your way to doing so!

Months Five, Six, Seven, and Eight: Work the Plan—and Invest!

You've done the work to put a plan into place. This might be the most mundane part of the year, because it's simply about working the plan. Barring any drastic losses or detrimental outcomes, we stress that you shouldn't deviate from a full execution of your plan for at least 90 to 120 days. This will give you solid metrics to examine during Month Nine. We know this will be difficult, especially if you don't see immediate results. This is one of the most common mistakes made by people who are entering financial freedom territory for the first time. The desire to abandon a plan that doesn't seem to be working will seem irresistible. But we're asking you to stay the course.

During these four months, we're also going to ask you to do something that may still have you on the fence: **invest**. We're breaking this down for two different groups: **those who haven't invested yet but want to add it to their personal EYL plan** and **those who are looking to expand their current investment portfolio**. For those who will be making their first investment, it's time to take out the research you completed in Months Three and Four and . . . make the investment! Hear us out: We're not telling you to sink your life savings into it, but we're also not telling you to take $5 and try to make something shake, either. This is the opportunity to make a comfortable initial investment that (1) reflects your commitment to your financial freedom and (2) can become the foundation of future investments, helping you establish healthy investment habits. Refer back to the chapter on investments for additional information.

Those of you who will be making another investment to add to your portfolio will need the research you did earlier in the year, too. Remember that we told you that different investments will require different levels of investment? This is where you'll put this knowledge into practice. A newly established investment is probably going to take more of your resources than one that's been working for a while. Be prepared for that, creating room in your investment budget to make the necessary changes and adjustments. And remember, seeing progress in this investment may take time—more time than your initial investments did. That's okay. Pace yourself and relax.

Out of all the EYL players' investments, Dre's might be the quickest and easiest to establish. At this point, he's making deposits into his brokerage account and leaving the account alone. Tracy will increase her investments, but like the Williams family, she wants to start a business, and that will take a bit of time to research and launch. Yet they all have a solid plan in place and are executing it. Corey made the decision to invest in an equity real estate investment trust, and with his financial adviser and Realtor, he located an investment property for sale. Having secured a loan, he's made the purchase, will complete the necessary renovations, and has hired a management company to handle the process of locating a tenant. Right now, Edwin can't make the investments he'd like because he's still building his savings. This would be a time for him to research the investment and entrepreneurial opportunities he's considering that will get him to that $500,000 EYL Baseline.

There may be some investments (such as real estate or company equity) that can't happen within a four-month window, for a variety of reasons. A sale can take longer than expected, and some companies may have a specific time of the year they set aside for establishing equity partnerships and investments. If this is the case for you, that's fine—as long as you're using the time to prepare to make the investment.

Month Nine: Evaluate! Evaluate! Evaluate!

To some people, a month to evaluate your financial plan and reevaluate your money goals may seem like too much time. To others, it's not enough. We think that four weeks is perfect for surveying your economic landscape and taking inventory of what is and isn't working. Don't worry, you'll be busy. Trust us.

Much of this may feel like the work you did in Months One and Two, and it is. But this time you'll have a minimum of three months of new transactions (and new behaviors, right?) to assess. This is the time to track how your spending is aligned with the EYL Money Principle. Where has your money been going? What adjustments do you need to make? Can you lower your expenses any more than you already have? Can you move more to your "Saving," "Sharing," and "Investment" budgets? This is the time to make those adjustments.

Additionally, revisit your progress toward your EYL Baseline, and take some time to look at your initial financial goals. Have they grown? Do you want to scale them down a bit? This may seem like a crazy question, but if you do, that's absolutely okay. Some people start with big financial goals because they think that's what they're supposed to have. But after sitting down and looking at their finances, they realize that they don't need all of it. There's nothing wrong with changing your mind. It isn't a failure, and it doesn't mean you're lazy. Your EYL Baseline and financial goals are all about you and your family—no one else.

Here are some activities we suggest for Month Nine.

1. **Schedule a meeting with your financial adviser** to evaluate the progress of your investments and what adjustments, if any, need to be made.

2. **Revisit your financial goals and EYL Baseline** and make any adjustments for possible major life events. Are you thinking about getting married or starting a family within the next year? Will you have to become the guardian or caretaker of a loved one? These life events will impact your financial circumstances, and it's important

that you begin to consider how they'll be affected and
forecast for it.

While Dre may have been a little frustrated by the drastic cuts he
had to make to his budget in the previous months, when he sees the
gains he's making in his investments, he's beginning to feel like an
adult. Additionally, with his second job, he's building up the resources
to move into his own apartment and create the financial structure
that will serve him well for the rest of his life. He can't believe he set a
budget and stuck with it. He's incredibly proud of himself, as he
should be.

Tracy's so glad that she started the 529 plan because she sees how
much it can grow in the next fifteen years to be ready for her daughter's freshman year of college. And she's proud of having started her
virtual admissions counseling business and establishing a clientele.
Now buying a home doesn't look as impossible as it did before. The
Williams family has learned a lot about investments, especially since
they had to engage in some asset allocation to create a high-yield
short-term investment to prepare for their oldest child's college fund.
It's on track to yield what they wanted to give each child. The investments for the other children can remain a longer-term investment
strategy.

With this being Corey's first investment property, he's been incredibly anxious. While it was a great investment, he underestimated his
renovation budget. That alone was enough to cause him to second-
guess the process. He'd begun to regret it when his property management company found a tenant. Now that he's gotten a tenant in his
home and is clearing $600 a month after monthly expenses, he doesn't
see the investment as a huge mistake anymore. However, spending the
time to reflect on the steps he took that caused him to miscalculate his
repair budget is important, especially since he wants to buy and rent
out more properties.

Edwin is really proud of himself. A jack-of-all-trades, he now uses his "off day" of Monday to do some graphic design contract work. Additionally, he's created some buzz at the restaurant and club with new menu offerings and themed club nights and events to attract more customers. It's worked. He's been able to bring more money into his household and his business. Coupling that with maintaining the personal budget cuts he's made, he's beginning to see progress in his savings goal.

Months Ten and Eleven: Finish Strong

After evaluating your EYL plan and making the necessary adjustments, there's nothing left to do but ensure that you finish the year strong! By the time you get to Month Ten, you'll see that there's really no secret to doing this. It's about creating a plan and working it. What's important here is that you've developed a mindset of ethics and behaviors that will enable you to achieve the financial freedom you desire. Now's the time to plug any holes you see in your plan or overall process.

Here are some activities to consider.

1. **Evaluate your financial team.** Is everyone playing their position? Are there other professionals you could've used before and are in a position to hire now?

2. **Take inventory of your financial habits and behaviors over the last few months.** Where can you go harder? You've done some great work these past few months. If you can do even better, you'll be in an even greater financial position.

By now, much as you have, all of our EYL players have discovered that the true cheat code involves hard work and discipline. Creating financial freedom is about doing the work and remaining committed to the process. At this point, everyone sees how well the process is working for them.

Month Twelve: Celebrate and Strategize

You've made it to Month Twelve of your EYL in a Year plan! How do you feel? We think the words you're looking for are *accomplished* and *proud*. And that's exactly how you should feel. A year ago, you weren't in this position. You didn't have these tools. And if you'd had them, you wouldn't have applied them in a way that would enable you to change your financial future. You've done that now. It's an achievement worth celebrating.

So celebrate! Take some of your savings, and buy something you've been eyeing or plan a trip. While this may seem counterproductive, this is one of the main themes of EYL. You don't *have* to wait until some arbitrary time to enjoy the riches (pun intended) of your labor. **You can do it—within reason—as you continue on the path of financial freedom.** Such celebrations are well deserved and warranted.

Here are some ways you might celebrate.

1. **Plan a joint celebration with your EYL in a Year accountability group.** Whether it's a girls' night out or a girls' trip, this is an opportunity to acknowledge your hard work during the past year and have fun! Plus, you can split the costs and save money.

2. **Plan a business trip that will be tax deductible.**

3. **Research commodities that will be both a celebratory purchase and an investment.**

Dre's gotten bit by the investment bug. He's celebrating by increasing the amount in his investment trust. His social media timelines aren't just following gamers and comedians anymore. He's actively engaging in financial empowerment communities and is sharing digestible content and advice on his timelines and with his friends.

Tracy had been grinding so much, saving for a home and for her daughter, that doing something for herself seemed out of the question. But her friends convinced her that she deserved to treat herself. She had always wanted to experience a spa day, so she took $750 and scheduled a day of pampering. She scheduled the day together with her girls, so whenever she told them she couldn't believe she had spent so much on herself, they quickly told her that they were not about to listen to that forever.

Gary and Morgan Williams are keeping their eyes on the prize: their first kid-free luxury vacation! To celebrate their hard work toward their financial goals, they added an additional $2,000 to the vacation budget. Wherever they decide to go, they will spare no expense.

Corey loves watches. To celebrate overcoming his investment fears, he took some of his earnings and purchased two new timepieces from a Black-owned business. At the beginning of the year, Edwin had only $200 in his savings account. Now it stands at $3,500. He didn't even think that was possible! To celebrate staying the course and keeping his eye on the prize, Edwin treated his family to a "Family Fun Day," doing everything his kids and wife wanted to do. Seeing them happy made him happy, and it reminded him who he's doing all of this for.

In addition to celebrating your accomplishments, it's time to begin strategizing for the next phase of your financial plan. Now is the time to revisit your goals from the top of the year and rate yourself. Have you achieved them all? Are there any that will require you to shift some of your focus and energy toward them? This is how you take a one-year plan and turn it into the blueprint for the rest of your life. The truth is that you should always spend some time at the start of your year planning how you intend to spend the year financially. This is the mindset of a winner.

As you've read this book, we hope that you've taken hold of the principles and strategies we've provided. Our greatest hope is that you've been able to realize just how close financial freedom is when you dedicate yourself to obtaining it.

◆ ◆ ◆

Loaded Bases

When we started the Earn Your Leisure brand, we had one goal: We wanted to provide our community with the tools and resources that have systematically been kept from us. The best way to describe it is that we saw a baseball game being played and the powers that be had all the bases loaded. The marginalized members of communities who were routinely shut out of opportunities were all on a team that reflected our plight in life. We didn't have proper bats or equipment—hell, we didn't even have uniforms. We were just out there scrapping.

The truth is that you can be a scrapper; you can have all the heart in the world. But when you don't have the financial means you need to be successful, it doesn't matter how much passion and will you have. When we looked at our community, some of our own family members, and others who were reaching out to us for help, we saw a lot of people with hunger and grit. They were ready for change, and they were willing to work for it. They just needed to learn what they didn't know about how to create it.

The more we kept improving the EYL platform, the more we realized that it was important to synthesize what we knew into a comprehensive financial literacy plan. If the ultimate goal is achieving financial freedom and creating generational wealth, we believe that offering the strategies and principles to do so in the most approachable way possible is the best way for everyone to win. This book is our attempt to do that.

We never wanted you to just read this book and put it down again. We hope you have processed it and truly engaged with it. Hopefully, you've highlighted paragraphs and concepts, you've bookmarked pages, you've written notes in the margins. Maybe you even got a notebook, as we suggested, and did all of the exercises. However you approached this book, we want you to be proud of yourself. Reading it and taking in our advice are the first steps to completely reshaping your financial future. Just know that if you lend this book to a loved one or friend, they're probably never going to give it back!

Revisiting the EYL Thesis for Wealth

At the beginning of this journey, we introduced to you the EYL Thesis for Wealth. Here it is again:

Increase income

Invest the Difference

Lower expenses

We believe that this principle is at the core of wealth building. Increasing your income is just the beginning. Whether it involves getting another job, maximizing your current investments, or pursuing entrepreneurship, making more money than you are right now has to be an objective. The more money you have, the more you have to create the future you deserve.

But it's not enough just to make more money. By now, we hope you can see that lowering your expenses is an essential part of your financial blueprint. You need to ask yourself the most important question: "What do I really need?" It may seem oxymoronic to make more money and not "show" it. However, if you do the right thing, you'll have something to show for it. This is a mindset shift, one that will stay with you. We guarantee that while you may purchase some expensive statement pieces and take luxury vacations, you will become more strategic with your spending.

One of our main objectives with this book was to demystify the process of investing. So many people in our community are afraid to do it, often because they lack the proper information or have been given the wrong information. In streamlining the steps to do so, we hope that we've been able to show that it's not as scary and stressful as many make it out to be. There is risk, yes, but anything that is worth having requires taking a risk. It may seem different because we're talking about money. But the principles of risk, loss, and reward are the same no matter what the variables are.

At the end of the day, we hope you got the overall message: You can't "save" your way into financial freedom. Your economic future depends on a combination of financial products, and the beauty is that there are enough of them that you can select what you need based on your personality and interests. You have the ability to control what your financial portfolio looks like. That power has always been yours, and utilizing it will require a little self-discipline. The good news is that if you buckle down now, you'll get to loosen your financial restrictions sooner rather than later.

There will be a time when your budget isn't as restrictive. You'll know when that time has come. But at this moment, everything has to be geared toward getting your house in order and stacking the deck for your future. We've been telling you all along that you deserve this. Now you know how to go get it.

All the Players Win

It is important to us that you be able to see how many of the EYL principles of financial freedom are applicable to people just like you. To accomplish that, we introduced you to six people who reflected many of those who make up our EYL community.

Dre

Dre had one goal: he wanted to move out of his parents' home and into a place of his own. It didn't even matter if he had a roommate; he just wanted to be out. But with two maxed-out credit cards, only $100 in savings, and a $17.50-an-hour wage, moving out didn't seem possible. It was going to have to require his taking a second job and saving aggressively.

In all fairness, EYL started because we wanted to get this message to young people such as Dre. Our hope is to educate them early so they can begin building wealth sooner than we did. It's not too late for kids like Dre. Youth really is on their side, and if they can begin putting the pieces of their personal financial plans together now, they'll sidestep many of the traps that have set us back.

At the same time, young people like Dre are going to need a lot of help. With costs increasing for everything, kids like him may need to stay at home longer. They may need their parents, guardians, or mentors to establish a whole life insurance policy that will create a safety net for them years down the line. They may even need a significant loan or a cosigner on a loan. Dre's obtaining his financial freedom will require someone to help him. In many other communities, kids are given a hand up and a head start. It's time to shift the narrative and do the same in ours.

Tracy

Tracy represents many single parents, single mothers especially, who truly make a way out of no way. Their ability to make magic with what they have is often celebrated and saluted. And while they know they work hard and are proud of the lives they can provide for their children, they want more. They believe that their children deserve more, but the truth is that they themselves deserve more, too.

Tracy's credit score is well below average, but she has a plan to increase it and purchase a home for herself and her daughter. Although she's proud that she started a business and has generated income to add to her budget, she's made the decision to pursue child support from her daughter's father. The extra income created the opportunity to pay for daycare, allowing her to get a second job. It also enabled her to pay down some debt and increase her credit score.

For some people, Tracy's decision to pursue child support will seem insignificant; it won't be that big of a deal. But Tracy's circumstances, like those of many single parents who don't receive assistance, reveal just how one person can impact another's financial future. Stepping into your power may include taking it back from people who have stolen it and are abusing it. Taking that power back doesn't mean that people will like the way you did it. But who cares? At the end of the day, the only thing that matters is moving forward in the purpose that will change your life and the lives of the people who matter the most to you.

The Williams Family

Not everyone approaches achieving financial freedom from a place of scarcity. The Williams family proves that. They are in a good position, one that has created an opportunity for them to keep their children from incurring mountains of student loan debt. Their mission was to amplify what they were already doing and maintain their position as they become empty nesters and fulfill their own dreams.

These two have done what many of our parents and grandparents couldn't do. They may have wanted to travel the world and vacation when we left the house. They may even have wanted to help us more financially than they did. But they didn't have that option. This is why we do this: Creating our own financial freedom and building generational wealth will foster a sense of pride that is unparalleled.

Should you find yourself in the same position as the Williamses are, the best thing to do is identify one or two areas in which your current financial plan can be strengthened. Gary and Morgan Williams are already on the doorstep of financial freedom. A mistake *can* set them back. To avoid that, having the strongest "money team" possible will be their game changer.

Corey

Corey is an investment dream. He has no debt, very few expenses, and the money to invest. He embodies the EYL Thesis for Wealth. All he has to do is take the final step: invest the difference. There are reasons for his fear and apprehension. He was taught, as most of us were, that investing is too dangerous. For those of you who were like Corey, we hope you've realized that that isn't true.

Though he has the financial resources to take a significant

leap, Corey and people like him might have to take responsible, mitigated steps toward investing. This may mean investing at or below our suggested minimums until they're comfortable. And though we understand why they may need to take this route at first, we don't recommend that they continue to do so. If you're making the decision to slowly wade into the investment waters, you need to have a plan for entering the deep end.

Corey is a prime example of what we mean by not being able to save your way into financial freedom. An employee benefits or savings plan won't do it alone. If you look at Corey's circumstances and can relate to him, we recommend sitting down with a financial adviser to create the kind of plan that will maximize all of your positive attributes. You've got the keys. It's time to unlock all of your potential.

Edwin

Edwin knows what it means to hustle. He's been doing it all his life; but Edwin was also ready to make a change and experience a certain kind of financial stability that didn't require the same level of hustle he'd been used to. Edwin has big dreams and they're all attainable. The first step was getting out of his own way.

For Edwin and others like him, a major mindset shift is needed. Edwin had gone into severe debt to appear like he was doing well. He thought he needed to do that to appeal to customers, but more than that, he was doing that to feel good about himself. He had a picture of entrepreneurship in his head, and he wasn't ready to let it go. If he was honest, full-time entrepreneurship probably wasn't the best move for him, but he's made it work. And while hindsight is perfect vision, it's time to move forward.

If you see yourself in Edwin, it's time to do some serious

reevaluation before things get too far out of control. Entrepreneurship is a journey with many detours. One for you, right now, might be considering additional employment to make ends meet. It also may mean reimagining how you saw your dream. What would it look like for Edwin to consider a partner or potential investors that could help him expand his current business even further? It's possible that you may have reached your capacity and need others to help you bring in new ideas and infrastructure. There's nothing wrong with that. A wise entrepreneur recognizes when they need help and welcomes it.

As we've offered you these profiles and glimpses into the various ways you can earn your leisure and achieve your dreams, we want you to understand this truth: **Financial freedom is for everybody**. And you are included in that everybody. From this moment forward, don't ever think that cultivating and maintaining your own economic power isn't possible. It's the work you must do now.

So What's Next?

We gave you our definition of financial freedom. For us, "earning your leisure" means having the active and residual income that affords you the ability to control your time and live a life on your terms. As our journey together comes to a close, we have one last exercise for you: **We want you to create your own definition of financial freedom**. What does that look like? What aspects of your financial future are nonnegotiable? Take some time and craft this for yourself.

The truth is that we can give you a definition—anyone can—but unless it's real to you, you'll never own it. And we want you to own it. If nothing else, we want you to walk away from the experience of reading this book knowing that you are meant to live the life of your dreams. As a matter of fact, your dreams aren't unrealistic, and they're not too far-fetched. The only reason you believed that was because the denial of access to tools and resources will make anyone think they're just a dreamer.

But you are not *just* a dreamer; you are someone with the vision and the tenacity to make your dreams a reality. You have the drive, the grit, and the determination. And now you have the tools! We titled this book *You Deserve to Be Rich* because you really do. You deserve every dime, every dollar, and every million dollars that will be attached to your name. So what are you waiting for? Go get it!

ACKNOWLEDGMENTS

◆ ◆ ◆

To my beloved wife, Danielle, for your unwavering support and love, which has allowed this unbelievable journey to flourish. Your understanding, flexibility, loyalty, and belief in me is the catalyst that drives me to be better every day. To my children, my legacy writers Jordyn and Christian, who inspire me every day with their boundless energy, intelligence, and curiosity. You are my why and the greatest blessing I could have ever dreamt of.

To my parents, Howard and Juliet, whose patience and guidance have shaped my journey. You provided a safe environment where thinking freely was encouraged, and family was a core principle. To my brothers, Howie and Gregory, for their constant encouragement and camaraderie. Before I had friends, I had brothers. Greg, thank you for being someone to learn from, model myself after, and help me unlock a deeper relationship with God.

To the Town of Greenburgh, where my roots are deeply planted and my dreams began to flourish. You've given me purpose, my family, my career, my business partners, and most important, a place to call home. I love education because of you, I love community because of you.

And finally to the supporters of Earn Your Leisure, whose belief and enthusiasm have made this journey possible.

With gratitude and love,
Troy

◆ ◆ ◆

To my beloved family, this book is dedicated to you.

To my son, Nasir, you are my greatest joy and the embodiment of limitless potential.

To my sister, Taheera, your strength and wisdom are a constant source of inspiration.

To my mother, Gail, and my father, Hassan, your love and guidance have shaped me into who I am today.

To my brother, Hassan, your unwavering support and camaraderie mean the world to me.

This work is a testament to the values and legacy we cherish together.

With all my love,
Rashad

LINER NOTES

◆ ◆ ◆

Chapter One: The Highest Level

41   **in 2021, the average:** National Association of Realtors, *2021 Home Buyers and Sellers Generational Trends Report,* 2021, https://www.nar.realtor/sites/default/files /documents/2021-home-buyers-and-sellers-generational-trends-03-16-2021.pdf.

42   **the national average cost:** Abha Bhattarai, Dan Keating, and Stephanie Hays, "How Much Does It Cost to Raise a Child?," *The Washington Post,* October 13, 2022, https://www.washingtonpost.com/business/interactive/2022/cost-raising -child-calculator.

Chapter Two: Dealing with Financial Trauma

50   **During Reconstruction, the Freedman's Bank:** John Steele Gordon, "The Freedman's Bank," American Heritage, December 1993, https://www.american heritage.com/freedmans-bank.

50   **In 2019, the median income:** Neil Bhutta et al., "Changes in U.S. Family Finances from 2016 to 2019: Evidence from the Survey of Consumer Finances," *Federal Reserve Bulletin* 106, no. 5 (September 2020), https://www.federalreserve .gov/publications/files/scf20.pdf.

50   **For Black families, it was:** Federal Deposit Insurance Corporation, *2017 FDIC National Survey of Unbanked and Underbanked Households,* October 2018, https://www.fdic.gov/analysis/household-survey/2017/2017report.pdf.

50   **A banking desert is defined:** Kenneth P. Brevoort and John D. Wolken, "Does Distance Matter in Banking?," in *The Changing Geography of Banking and Finance,* ed. Pietro Alessandrini, Michele Fratianni, and Alberto Zazzaro (New York: Springer Verlag, 2009), 27–56.

54   **adults who grew up:** Cynthia L. Harter and John F. R. Harter, "The Link Between Adverse Childhood Experiences and Financial Security in Adulthood," *Journal of Family and Economic Issues* 43, no. 4 (2022): 832–42, https://www .ncbi.nlm.nih.gov/pmc/articles/PMC8428486.

57   **In 2022, the Pew Research Center:** Monica Anderson, "Payment Apps Like Venmo and Cash App Bring Convenience and Security Concerns to Some Users," https://www.pewresearch.org/short-reads/2022/09/08/payment-apps-like -venmo-and-cash-app-bring-convenience-and-security-concerns-to-some-users.

58   **Merriam-Webster defines trauma:** "Trauma," Merriam-Webster, https://www .merriam-webster.com/dictionary/trauma.

61   **77% of adults say:** Annie Atherton, "77% of Us Lose Sleep Over Financial Worries. How Do We Earn It Back?," Sleep Foundation, https://www.sleep foundation.org/sleep-news/77-percent-lose-sleep-to-financial-worries.

61   **people experiencing financial stress:** "Significant Financial Stress Associated with 13-Fold Higher Odds of Having a Heart Attack," *Cardiovascular Journal of Africa* 29, no. 4 (2018): 217, https://www.ncbi.nlm.nih.gov/pmc/articles/PMC 6291807.

61   **Doctors have discovered connections:** "The Impact of Financial Stress on Health," Tufts Health Plan, https://tuftshealthplan.com/employer/work-well,-live -well/covid19/impact-of-financial-stress-on-health.

61   **Americans listed finances as:** The Harris Poll, "Research Method and Reading the Report," *Stress in America 2023,* November 2023, https://www.apa.org/news /press/releases/stress/2023/november-2023-topline-data.pdf.

Chapter Three: Creating Annual and Monthly Budgets

74   **the 15% the average American was saving:** "Personal Savings as a Percentage of Disposable Income in the United States from 1960 to 2023," Statista, 2024, https://www.statista.com/statistics/246234/personal-savings-rate-in-the-united -states.

87   **per capita credit card debt:** Matt Schulz, "2024 Credit Card Debt Statistics," LendingTree, June 13, 2024, https://www.lendingtree.com/credit-cards/study /credit-card-debt-statistics.

87   **while fewer members of Black:** Kendall Little and Christopher Murray, "Credit Card Statistics by Race and Ethnicity," Bankrate, June 7, 2023, https://www.bank rate.com/credit-cards/news/credit-cards-and-race-statistics.

Chapter Four: The Keys to the Kingdom

103   **Barbara Hudson offers:** "Four Stages of Wealth," SF Money Coach, https:// www.sfmoneycoach.com/blog/four-stages-of-wealth.

Chapter Five: The EYL Investment Blueprint

129 **average cost of U.S. farmland:** "2023 Agricultural Land: Land Values and Cash Rents," *NASS Highlights,* no. 2023-6, October 2023, https://www.nass.usda.gov /Publications/Highlights/2023/2023LandValuesCashRents_FINAL.pdf.

Chapter Six: Risky Business

165 **only 62% of landlords collected:** Elijah de la Campa and Vincent J. Reina, "How Has the Pandemic Affected Landlords?," Joint Center for Housing Studies of Harvard University, August 25, 2021, https://www.jchs.harvard.edu/blog/how -has-pandemic-affected-landlords.

165 **62.7% of their respondents:** Marin Scott, "Going Into 2021, Renters and Landlords Are Still Hurting from COVID Consequences," Avail, February 7, 2022, https://www.avail.co/blog/going-into-2021-renters-and-landlords-are-still -hurting-from-covid-consequences.

166 **investments with the greatest potential:** Marianne Hayes, "Which Type of Investment Has the Highest Risk?," Experian, January 18, 2022, https://www .experian.com/blogs/ask-experian/which-investment-has-highest-risk.

166 **In March 2024, its value:** John Edwards, "Bitcoin's Price History," Investopedia, May 26, 2024, https://www.investopedia.com/articles/forex/121815/bitcoins -price-history.asp.

166 **At the end of April:** Billy Bambrough, "$300 Billion 'Perfect Storm' Bitcoin Price Crash Under $60,000 Suddenly Accelerates as Ethereum, XRP and Crypto Brace for Shock Fed Flip," *Forbes,* May 1, 2024, https://www.forbes.com /sites/digital-assets/2024/05/01/perfect-storm-bitcoin-price-now-braced-for-a -shock-fed-inflation-flip-as-ethereum-xrp-and-crypto-crash-back/?sh=3a89c1 e0df21.

167 **in March 2024, CNBC noted:** Greg Iacurci, "Bailing on the Stock Market During Volatility Is a 'Loser's Game,' Financial Advisor Says. Here's Why," CNBC, March 7, 2024, https://www.cnbc.com/2024/03/07/why-bailing-on -the-stock-market-is-likely-a-losers-game-cfp-says.html.

169 **the stock market did extremely well:** Emily Stewart, "Why Stocks Soared While America Struggled," Vox, May 10, 2021, https://www.vox.com/business-and -finance/22421417/stock-market-pandemic-economy.

169 **Two years later, the stock market:** Nicole Goodkind, Julia Horowitz, and David Goldman, "Goodbye 2022—and Good Riddance. Markets Close Out Their Worst Year Since 2008," CNN, December 30, 2022, https://www.cnn.com /2022/12/30/investing/dow-stock-market-2022/index.html.

Chapter Seven: Entrepreneurship (A Beautiful Struggle)

203 **60% of the world's population:** Brian Dean, "Social Media Usage & Growth Statistics," Backlinko, February 21, 2024, https://backlinko.com/social-media -users#social-media-usage-stats.

Chapter Eight: Love and Money

225 **In 2019, a study found:** Ramishah Maruf, "Prenuptial Agreements Aren't Just for the Rich. Here's What You Should Know," CNN, March 29, 2022, https://www.cnn.com/2022/03/29/success/prenuptial-agreement/index.html.

227 **In 2024, *Newsweek* published:** Suzanne Blake, "Childcare Now Costs More Than College As Parents Fork Over $36,000 a Year," *Newsweek,* January 19, 2024, https://www.newsweek.com/child-care-costs-more-expensive-college-1862309.

230 **Black children are less likely:** Timothy Grall, "Custodial Mothers and Fathers and Their Child Support: 2017," U.S. Census Bureau, May 2020, https://www.census.gov/content/dam/Census/library/publications/2020/demo/p60-269.pdf.

230 **no universal formula for calculating:** "How Much Child Support Do Parents Actually Receive?," USAFacts, March 28, 2023, https://usafacts.org/articles/how-much-child-support-do-parents-actually-receive.

Chapter Nine: Legacy, Legacy, Legacy

242 **His widow, Vanessa Bryant:** Dawn Onley, "Vanessa Bryant Asks Judge to Amend Kobe's Trust to Add Their Baby, Capri," TheGrio, March 19, 2020, https://thegrio.com/2020/03/19/vanessa-bryant-kobe-trust.

INDEX

✦ ✦ ✦